Florida A&M University, Tallahassee
Florida Atlantic University, Boca Raton
Florida Gulf Coast University, Ft. Myers
Florida International University, Miami
Florida State University, Tallahassee
University of Central Florida, Orlando
University of Florida, Gainesville
University of North Florida, Jacksonville
University of South Florida, Tampa
University of West Florida, Pensacola

Enlightenment Fiction in England, France, and America

*

William Donoghue

University Press of Florida
Gainesville · Tallahassee · Tampa · Boca Raton
Pensacola · Orlando · Miami · Jacksonville · Ft. Myers

07 06 05 04 03 02   6 5 4 3 2 1

Library of Congress Cataloging-in-Publication Data
Donoghue, William, 1949–
Enlightenment fiction in England, France, and America /
William Donoghue.
p. c.m.
Includes bibliographical references and index.
ISBN 0-8130-2481-1 (acid-free paper)
1. English fiction—18th century—History and criticism. 2. Skepticism
in literature. 3. French fiction—18th century—History and criticism.
4. American fiction—18th century—History and criticism. 5. Literature,
Comparative—English and French. 6. Literature, Comparative—French
and English. 7. Philosophy in literature. 8. Enlightenment. I. Title.
PR858.S53 D66 2002
823'.509384—dc21   2002016590

The University Press of Florida is the scholarly publishing agency
for the State University System of Florida, comprising Florida A&M
University, Florida Atlantic University, Florida Gulf Coast University,
Florida International University, Florida State University, University
of Central Florida, University of Florida, University of North Florida,
University of South Florida, and University of West Florida.

University Press of Florida
15 Northwest 15th Street
Gainesville, FL 32611–2079
http://www.upf.com

To Xianmei

Deception and survival resemble one another closely.

CHRISTA WOLF

Contents

Acknowledgments

Support comes in many forms. I owe a debt of gratitude to some excellent thinkers and close readers for their help with this book before it was one: John Bender, Terry Castle, and Bliss Carnochan all read and commented on the project in its earliest stages. Mel New, Anne Vila, and Susan Fernandez made valuable suggestions as the book came to term. I have also benefited from the encouragement of David Halliburton, whose work on philosophy and literature is a model for the sort of interdisciplinarity I pursue here. Special thanks to Jay Fliegelman, whose energetic support always came along when I needed it. I want to thank Emerson College for granting me the necessary course relief and time to complete the manuscript. Finally, special thanks to Xianmei, whose support made everything possible.

Skepticism, Sensibility, and the Novel

This book is an examination of the relationship between two eighteenth-century intellectual events: the rise in popularity of the novel and the rise of philosophical skepticism. I say "rise in popularity" rather than "rise of the novel" because I want to focus on that popularity and suggest that one reason for it was the novel's perceived ability to act as an antidote to the anxieties and uncertainties of skepticism—to palliate what has been called the "epistemological crisis" in the century.[1] *Crisis* is a strong word, since there has probably never been a time in the history of Western thought when the status of knowledge was not an issue to one degree or another. I would suggest, however, that there are three particular periods when philosophical skepticism casts an especially long shadow: Classical Greece, the British and French seventeenth and eighteenth centuries, and our own age, which in the last thirty years has experienced its own epistemological crisis under the banners of deconstruction and post-Nietzschean antifoundationalism.[2] Indeed, part of my motivation for writing this study is to suggest that the tenacity of literary realism today has something to do with its operating the same way against skepticism as it did in the eighteenth century.[3] I am not suggesting that wherever and whenever in history skepticism has been a problem one should expect to see forms of aesthetic realism arise, but I do want to suggest that the popularity of the literary form in the age of Hume is no coincidence.

We have no surveys for the early period that might tell us what readers thought they were getting out of novels, but we do have them for our own day. Shirley Brice Heath, the Stanford linguist, conducted one such survey in the 1980s and received some responses that stress what I will argue here on behalf of the cognitive and ethical valence of novels. Heath went around polling readers in "enforced transition zones" such as airports, subways, and resorts who were reading "substantive works of fiction" and asked them what they were getting out of these books. The readers told her that what they liked was the way the novels presented unpredictability and its resolution. Heath found that most of them had had some experience with unpredictability in their own personal lives. As in the eighteenth century, most buyers and readers of novels today are women. Heath comments: "There is a certain predictability to literature's unpredictability . . . and *that* predictability is what readers tell me they hang onto." This is the cognitive, Kantian aspect of literary realism—its purposiveness. Heath cites a typical response that makes the ethics connection: "Reading enables me to maintain a sense of something *substantive*—my ethical integrity, my intellectual integrity."[4] I would suggest that novels probably produced much the same sort of Kantian effects in their readers, men as well as women, in the eighteenth century. The discourse *on* the novel in the eighteenth century, when it is positive, almost always takes this approach, linking the novel's cognitive or epistemological valence to its ethical and moral power.

Given the importance of both skepticism and the discourse of and on the novel in the eighteenth century, it is surprising that so little has been written on how the two were articulated—not only given voice but also worked out together, as I want to do here, like sets of interlocking muscles. Michael McKeon's *Origins of the English Novel 1600–1740* and Eve Tavor's *Scepticism, Society and the Eighteenth-Century Novel* both appeared in 1987, but they take a Marxian approach to literature that rules out the formal, aesthetic agency of literary realism that I want to examine. They make the novel belated, a consequence of precedent base issues of "categorial instability" (McKeon), or a symptom of epistemological *Angst* (Tavor). At best, McKeon sees the novel as a mediator of the "change in attitudes" in the century toward problems of truth and virtue, whereas Tavor, for her part, sees a direct cause and effect relation between base and superstructure where skepticism is the cause and the novel is the effect.[5] Neither grant realist fiction the sort of social power I will argue for here. As for sensibility and its cult, I would modestly propose that the language of feeling is the principal manifestation of skepticism in the eighteenth century. I will devote considerable time to describing its literary appearance, with special emphasis on Sterne, Diderot, Radcliffe, and Sade.

In terms of methodology I want to borrow some of the language of discourse analysis and systems theory to discuss skepticism and the novel as two systems of expression operating within the larger intellectual discussion of the century—two dissonant language games that are part of the polyphony rather than the symphony of the eighteenth-century sound track. Robert Mayer writes that scholars of the novel in the last decade or so "have tended to see novelistic discourse in relation to, or as part of, larger discursive formations."[6] This is a relational rather than causal model that is particularly well-suited to the interaction of the skeptical and realist discourse systems I want to describe.

The larger discussion is the discourse on knowledge in the eighteenth century as a whole—questions and answers about the sources and formation of knowledge, the criteria for truth, the ethics and aesthetics of knowledge, and so on. The novel's place in this conversation has not been well understood. Bakhtin popularized a view of the novel as a kind of collection of voices, mute in itself, acting as host to a variety of others. Indeed, in the eighteenth century the novel acts often enough as a kind of host blackboard to the discourse of skepticism itself, to sentimentalism, and even to attacks directed against its own practice. But novels also contain their own comments on that practice—their own discourse on the novel, so to speak—and how it contributes to both epistemology and ethics. They host, that is to say, a self-reflexive meditation on their own practice; and it is one, I would suggest, that contradicts the language of skepticism and sentiment. Let me begin by expanding first on what the discourse of skepticism and its sentimental adjunct looked like in the eighteenth century, then discuss in more detail the novelistic response. I will conclude with a summary of how my readings bear on the topic.

The first question to answer is, was there in fact an epistemological crisis in the eighteenth century? Surely the phrase overstates the case in a century with a so-called Age of Reason and an Enlightenment.[7] Berkeley, after all, was never taken seriously, and Hume's *Treatise*, as he tells us, fell dead-born from the press. Nor did Hume feel there was any crisis, if we are to judge by his behavior after philosophizing, when he would go off happily to his dinner and a game of backgammon. The answer to this question must take us into a brief overview of skepticism itself.

Skepticism is a kind of cognitive virus that works on a sliding scale of seriousness. McKeon and Damrosch in their "crisis" comments (see n. 1) are concerned with the least painful manifestation, where we doubt the factuality of the Countess's memoirs, for example, or of romance adventures like the slaying of dragons. This is something I would call first-order skepticism: we are skeptical of what people tell us until we see some empirical evidence for what they are claiming. This is the sort of skepticism McKeon, for instance, is concerned with in his dialectics; this everyday, ordinary-language skepticism is like an epistemological defoliant that clears the camouflage and weeds. It is a comfortable part of the discourse of science and reason, as it was in the Enlightenment. We doubt until Newton shows us his proofs, doubt miracles, or the existence of God, as the philosophes did, all in the name of Reason.[8] It was this positivist brand of skepticism that many eighteenth-century churchmen complained about when they "rebuked the *spirit of the age*," as Joseph Milner the ecclesiastical historian did at the end of the century, "as one of *reasoning to excess*."[9] Joseph Butler has this discrimination in mind when he complains in the "Advertisement" to his *Analogy of Religion* (1736) that Christianity had already come to be seen as "fictitious" by people of supposed "discernment."[10] For Butler it is a matter of right and wrong and getting things straight. The existence of truth itself is not in question. Tillotson does not bother to distinguish when he generalizes that Butler's aim was "saving . . . man from the skeptical philosophers" per se.[11] James Beattie also identified skepticism in general as the problem as late as 1770, titling his refutation of Hume *The Nature and Immutability of Truth in Opposition to Sophistry and Scepticism*. "England's divines," as B. W. Young puts it, "were aware of an intellectual tendency which was especially characteristic of their knowing age," and this was the tendency no longer to take the claims of religion on faith.[12] In this least serious of its manifestations, skepticism throws doubt on a limited number of things—granted, often very important, even fundamental things—but accepts that much else is true.

Skepticism of course, in whatever form, was not the only factor in the falling off of religious observances in the century; much of the trouble came not from skeptics but from a general indifference to matters of religion under George I and from feuds within the church itself: from corrupt clergy and an ecclesiastical "system," as J. H. Overton puts it, that "had become mechanical and dead."[13] And even with this, the age was hardly atheistic. As Johnson noted, there were few infidels.[14] But skepticism was a factor and was identified early on as a threat. Stillingfleet shared Berkeley's view that their age was one of doubt and relativism in its first years. Berkeley targeted "Scepticism" and "Atheism" as a common enemy in his 1710 *Treatise Concerning the Principles of Human Knowledge*; he aimed again at "Sceptics and Atheists" in his 1713 *Three Dialogues Between Hylas and Philonous*.[15]

But something a little more serious was happening in the century, and it has to do with what I would call second-order skepticism—a more unstable, philosophical and dangerous hybrid than the everyday strain. Second-order skepticism has its roots in Protagoras and Epicurus. Protagoras claimed that because all knowledge begins in sensation, and sense perceptions are different at different moments and for different people, everyone is right at all times. A hundred years later Epicurus insisted on the absolute dominion and reliability of the senses. Knowledge was possible, but it was the knowledge of the senses. Sensationism, empiricism, and materialism are all forms of a second-order skepticism that grounds knowledge in the senses. Reason is a function of the senses, if not a sense itself, and is therefore heavily circumscribed in its powers. This was the type of skepticism Locke and fideistic Christian skeptics like Montaigne gave voice to in an attempt to establish the grounds of faith as suprarational. By circumscribing the powers of human reason, one establishes the domain of what exceeds it. Indeed one might look at this level of skepticism as reason's ultimate victory: the self-effacing illumination of its own limits.[16] This is Locke's hope in his *Essay Concerning Human Understanding*, and it is what Philo has in mind in Hume's *Dialogues Concerning Natural Religion* when he says to Cleanthes: "To be a philosophical sceptic is, in a man of letters, the first and most essential step towards being a sound, believing Christian."[17] Needless to say, this was not the conclusion that materialists like Diderot or Epicureans like Lucretius came to, but the sensationist basis of the category makes them all members of the same club.

Nor should Hume be too closely identified with Philo's second-order skepticism; his own version often has more in common with Pyrrhonism, the third and most corrosive form of skepticism. We probably owe the beginnings of this more extreme third-order skeptical strain to the logical development of Protagorean thought into pure subjectivism and to the flux theory of Heraclitus. In Protagoras the claim that because we all have our own sense impressions, and since they are foundational, we are all always right, empties the word *right* of any universality and hence of any real meaning, and does the same to *knowledge* and *truth*, all of which demand something more than personal vouching. So in effect no one is right. This is what Heraclitus said. For Heraclitus, everything is in flux, so any predicative assertion about the world is instantly outdated and wrong. For Heraclitus we are all wrong all the time. Plato saw how serious a position this was. He believed that Protagoras and Heraclitus were essentially saying the same thing, and he devotes a large part of his *Theaetetus* to proving it and refuting them.

Aristippus, who studied with Socrates and founded the Cyrenaic school, continued nonetheless to insist on the epistemological primacy of feeling—as did Epicurus in the next century. However, it is with Pyrrho of Elis (360–272 B.C.E.), and later, Sextus Empiricus (ca. 200 C.E.), that the third level of skepticism is usually identified. From this perspective, first- and second-order strains look almost benign—what Hume ends up calling "mitigated" skepticism.[18] Pyrrhonism is the last word in disbelief in that it denies our very ability to make the determinations necessary to doubt. The Pyrrhonist believes that there is insufficient evidence to determine that anything is true or untrue, including sense knowledge and of course the Pyrrhonist's own claim that this is the case. Pyrrhonism tells us that we cannot say, *Since all knowledge depends on sense impressions, we are all right all the time,* or that we are all wrong, since both claims rest on the same illusory ground and are therefore equally untenable. Stanley Cavell calls Pyrrhonism "the recoil of demonic reason."[19] Its classic Pyrrhic victory is the self-annihilating assertion of the Liar's Paradox that *All statements are untrue.* The result of this ultimate doubt, according to the followers of Pyrrho and Sextus Empiricus, is peace of mind (ataraxia)—the peace of mind that follows the suspension of judgment. Pyrrhonism is thus politically conservative. Sextus Empiricus advises reformers that since nothing can be known for certain, the best thing to do is fall back on tradition and custom.[20]

To come back to Hume for a moment, and the question of whether there really was a skeptical crisis of belief in the century, we should remember that an epistemological crisis that had anything to do with Pyrrhonian doubt would not have had any overt consequences. Hume's famous good humor and geniality, along with his politics, seem very much in keeping with a Pyrrhonian ataraxia—just what was needed to put the "bon" in "le bon David." Pyrrhonism does not produce crises or change the world or the way we live. Some of the Enlightenment philosophes, including Diderot, were unhappy with Hume in the 1760s and saw him as a great reactionary.[21] He was noncommittal, choosing to follow the customary way, and eventually turned to other pursuits than philosophy. Paradoxically, Hume's praise of common life is sometimes cited as proof that he was *not* a Pyrrhonist, as if Pyrrho and Sextus Empiricus had been so convinced of the truth of their philosophy that they had retired from the world. But this is a misconception. Pyrrhonism leaves everything as it is, and is nothing if not the philosophy of common life. The same kind of misprision of the specific meaning of Pyrrhonism is often read into Montaigne—and into Bayle, the great skeptic at the end of the seventeenth century who was so strong an influence on Diderot. Bayle thought of himself as a Pyrrhonist, but like Montaigne and Diderot he was much too opinionated, active, and committed to causes to be worthy of the name. Bayle was an important influence on Hume, but Hume was the better Pyrrhonist.[22]

Hume himself contributed to the misuse of the word *Pyrrhonism*. Montaigne and Bayle used it loosely for second-order skepticism; Hume, for his part, understood Pyrrhonism as a kind of madness. "The great subverter of Pyrrhonism," he writes in *An Enquiry Concerning Human Understanding*, "is action, and employment, and the occupations of common life"—as if, again, Pyrrho and Sextus had believed rather than doubted their own conclusions and gone to live in caves (158–59). A Pyrrhonian, Hume writes, must acknowledge "that all human life must perish, were his principles universally and steadily to prevail. All discourse, all action would immediately cease; and men remain in a total lethargy" (160). But remaining speechless, unmoving, in a state of lethargy would require the sort of conviction that Pyrrhonism renders impossible. In the *Treatise* Hume refers to Pyrrhonists as "that fantastic sect," but the section that contains the remark is itself a perfect example of Pyrrhonism. Here, in part 4 of book 1, Hume first sets out the standard skeptical arguments on the inevitable fallibility of judgments, then states that "neither I, nor any other person was ever sincerely and constantly of that opinion" (183). No good Pyrrhonist could be devoted to that opinion—or any other. That is what the suspension of judgment involves.

When Hume begins speaking the language of feeling, however, he shifts into a "mitigated" or what he also calls "academical" second-order skepticism that is more in tune with Protagoras and the Epicureans. He does so in the *Treatise* when he dismisses reason as a specific faculty and source of conviction and replaces it, like Protagoras, with feeling. Hume is the best example in the century of the symbiotic relationship of the discourse of feeling and that of skepticism. "Belief is more properly an act of the sensitive, than of the cogitative part of our natures" (183). This is Hume the "homme de sensibilité" speaking. In the *Treatise* Hume clearly prioritizes Nature over reason. "Nature, by an absolute and uncontroulable necessity has determin'd us to judge as well as to breathe and feel" (183). Reason becomes a sense. And when Hume speaks of morality in book 3, feeling is fully in charge. Things change slightly in the *Enquiry Concerning the Principles of Morals*, however, where reason is rehired, although at lower wages, to establish what action is useful and what pernicious. But only sentiment determines the choices we make in terms of actions. Reason sets the table, so to speak, but sentiment tells us what to eat.[23] This kind of personal ethics of feeling is solipsistic and cannot ground the kind of claims for universality needed for prescriptive moral judgments. It is not really different from Hutcheson's moral sense theory. Like Protagoras, Hume's individual moral agent can only say: I feel, therefore I am right. Unfortunately, so is everyone else; or no one is.

The discourse of skepticism in European thought all but disappeared after Sextus Empiricus, but was revived in the sixteenth century with the rediscovery of his writings. It appears in Erasmus and most prominently in Montaigne, who had Sextus's maxims carved on his rafters. It simmered on into the seventeenth century with Charron's secularizing On Wisdom (1601), which touted Montaigne as its Muse, until it had finally become alarming enough once more for Descartes to take up Plato's cudgels and again try to establish the conditions for knowledge outside its grasp.[24] He saw his "Cogito, ergo sum" as the first principle in doing so; and the notion of clear and distinct ideas—innate ideas that could not be doubted—were his proofs. And Descartes believed that he had succeeded in his task: that he was the first philosopher in history, as he said, to refute "the Skeptics."[25] Since the skeptical claim had always been that sense-based knowledge was unreliable, Descartes abandoned body for mind where, in his view, apodictic certainty and a priori truths were unassailable.

The reaction from empiricists to his claim for innate ideas found expression in a restatement of Epicureanism by Gassendi in his Syntagma Philosophicum, published posthumously in 1658, and then in Locke's Essay in 1690, which followed Gassendi's work closely but quickly surpassed it in influence. Gassendi offered the materialist response to Descartes, discrediting once again the powers of reason and reaffirming the Epicurean credo from Lucretius that, Nihil est in intellectu quod non prius fuerit in sensu [There is nothing in the mind that was not first in the senses]. The senses are absolutely reliable and tell us all we can know. Gassendi needed to counter the skeptic's point that this reliance on sense equated to subjectivism, and he did so by rehearsing the Ten Tropes of Sextus Empiricus, then offering his solution. In chapter 14 of his Outlines of Pyrrhonism, Sextus Empiricus goes through ten instances of how sense perception cannot produce knowledge: the same object produces different impressions in different animals; the same object produces different impressions in the same man at different times, and in different circumstances; the senses disagree among themselves: something like perfume smells good but tastes bad; and so on. Gassendi counters with the pragmatic solution of accepting the truth that best fits the occasion.[26]

Locke begins his discussion of primary and secondary qualities with a similar gesture toward the Ten Tropes and cites situations where a thing has different qualities, where water can feel hot to one hand, cold to another, for example.[27] He was probably familiar with the Tropes, perhaps through Diogenes Laertius who sketches a version of one of them in his *Lives*, which Locke had in his library. But he also had Gassendi.[28] Gassendi died in 1655, but Locke probably met his disciple, François Bernier, when he visited France between 1675 and 1679. The doctrine of primary and secondary qualities does not appear in drafts of the *Essay* until after the visit. Henry Lee in his 1702 *Anti-Skepticism* wrote that Locke might as well have said, like Gassendus, "Nihil est . . ." et cetera; and Leibniz identified the author of the *Essay* immediately as a Gassendist.[29] Locke's *Essay* is thus located within a discourse on knowledge whose sensationism links it to the Ancients and skepticism.

Locke's focus, however, was theological rather than epistemological; and although he authored the English language's single most influential work of epistemology, it was out of a desire "to lay down the measures and boundaries between faith and reason" and so put an end to disputes dividing the church. Such a thing was hardly Gassendi's intention, let alone that of Lucretius, who referred to the sacrifice of Iphigenia as the first in an endless string of religion's "sinful and unholy" deeds.[30] Locke has a different attitude toward religion; he writes in book 4: "I find every sect as far as reason will help them, make use of it gladly: and where it fails them, they cry out, It is matter of faith, and above reason. And I do not see how they can argue with any one, or ever convince a gainsayer who makes use of the same plea, without setting down strict boundaries between faith and reason; which ought to be the first point established in all questions where faith has anything to do" (2.415–16).

In attempting to establish the limits of reason, Locke's argument necessarily partakes of the historical discourse of skepticism—in particular the second-order skepticism of Montaigne, whose own doubts had the same theological purpose as Locke's. When Locke writes that he wants "to prevail with the busy mind of man to be more cautious in meddling with things exceeding its comprehension; to stop when it is at the utmost extent of its tether; and to sit down in a quiet ignorance of those things which, upon examination, are found to be beyond the reach of our capacities" (1.28) he sounds like Sextus Empiricus recommending Pyrrhonian ataraxia and a quiet suspension of judgment, when in fact his focus is very much on "things exceeding" and "beyond" human reason. Many readers misunderstood this and took the discourse of skepticism in the book out of context, as if it were a kind of first-order skepticism denying the mysteries of Christianity because they lacked empirical proof.[31] Stillingfleet had reservations along these lines, as did Henry Lee, who made the charge explicit with regard to book 4 in his *Anti-Skepticism*. This mistaken view vexed Locke greatly, as we know, and he devoted much time and energy (for example, in his elaborate correspondence with Stillingfleet) to correcting it. Skepticism is in the enemy camp for Locke. It is not officially listed as such in the *Essay*, but Locke nonetheless associated it, as Descartes had, with the problem of re-establishing the foundations of knowledge. In the introduction to the *Essay* he refers to it as inextricably wound up with the disputes that concern him: "Thus men, extending their inquiries beyond their capacities, and letting their thoughts wander into those depths where they can find no sure footing, it is no wonder that they raise questions and multiply disputes, which never coming to any clear resolution, are proper only to continue and increase their doubts, and to confirm them at last in perfect skepticism."[32]

In France, the discourse of skepticism was more far-reaching, extending into the materialism of La Mettrie and D'Holbach. Locke again was a key figure, surpassing Gassendi in influence as the principal critic of Descartes and the doctrine of innate ideas. The discourse of skepticism in the *Essay*—which was translated into French under Locke's supervision in 1700—at first prompted the familiar outcry that its author was out to destroy religion, and this brought down on Locke's head the same accusations of Deism, Socinianism, and even atheism made against him in England. Misread on one hand by believers, he was now promptly misread on the other by skeptics like Voltaire, who insisted that the *Essay* in fact had no bearing at all on religion. Voltaire's reaction was close to the norm in Enlightenment circles. The secular empiricism and discourse of skepticism in the *Essay* were identified by the philosophes as the language of their own enquiry and singled out for attention.[33] Locke's empiricism corresponded to their rejection of innate ideas in favor of science; and his language of skepticism, which they read as first-order skepticism, served their critique of metaphysics and religion. Thus Locke was quoted everywhere, especially by Condillac, who in the 1740s became Locke's most influential exegete on the Continent, following and expanding Locke's sensationist epistemology in his *Treatise on Systems* (1749) and *Treatise on Sensations* (1754) and announcing his own *Essay Concerning the Origin of Human Knowledge* (1746) as a supplement to Locke's essay.

Skepticism among the philosophes was often expressed as a simple first-order skepticism articulated within the discourse of reason and aimed at the church and metaphysical systems-builders like Descartes and Malebranche. The two more serious strains of skepticism were limited. The Roman Catholic bishop, Pierre-Daniel Huet, knew Locke, understood him, and shared both his sensationist theory of knowledge and his fideistic second-order skepticism; but there were few like him. Instead there were the thinkers of the D'Holbach circle who followed Epicurus, Lucretius, and Spinoza and pushed second-order skepticism to its limit in an atheistic materialism. Third-order Pyrrhonism, however, was too socially disenabling for the reform-minded *encyclopédistes* (witness their chilly reception of Hume), although Diderot was not always immune to its omnivorous spirit. Voltaire occasionally also seems to have felt that all knowledge was an illusion. In 1738, for example, he writes: "[E]very substance is unknown to us. We see appearances only; we are in a dream."[34] This is closer to Pyrrho than to the spirit of the *Encyclopedia*.

And yet even in that scientific undertaking, as Robert Darnton points out with regard to the *Prospectus*, one senses a certain "epistemological *Angst*."[35] Empiricism is attractive when one is trying to get past the notion of innate ideas and put knowledge of the world back on a solid footing, but a sensationist epistemology, as Plato noted, cancels the possibility of certainty, and hence, cancels the possibility of truth and knowledge. And knowledge was the object of the *Encyclopedia*. D'Alembert, in his *Preliminary Discourse*, says that the two-fold intent of the *Encyclopedia* is "to set forth as well as possible the order and connection of the parts of human knowledge," and function as a *dictionnaire raisonné* [systematic dictionary] of the sciences, arts, and trades. Newton and Locke were the Muses, and the project was grounded in the primacy of the senses. "All our direct knowledge," D'Alembert writes, "can be reduced to what we receive through our sense" (4, 6). For D'Alembert the system of the *Encyclopedia*, its mapping and genealogical tree approach to knowledge, was not like the systems Condillac condemned in his *Treatise on Systems*—a work D'Alembert praises for delivering the "death blow" to such structures (94). But it is not always clear how knowledge is to be categorized other than systematically. This produces some tension in the language surrounding the *Encyclopedia* project. Science is the goal, but then it is not. In the *Prospectus*, for example, Diderot seems to see the *Encyclopedia*'s contribution more in the domain of epistemology, lying in the *way* knowledge is presented rather than in its content. What matters is the way the articles are connected, their *enchaînement* [linkage] through the *renvois* [cross-references], a chancy, free-association mode that has much in common with materialist philosophy. There is no map or system for this movement; the reader's path through the articles is indeterminate and based on feeling and taste. Voltaire is reported to have said the result was more like a Tower of Babel than an encyclopedia. The "epistemological *Angst*" Darnton talks about is a product of this kind of tension—in both Diderot and D'Alembert—between their belief in the primacy of feeling and a need for system. Thus, the discourse of skepticism manifests itself even in the *Encyclopedia* project.

It is interesting to note that in the *Preliminary Discourse*, D'Alembert goes from a condemnation of systems directly into a long excursus on literature and the fine arts, which he calls products of the passions and sentiment. Sentiment, D'Alembert tells us, "has principles completely different from those of ordinary logic." Feelings cannot be analyzed, only surrendered to (96). This juxtaposition of the language of skepticism and that of sentiment seems like a good place to make the same shift and say a few brief words about the discourse of sentiment and sensibility before moving on to the novel.

The common cause of sensibility and skepticism in the eighteenth century is evident in Hume's comment in the *Treatise* about "Belief" being "more properly an act of the sensitive, than of the cogitative part of our natures" (183). The discourse of feeling goes back to Protagoras, Heraclitus, and Epicurus and their emphasis on the primacy of the senses. Eventually, words like *feeling* and *sensitive* became abstract and took on an emotional and psychological rather than physiological connotation. As such the language of feeling has had its own long history, predominantly in the arts—the language of love, for example, is obviously far more ubiquitous in literature than the discourse of skepticism per se; but also outside literature. R. S. Crane first argued that the forerunner of eighteenth-century sensibility was the language of benevolence and good nature in the latitudinarianism of seventeenth-century divines like Tillotson and Clarke, and in the anti-Puritanism of the Cambridge Platonists.[36] The accents are diverse, but in all cases feeling is in the ascendant.

Nonetheless, it was with the philosophical revival of sensationism in Gassendi and Locke that the discourse of feeling took on new life in the century. It was expressed as such in the literature of sensibility in both England and France. The Locke connection appears in the Abbé du Bos, who visited Locke in England in 1698, corresponded with him, and knew the *Essay* well. In his *Réflexions critiques sur la poésie et la peinture* [*Critical Reflections on Poetry and Painting*] (1719) he drops reason as a guide and replaces it with feeling (*le sentiment*).[37] Outside of literature, Shaftesbury used Plato's language of the beautiful and the good to give sentiment an ethics, which by midcentury dominated in both England and France and became the standard in Hutcheson and Hume.[38] In Hume's writing, as mentioned above, sentiment is articulated within the discourse of skepticism.[39] The public's belated recognition of this affiliation probably contributed to the reaction against sentiment that took place later in the century.[40]

Another reason for the demise of sensibility, at least in Britain, was that it quickly became gendered female—what Markman Ellis calls "a distinctly feminine field of knowledge"—until it was finally rejected by women themselves.[41] Why it became gendered female in the first place has never really been explained. But it is at least more understandable if we ask, not how the "field" developed, but where it stood in relation to adjacent discursive fields. The identification of women with a discourse (of their own) in which reason is discredited is convenient for those who lay claim to the powers of reason (as their own), especially if this discourse is hegemonic, which in patriarchy it always is. The association of women with the literature of sentiment buttresses patriarchy if arguments from sentiment are subjective and therefore politically void—which they have been since Protagoras.

In France, by contrast, qualities associated with sensibility like delicacy and tenderness were not considered the private holdings of the "weaker sex" but rather attributes of aristocracy. As Anne Vila points out, sensibility, at least in the first half of the century, was a class rather than gender issue.[42] Vila notes that *sensibilité* in France was never de-realized and stripped of its original physical meaning (as it was in England)—and that in fact after 1750 the original physical meaning of words like *sensation* and *sensibilité* was reaffirmed by their presence in the adjacent discourses of medicine and physiology that had begun to flourish in the 1740s: "Sensibility's sociomoral connotations were not so much replaced as broadened in the 1750s, when novelists began to transcode the notion's recently acquired physio-philosophical overtones into their fictional writings."[43] Vila's juxtaposition of a physical and even medical discourse of sensibility in France to its abstracted literary analogue throws considerable light on the puzzling role of sensibility in Sade, who reminds us of the original physical meaning at every opportunity.[44] Chapter 6 discusses this aspect of Sade in detail. For the moment, let me end the description of these two sibling systems by saying that regardless of the accents of sensibility, it is always expressed in the language of skepticism. Locke's importance to the development of sensibility in the century, in both England and France, is a matter of record; but sensibility itself is only understandable as part of the discourse of skepticism.

This book, however, is not exclusively about eighteenth-century skepticism, or the cult of sensibility; it is about the way the discourse of the novel relates to these two systems and contradicts them. As I mentioned earlier, the novel also contributes something to the discourse on knowledge in the century, and this contribution comes in the form of the novel's self-reflection on its own practice, its own discourse on the novel—a self-reflexive meditation that contradicts both the language of sentiment and that of skepticism. What does it mean, then, to say that part of the discourse of the novel is a self-reflexive meditation on its own practice? And if, as Aristotle tells us in chapter 4 of his *Poetics*, mimesis has to do with knowledge, should we not expect that realist fiction *would* in principle contradict a philosophy like skepticism that denies the possibility of that knowledge? Let me begin with the first question. Today it is a truth generally (if not universally) acknowledged that since realist fiction has no referent in what we loosely call reality, it cannot be discussed as if it had. Novels refer, but refer to themselves, their own fictional status, their *relation* to other language games and discursive systems rather than to the world. What realist fiction in particular does, as Fredric Jameson claims in *The Political Unconscious*, is produce the referent it claims to reflect, making it inevitably self-referential. Regardless of what else a novel may be doing, the act of self-reference, in such an understanding, is central. Roland Barthes claims that realist fiction is not based on any correspondence of signifier and signified, but on their divergence, so that the subject of realist fiction will always necessarily be that divergence—the relation of mimesis itself, in other words, to an ostensible world. As one critic of modernity writes, "mimesis is the ultimate subject of every so-called realistic text."[45]

We know what this self-reflexive awareness looks like in metafiction when writers decide to forgo illusionism and make the self-reference overt. Pirandello, Nabokov, Gass, Barth, Gide, and a host of others in our century have given us examples of work in this vein, where the subject is fiction-making itself, and where the (often Brechtian) message is that realism is a form of ideology—an Althusserian thought that became especially persuasive in the 1970s when it was formulated by the writers at *Screen* magazine. And although we sometimes think that the idea Jameson refers to is a modern one, since it does not seem to have been available to Matthew Arnold or F. R. Leavis, it is not. Thinkers from Kant back to Aristotle saw form-giving as more than imitation. Kant looked on it much the way Shirley Brice Heath's survey respondents do, as a cognitive act related to our ethical life, more a way of knowing, an organ of knowledge as Ernst Cassirer puts it, than a mirror held up to the world. And self-reflexivity in literature goes back at least to *Don Quixote*, where Cervantes puts the narration into a series of Chinese boxes, shuffling the narrative cards so often that the reader ends up wondering whether, as in Pirandello, it is not the character himself who has written his author.[46] *Don Quixote*, in turn, was rediscovered in England in the eighteenth century and was particularly important to Fielding and Sterne. After *Don Quixote*, *Tristram Shandy* may be the best early example of overtly self-reflexive fiction (metafiction) in the Western tradition. I discuss Sterne's novel in chapter 3 as an example of what happens when the discourse of sentiment is isolated and removed from the discourse of the novel. But what we often tend to overlook is that the same sort of self-reflexivity, albeit to a different end— the valorization of a realist epistemology—is evident elsewhere, in a variety of places, in texts that are neither manifest fiction of the sort Fielding wrote, nor overt metafiction like Sterne's. I will examine such occurrences in texts across the century, principally in novels, but also in the writings of Pope and Diderot.

The second question is whether we should really be surprised to learn that skepticism and the realist novel are antithetical. Verisimilitude in fiction entails a correspondence theory of truth that presupposes the possibility of knowledge of the world. Narrative is predication (in the way we state that A is B or A causes B), and this is how knowledge, certainly in ethics, is constructed in language. If knowledge and narrative are so closely tied to one another it should hardly be surprising to discover that skepticism, being antithetical to knowledge, will also be antithetical to narrative. It is not surprising, and yet critics of the novel in the eighteenth century did not see it this way; they saw the new realist form as *part* of the discourse of skepticism. Mark Kinkead-Weekes puts it this way: "To project oneself imaginatively into radically differing points of view is to embark on a road which leads to relativity. For the more convincingly these are *done*, the more it may come to seem that there is no such thing as *the story*, only stories, only points of view, only ways of looking."[47]

José Ortega y Gasset writes that the realist novel participates in the dehumanization of art by obscuring any ethical or didactic component the work might have in a deluge of physical detail.[48] A work's ethical valence, in this view, is lost in its formal qualities—and content somehow sacrificed to form. Ronald Paulson, in his discussion of satire and the novel, agrees with Ortega y Gasset on the effects of an attention to detail and adds that the fluidity of consciousness and the emphasis on inwardness in the novel obscure the kind of "emblematic character" satire used—a "sitting duck" that made telling right from wrong an easy matter. Paulson sees Lockian empiricism—and Hume's insistence that moral feelings are only feelings, hence subjective—as good reasons for adopting a view of the novel as a subjective form unable to support an ethical standard.[49] Despite the firm intentions of its author, in other words, a novel like *Clarissa* is trapped in a world of morally neutered realia, upon which it is impossible to ground any ethics.

This was more or less the objection made to the form in the eighteenth century by its critics.[50] The novel was seen as part of the discourse of skepticism because its very polyphony, one might say, produced an ambiguous universe where moral truths, as in *Moll Flanders*, were impossible to sustain. The "Spiritual Barometer" in the *Evangelical Magazine* in 1800 tallied up the century from a salvational plus seventy (Glory) at the top to a perditional minus seventy (Death) at the bottom and put "novels" and "skepticism" together: they came in at a sad minus forty, one step above "drunkenness" and "lewd songs."[51] Relativism and knowledge were the issues, and morality the concern. Objections often relied on and referenced different language systems, but were almost always related to the discourse on knowledge. We have Locke's warning, for example, that while judgment deals in distinctions, *wit* deals in similarities. The danger is error. Avoiding wit means avoiding "being misled by similitude."[52] Hume's comments are interesting because they are not skeptical but rather formulated in the language of knowledge. In the *Treatise* poets are liars whose fictions derive from sentiment rather than knowledge and can thus command only a weakened assent or belief.[53] In the *Treatise* at least, Hume sees no contradiction in believing at the same time, as Shaftesbury did, that only feeling can ground ethics. But here he criticizes poetic fictions as part of a discourse of sentiment he abjures. Other objections came in the older language of antitheatricalism, where the danger (duplicity) involved the confusion of copy and original—what Jonas Barish calls "the ontological malaise." Barish suspects that drama from the beginning was the target of antitheatricalists because it was "the mimetic art par excellence" and that what was always at stake for antitheatricalists from Plato to Law was mimesis itself.[54] Chesterfield has recourse to this language when he writes that "Mimickry, which is the common and favourite amusement of little, low minds, is in the utmost contempt with great ones. It is the lowest and most illiberal of all buffoonery."[55] And Georges May writes that in spite of the non-Puritan tradition in France, antitheatricalism there made the same transition from the stage to attacks on the novel.[56]

When we listen to the discourse on the novel in the century, these are often the voices we hear—echoes of Plato from *Ion* and *The Republic*. But if we move our receiver slightly there is another voice to be heard, and it is singing a different tune—one from chapter 4 of the *Poetics*. It occurs not just in realist works themselves but in a variety of places and forms, appearing sometimes more directly as claims for the necessity and even juridical power of mimicry (think of *The Mousetrap* in *Hamlet* and its analogue in *Caleb Williams*), sometimes in a mediated fashion in the guise of claims for the cognitive value of artifice, the *judicious lie*, or even deception, and sometimes as an attack on romance.

Why do realist forms give readers pleasure? First of all, as a simulacrum or second-order reality (to use Baudrillard's terms), the novel world is immune to real-world doubt; the suspension of disbelief is the suspension of that doubt, and this gives pleasure. This is what the respondents to Shirley Brice Heath's survey are experiencing, and what all lovers of Balzac or Joyce Carol Oates experience when they read these writers. A deeper, but related reason has to do with the Kantian effect—a sense that form-giving itself, especially in more highly wrought works ("substantive" novels as Heath calls them), is a kind of ethical act that resolves epistemological dissonance. This is what Heath's respondents are enjoying and calling the resolution of unpredictability.[57]

Roman Ingarden uses the phrase "quasi-judgments" for the cognitive acts readers perform in fictive worlds to distinguish them from real-world judgments.[58] The two-world paradigm has been hotly contested—Peter McCormick, for example, writes that "aesthetic experience theories cannot finally resist determined criticism."[59] This is true, but there may be other reasons for believing them, just as there are for believing in Hamlet. A pragmatist might wonder if a kind of canteen theory of truth is not at work in a comment like McCormick's: the point of theories is not to carry water. What matters is that a reader's identification of an experience as "aesthetic" need only equate to her belief that what she is reading is a novel.

Whether she can logically defend her experience as an aesthetic one is, at least for her, irrelevant. Once she makes the determination Ingarden's point is gained, and the terrain in which quasi-judgments and literary truths reside is effectively established. Skeptical doubt then makes no more sense than doubting that Lady Macbeth loved her husband. Surely this is what Sidney meant when he said that the poet nothing affirmeth. This is the basis on which the discourse of the novel founds its resistance to skepticism and the place from which it makes its epistemological claims.

Hume, as we know, may have objected to poetic fictions, but he considered logical fictions like identity (the fiction of continued existence), or the artifice of justice (as he calls it in book 3 of the *Treatise*) indispensable. For Hume, poetic fiction was an abuse of the drug—like using it to flavor soft drinks instead of cure the sick.[60] Although the examples I discuss in the chapters below come not just from novels, the claim is always the same—realist forms are a highly wrought product of the mind that help us know ourselves and the world. And this is the source of the pleasure we get from believing in them. Symbolic forms in general, as Cassirer writes, "are not imitations, but organs of reality, since it is solely by their agency that anything real becomes an object for intellectual apprehension, and as such is made visible to us."[61] Cassirer writes this, as he wrote everything, with one eye on Kant, but I think it is something novelists today would still agree with.

Deception—and illusionistic fiction is a kind of deception—had been recognized since Machiavelli as a means of dealing with the irrationalism of human behavior, and it entered the eighteenth-century discourse on knowledge via Spinoza and Hobbes.[62] De la Rochefoucauld, in the mid-seventeenth century, argued that Machiavellism was a way of managing knowledge that was essential not only to successful politics but often enough to survival itself, especially at court. Man, as Swift put it, was not a rational creature but merely *rationis capax*, only *capable of rationality*, or worse yet, as Gulliver's Master puts it, "pretending to reason"; therefore, pretense, deception, and deceit were fair ways of dealing with him. This is Machiavelli's position (take Man as he is) and the foundation of the moral realism of Spinoza and Hobbes.[63] Intrigue—what Rochefoucauld calls *les finesses*—is a kind of deception, like poetic fictions, that changes the rules of the language game in order to rationalize the otherwise inchoate, irrational motives, actions, and beliefs that constitute *animale irrationale*. The artifice of the novel in this sense has the same positive epistemological valence it has for Hume or Adam Smith in their logical fictions, and it operates within the same parameters of reason.

In literature, dragons and monsters indicate that we have stepped outside this discourse and are operating outside the laws of probability. Romance improbabilities were condemned in different ways in the eighteenth century, but the indictment was usually written in the language of knowledge and truth (Nature), against which the romance offended. "Here you see Romances," writes Rica's guide in *Persian Letters*, "whose authors . . . spend their lives chasing truth and never catch it; their heroes are as strange as winged dragons and hippo-centaurs."[64] Pope makes the bold claim in his *Dunciad* that a like failure of realism on the stage is a direct result of a failure of knowledge in the century. I begin with Pope in the next chapter for this reason. His *Dunciad* (1743) embodies the terms of my argument more clearly than novels themselves: in his poem the question of verisimilitude in art as a form of knowledge, and its relation to skepticism, is foundational to the novel's project in the century. I juxtapose him to Richardson in the chapter because Richardson shows us how a writer who shares the novel phobia of his time still embeds a language of legitimation for that fiction in his own.

In chapter 3 I look first at Sterne's *Tristram Shandy* (1759–67) and *Sentimental Journey* (1768) as seminal documents of both sentimentalism and skepticism, and then juxtapose to them a reading of Laclos's *Les Liaisons Dangereuses* (1782), a work that follows Richardson in its expert use of illusionism. Laclos's novel takes up a moral position similar to Richardson's, but offers us at the same time a claim for the epistemological power of artifice that is one of the most persuasive in the century. In chapter 4 I then look at the relation of skepticism to the discourse of and on realism in the work of Denis Diderot, a writer who at various times in his career was both a fervid supporter of mimesis and an equally fervid critic of it.

In chapter 5 I discuss three novels. Ann Radcliffe's *The Mysteries of Udolpho* (1794) attacks sensibility and purges its own romance elements in favor of a realist aesthetic, while William Godwin's *Things As They Are; or, The Adventures of Caleb Williams* (1794) dramatizes the same transformation as a battle of genres. Godwin's novel strives to portray romance as the villain while making one of the strongest moral claims in the century for the discourse of the novel. I conclude the chapter with a few comments on Goethe's treatment of nature in *The Sorrows of Young Werther* (1774), since this text is the first to identify the discourse of sentiment in the century with death. In chapter 6 I pursue this connection with a concluding look at violence in works by Charles Brockden Brown and the Marquis de Sade. Brown's *Wieland; or, The Transformation: An American Tale* (1798) begins in the skeptical mode then transforms itself into a powerful statement on behalf of mimetic art, while Sade takes sensibility back to its roots in physical sensation, making the discourse of feeling a de facto physical nightmare.

Of all the writers I look at here who are interested in the articulation of skepticism and literary realism, only Diderot praises the novel outright, and as we shall see, he takes the praise back. But others, even those who echo and re-present the skeptical, antinovel sentiments of their time, also stage the novel as an antidote to those skeptical sentiments. Of this, one can only say what de la Rochefoucauld said in 1665 about intrigue: "The shrewdest always pretend to hate it, only in order to use it."[65]

Pope and Richardson on
the Epistemology of Artifice

One dark and stormy night back in December 1740 a small hunchbacked man got into a carriage in Bath after taking the waters and instructed the driver to convey him out to the Allen house on the edge of town. Back in his rooms, Alexander Pope ate a solitary late dinner then stayed up all night finishing a titillating new novel he had been reading about a serving girl held in a breathless state of expectancy by a master with designs on her virtue. Pope liked the story and told George Cheyne to pass on his compliments to Richardson.[1] Born within a year of each other, Pope and Richardson were fifty-two and fifty-one respectively in 1740, and despite their many serious differences, they held similar views on the potential of literary realism for promoting moral improvement.

Chapter 1 describes this potential as inhering in the novel's status as a form of cognition whose second-order realizations are immune to skepticism, and I suggested that this was what attracted, and still attracts readers. As Shirley Brice Heath's respondents put it, the pleasure resides in the resolution of unpredictability. In Richardson, for example, this resolution is what powers his first two novels. Lovelace, as William Warner argued, is a deconstructionist, an epistemological villain, a nominalist, skeptic, and relativist whose game, as Pope might say, is words and words alone, and whose job it is to undermine Clarissa's inner certainty. Witnessing his fall has a cathartic effect on readers even today. Pope's satisfaction with *Pamela* probably had a similar basis since Mr B is cut from the same epistemological cloth. In skeptical times it is particularly difficult to resist the appeal of a resolution of the kind Richardson offers, where a semiotic sleight of hand is highlighted, given free play, and then resolved.

Openly claiming too much for the novel in this respect in 1740 would have been risky. The word *artifice*, for example, had picked up a negative connotation in the century that it had not had before, and novelists like Defoe and Richardson knew very well that they were artificers. They protested too much, as we know, in their prefaces and title pages, that what they were laying before the public was history not romance, fact not artifact. But readers like Pope were not fooled. The OED entry for *artifice* tells us that the word comes from *ars* [skill] and *fex*, from *facere* [to make]. Artifice originally had the moral neutrality of artifact, or the more positive sense of the means of constructing an artifact: ingenuity or skill. But by the early eighteenth century it was also being used in a derogatory way. Defoe uses it both ways: artifice means manufactured product or invention in *The Great Law of Subordination Consider'd* (1724) but sleight of hand in the *Complete English Tradesman* (1726). By Johnson's day the negative sense is primary: in the *Dictionary* artifice means "trick; fraud; stratagem." So making too strong a claim, or too outright a claim for the new literary form would have been difficult.

Pope and Richardson in fact voice conventional negative views of artifice, especially in relation to the corrupt stage practices of their time. What is interesting, however, is that their work also contains a quite different claim for the artifice of the novel. Pope's *Dunciad*, for example, which went back as a project to 1725 but did not receive its final addition in the form of book 4 until 1743, is a long-term and powerful polemic on behalf of realism as a form of knowledge. Missing this fact can make the poem look hyperbolic, or even petty.[2] The *Dunciad*, in fact, contradicts the claim often made, both then and now,[3] that the novel is a skeptical form that cannot support a system of moral beliefs. As such, it makes a good starting point for my discussion.

The *Dunciad*'s two nominal subjects are abuses of knowledge and abuses of the stage; and it is the way Pope links them that carries the weight of the argument. To put it simply: by 1743 the public taste for spectacle and entertainments struck Pope as symptomatic of a general failure of knowledge that he characterizes famously at the end of book 4 as "Universal Darkness." The abuses of the stage he catalogues are described unambiguously as the creatures of that "Darkness." Their sin is that they are nonmimetic and irrational. Did Pope have skepticism in mind, specifically, as the root cause of the darkness? The answer seems to be, no; there is no indication that Pope consciously associated the failure of knowledge he characterizes as universal darkness with skepticism. The word *Sceptic* appears only once in his poetry;[4] and he shows no explicit awareness either of

Hume's *Treatise* or the skeptical legacy in general. Nonetheless, his concerns are clearly with its effects.

In a way it is odd that Pope was not more concerned with identifying the root cause of the problem; Berkeley certainly had identified it, and by 1743 Berkeley was an old acquaintance whom Pope had known for thirty years. Berkeley's early 1710 *Treatise* had made it clear that philosophical skepticism was already at that early date a powerful force to be reckoned with, and that its refutation was a matter of some urgency. And in 1713, the year Berkeley probably met Pope, he reiterated the problem in his *Three Dialogues between Hylas and Philonous*, claiming it was written "in opposition to Sceptics and Atheists."[5] Berkeley's discussion, however, in which skeptical arguments are given voice if only to identify, convict, and silence them, remained essentially isolated, not only from Pope but also from public discourse at large. In the first half of the century few noticed Berkeley's ideas, and those who did dismissed them as slightly mad— which testifies to their danger. Berkeley himself, his loud protestations notwithstanding, met a peculiar fate at his own hands, for in engaging the discourse of skepticism he found it too much for his own counterarguments, and this earned him the reputation of being a skeptic in spite of himself. Hume's note in *An Enquiry Concerning Human Understanding* makes the point:

> This argument [immaterialism] is drawn from Dr. Berkeley; and indeed most of the writings of that very ingenious author form the best lessons of skepticism, which are to be found either among the ancient or modern philosophers, Bayle not excepted. He professes, however, in his title-page (and undoubtedly with great truth) to have composed his book against the sceptics as well as against the atheists and free-thinkers. But that all his arguments, though otherwise intended, are in reality, merely sceptical, appears from this, *that they admit of no answer and produce no conviction.* (155 n.)

Instead of taking this as evidence of the power of skeptical thought, Berkeley's readers, with the notable exception of Hume, chose to take it as proof that Berkeley was a kind of lunatic. Tagging the discourse of skepticism as an example of mental, or at least intellectual instability (Hume's response to Pyrrhonism), was perhaps enough to keep it from even Pope's ears. And yet, Berkeley was as much a skeptic and devotee of metaphysics as any Pope could have hoped to pillory in his poem. But Pope read him as the self-declared opponent of all that was wrong. He grants "To *Berkeley*, ev'ry Virtue under Heav'n,"[6] and attacks "*Minute Philosophers* and *Free-thinkers*" in his argument to book 4 much the way Berkeley had in his 1732 *Alciphron: Or, The Minute Philosopher*. So although Pope felt the same dangers Berkeley did, he did not diagnose the breakdown of knowledge in the same way. Pope aims his attack instead at metaphysics and then contents himself with painting the picture of dullness on the faces of his dunces. In doing so, however, he portrays the failure of knowledge in the unmistakable garb of skepticism.

Truth and error in the *Dunciad* are cast in the familiar imagery of light and darkness; truth, however, is a matter of poetic or universal vision while error is indentured to an empiricist epistemology and dependence on physical sight. When the sun is sick, night descends "To blot out Order, and extinguish Light" (B 4.11–14); darkness triumphs over light, dullness and night over learning, until, at the end of the poem, "the Great Mother bids Britannia sleep" and "Universal Darkness covers all" (B 4.642, 656).[7] In one way the imagery is thoroughly conventional, and even topical, since words like *vision*, *clarity*, and *light* had a particularly high charge at the time. Newton's *Opticks* (1704) had given sight and observation a new, almost religious legitimacy that lasted through midcentury; and even Berkeley wrote a treatise on vision in 1733. Locke placed the highest premium on sense impressions; and clarity had been a trope for knowledge in Descartes' proposition on clear and distinct ideas. This was all, by Pope's day, a familiar part of the general discourse on knowledge. But the particular reliance on the senses in Pope's characterization of error is also a traditional cornerstone of the discourse of skepticism. Given that reliance, darkness indeed means the end of knowledge.

Pope's admiration for Newton is expressed in a way that makes this clear. The famous couplet on Newton that first appeared as article 42 in *The Present State of the Republic of Letters* (1730), three years after Newton's death, reads: "All Nature and her laws lay hid in Night: / God said, *Let Newton be*: And all was Light!" But then there is everything that neither Newton nor anyone else can ever see. The telescope and microscope show us new worlds, but also hint at how many others must yet remain invisible. In *An Essay on Man* (1733–34), Pope mocks the overweening self-assurance of Newtonians much the way Swift had satirized the empiricism of the Royal Society in his projectors of Lagado. Pope reminds them of the invisible, and of the difference between physical and spiritual vision by speaking of Newton:

Could he, whose rules the rapid Comet bind,
Describe or fix one movement of his Mind?
Who saw its fires here rise, and there descend,
Explain his own beginning, or his end?[8]

The short note by Pope and Warburton to the line quoted above on night descending "To blot out Order, and extinguish Light" (B 4.14) indicates that a deeper malaise than pedantry or stupidity underlies Pope's complaints. The note reads: "Order here is to be understood extensively, both as Civil and Moral, the distinctions between high and low in society, and the true and false in Individuals." The issue is not particular instances of the breakdown of order, such as the mixing of high and low in society, but something more extensive. All order, civil and moral, is threatened by the "Darkness."

Pope comes closest to addressing skepticism directly in his attack on scholastic nominalism in book 4. The schoolmaster's phrase is, "Words are Man's province, Words we teach alone" (B 4.150); his attitude to students is to "keep them in the pale of Words till death" (B 4.160); "Give law to Words, or war with Words alone" (B 4.178); "'Tis true, on Words is still our whole debate" (B 4.219). Nominalism, in the philosophy of William of Ockham in the fourteenth century, was designed to set the limits of human knowledge much the way second-order skepticism does, in order to confirm the domain of faith in guaranteeing statements of God's existence. Its adherents attacked essences the way empiricists attacked innate ideas, discounting universal or general terms and claiming that there was nothing in the actual world corresponding to *Human Nature*. Nominalism and second-order skepticism come to the same conclusion on the epistemological priority of sense data and hence the limits of human knowledge. So in attacking nominalism Pope is indirectly attacking skepticism.

Since skepticism is allied to an empirical reliance on sight, it is no surprise that Pope's attack on nominalism is where he shifts to the attack on Newtonians and their skewed *vision*. The shift is from a mental error to one expressed as a failure of vision, and from the voice of the pedant to the voice of Pope. "'Tis true, on Words is still our whole debate," says Pope's pedant; and he goes on for thirteen lines in ironic self-praise, concluding:

For Attic Phrase in Plato let them seek,
I poach in Suidas for unlicens'd Greek.
In ancient Sense if any needs will deal,
Be sure I give them Fragments, not a Meal;

What Gellius or Stobraeus hash'd before,
Or chew'd by blind old Scholiasts o'er and o'er.

Then comes the change of pace:

The critic Eye, that microscope of Wit,
Sees hairs and pores, examines bit by bit:
How parts relate to parts, or they to whole,
The body's harmony, the beaming soul,
Are things which Kuster, Burman, Wasse shall see,
When Man's whole frame is obvious to a *Flea*.
(B 4.218–23, 33–38)

The Newtonian, like the nominalist, cannot see the forest for the fleas; and for Pope it is the forest that counts. He believes in it, and in our ability to *see* it, but the vision is of a universal rather than particular kind: the relation of parts to whole, harmony, and soul. Newtonians and nominalists, by contrast, are trapped like fleas in the particular, terminally minute philosophers who are unable to see the bigger picture, victims of their own reliance on sight. The question of vision then serves as a transition to the stage, where its poetic sense is even more conspicuous by its absence.

One might note in passing that the specular language in book 4 was originally intended to work in an illustrative, exemplary way linking together the argument of a follow-up poem to *An Essay on Man*. Sutherland quotes a letter to Swift, dated March 25, 1736, where Pope sets out the parts of this projected poem:

1. Of the extent and limits of human reason and science. 2. A view of the useful and able, arts. 3. Of the nature, ends, application, and use of different capacities. 4. Of the use of learning, of the science of the world, and of wit. It will conclude with a satire against the misapplications of all these, exemplified by pictures, characters, and examples.[9]

Misapplication through a reliance on pictures; the "limits of human reason"—the language is similar to the discourse on knowledge in Locke's *Essay*. Much of it finds its way into the 1743 *Dunciad*, and the ominous attitude to "pictures" and "characters" will become part of its attack on abuses of the stage. Pope of course held the Horatian view that art had to both instruct and delight and shared the utilitarian aesthetic that discriminated art from nonart on the basis of its good or bad effects. Priority of place was reserved for the instructive aspect, so obviously the question of knowledge was paramount. Poetry, or drama, that promoted right thinking and proper knowledge would naturally be delightful. This was the problem with the vulgar stage entertainments of his day: they were not art because they did not display the requisite erudition and learning; they offered delight without "sense." The particular complaints, including Pope's attack on Cibber and the Licensing Act, make it clear that Pope saw realism and knowledge as a union that was being travestied.

In book 2, for example, the Goddess tells her sons to learn "the Wond'rous pow'r of Noise"—to forget the true art of a Shakespeare or Jonson and instead "shake the soul, / With Thunder rumbling from the mustard bowl." Horns and trumpets "now to madness swell"; and She comments: "Such happy arts attention can command, / When fancy flags, and sense is at a stand" (B 2.222–230). Noise, audio or visual, means the lack of distinctions, the collapse of thought, sensory chaos, the triumph of nonsense over reason. Empty spectacle is characterized by "braying" and the senseless chatter of a "thousand tongues . . . heard in one loud din" as "[t]he Monkey-mimics rush discordant in." "Dissonance" means "captious Art" that has nothing to offer but "Snip-snap short, and Interruption smart" (B 4.234–40). And Pope has no trouble lining up these abuses as abuses of knowledge—more effects of its general breakdown. The second line to book 1 in the 1729 Variorum Edition contains the Smithfield muses, but the first contains Books and the Man: "Books and the Man I sing, the first who brings / The Smithfield Muses to the Ear of Kings." Ignorance here goeth before a fall; the failure of knowledge leads to the collapse, in theater, into the howling improbabilities and nonsense of Smithfield. Pope's own personal outrage at the sea of ignorance breaks out in the first note to the first line, where he jabs at the misinterpretation by critics of the "Man" in his opening: "Wonderful is the stupidity of all the former Criticks and Commentators on this Poem! It breaks forth at the very first line" (A 1.1 n).

When night descends, boundaries disappear—between high and low, true and false. The world can be upside down without knowing it. Like Swift, who describes in his 1710 "A Description of a City Shower" a torrent of turnip tops, dead cats, and sewage tumbling down the flood from Smithfield into the city, Pope sees the Bartholomew Fair drolls of writers like Elkanah Settle following a similar course in 1725. Settle, who had been City Poet of London and died in 1724, plays Anchises in the poem first to Theobald's and then to Cibber's Aeneas in the descent into the underworld in book 3. Settle was famous for his elaborate stage machinery and effects in Smithfield pieces like *The Siege of Troy*. He is mentioned several times, with a particular reference to his *St. George for England*, in which, Pope makes a point of telling us in a note, Settle "acted in his old age in a Dragon of green leather of his own invention" (A 3.181 n). In 1743 he is mentioned as an author "famous for unintelligible flights in his poems on public occasions, such as Shows, Birth-days, etc." (B 1.146 n). The key word for Pope is "unintelligible." Intent on making sense where it cannot be found on its own, Pope gives up on Settle.

Lewis Theobald is as guilty as Settle. Pope mocks the visual chaos of his farces, in which gorgons and dragons mix with fiends, giants, gods, and imps "till one wide Conflagration swallows all" (A 3.231–36). When there is no vision, but only a desire for sensual pleasure, the mind will fail to discriminate; what follows will be a torrent of turnip tops, and an open commerce between the lower, middle, and upper regions. This is what happens in Theobald's *Rape of Proserpine*. In one scene the heavens open to reveal Jupiter, then the earth opens and Pluto and Proserpine rise from hell. The event earns a special mention in the catalogue of Tibbald's sins: "Hell rises, Heav'n descends" (3.233). Pope's note to the line calls it a "monstrous absurdity." The play features other absurdities: there is an earthquake, a building falls, Mount Etna erupts, a giant rises, the earth opens, and Pluto's chariot rises.[10] The complaints echo those made in general in the century against the absurdities of romance. Pope makes conflagration, fire, and the fusion of what should forever remain separate, characteristic of both the stage and ignorance. The lines that open the list of gorgons and dragons refer to Faustus: "He look'd, and saw a sable Sorc'rer rise" (A 3.229). Pope's note, identifying the sorcerer as Dr. Faustus, states that there was a wave of new interest in Faustus in 1726 and 1727. Sutherland dates the "vogue" back to 1723 (A 3.229 n). Pope mentions that in Tibbald's play a cornfield is set on fire and that the two patent houses "rival'd each other in showing the Burnings of Hell-fire, in Dr. Faustus" (A 3.310 n). This does not seem to bother Pope on religious grounds. His reference to Dr. Faustus draws attention instead to the abuse of knowledge.[11] "He look'd, and saw a sable Sorc'rer rise, / Swift to whose hand a winged volume flies: / All sudden, Gorgons hiss, and Dragons glare, / And ten-horn'd fiends and Giants rush to war" (A 3.229–32). False knowledge, as Faust should have known, is no knowledge at all. Like the sleep of reason, it produces the unrealistic monsters of Tibbald's plays.

In the argument to book 3 in the 1743 edition, Pope makes his only explicit reference to a possible cause for the abuses he catalogues, linking them in a whimsical way to something like Hamlet's "fair thought." Even here the obsession is with knowledge. The Goddess of Dulness carries King Cibber to her temple "and there lays him to slumber with his head on her lap." The result is "raptures" that "the seat of Sense o'erflow" and "only heads refin'd from Reason know" (B 3.4–5). The word *know* is ironic since knowledge, like Reason and Sense, are voided in the sketch. The "visions" in question are those of Bedlam—irrational, perhaps exalted, but delusions. Cibber is conveyed down into the underworld by a mad, unwashed, "slip-shod Sibyl" with "tresses staring from Poetic dreams" (B 3.15–18). Warburton's note on the Sibyl is interesting: "Hence we find the religious (as well as the poetical) Enthusiasts of all ages [who] in their natural state [are] heavy and lumpish; but on the least application of *heat*, they run like lead, which of all metals falls quickest into fusion. Whereas *fire* in a Genius is truly Promethean, it hurts not its constituent parts but only fits them (like well-tempered steel) for the necessary impressions of art" (B 3.15 n).

In Warburton's critical and fiery analogy fusion is again the issue; at night all cats are black. Even the *divine afflatus* can mix things up when it blows through the leaden soul of a dunce. The true Promethean, by contrast, deals in steel not lead, and steel does not run. Fusion in the poem is a particularly telling trope for confusion when it comes to Colley Cibber and his promotion to Laureate. When Pope brought out the 1743 *Dunciad*, he added a mock proclamation to the already extensive footnotes and prefatory matter that had been in place since the revised Variorum Edition of 1729.[13] The proclamation crowns Cibber through a burlesque of the 1737 stage Licensing Act, which had placed the London stage under the censorship powers of the Lord Chamberlain.[13] "By virtue of the Authority in Us," the mock proclamation begins, "by the Act for subjecting Poets to the power of a Licenser, we have revised this piece." The author states that "the style and appellation of King" in the poem had previously been given to a "Pretender," namely Tibbald; "and apprehending the same may be deemed in some sort a reflection on Majesty, or at least an insult on that Legal Authority which has bestowed on another Person the Crown of Poesy," the said pretender is to "vanish" and be replaced by "the Laureate himself," namely Colley Cibber.

The proclamation carries a signature consisting of two back-to-back C's and "Ch." where the "Ch." is probably a reference to the Lord Chamberlain, the Duke of Grafton. Grafton's grandfather, Charles II, had a monogram of two interlocking C's, with the first reversed, that resembles the

signature; and since Grafton himself was a Charles, there is plenty of significance in the mirrored C's. But the proclamation can also be Cibber's: he
is banishing Tibbald the "Pretender" and replacing him as Laureate.[14] The
mirrored C's can be read as Cibber's monogram, which is not only logical
but appropriate as well: the Janus-faced Cibber, with one eye on the main
chance, represented by his government and its Lord Chamberlain, while
the other is looking back over his shoulder—quite properly since Pope is
behind him with a dagger. Pope might have left the two C's interlocked,
since that is how they appear in the original royal monogram. But to do so
would have been not only dangerous, it would have also proposed a kind of
legitimacy, genealogy, and even aesthetic quality quite foreign to both the
new Laureate and the act. Cibber, however, is for Pope something that
could only pass in the dark; he represents the collapse of distinction and
the disintegration of a legitimate line of great poets and kings, all of whom
have come to nought in an age of philistinism. The integrity of two properly interlocked royal C's is replaced with a game of mirrors and mimicry
better symbolized by the double-backed beast of Pope's double C's—C's
that, like so much more in the age, in Pope's view, are falling apart.

Cibber writes his own charter in this senseless proclamation, proclaim-
ing himself the new king through a performative speech act of indepen-
dence. The mock proclamation attempts to produce legitimacy by declaring
it and even succeeds in passing some of it on to the poem that follows—a
side effect Pope would not have objected to. At the same time, Pope turns
its author into a dupe who, like Shakespeare's Touchstone, is so completely
a nominalist that he fails to notice that his words, like his head, are empty:
a dunce whose crown will be a cap. Cibber is the living incarnation of the
mindlessness that has invaded theater.

Pope's criticisms of the stage remain in this secular, occasionally ad
hominem vein, and as such are closer to Jeremy Collier's reformism of
1698 than William Law's later apocalyptic abolitionism. Collier, we should
remember, wanted only "to distinguish the right use of a thing from its
abuse," which is what Pope wants to do. William Law, by contrast, in his
1726 *The Absolute Unlawfulness of the Stage-Entertainment Fully Demonstrated*, had insisted that abuses of the stage came about not "through
any accidental Abuse, as any innocent or good thing may be abused; but
that Corruption and Debauchery are the truly natural and genuine Effects
of the *Stage-Entertainment*."[15] Law's bias is purely antimimetic and his
religious fervor leads him toward the older biblical fear of iconicity and

doubleness; Pope's concern, by contrast, is on the epistemological and cognitive side of things—on whether a spectacle makes sense or not.

The Licensing Act served as one lightning rod for Pope's unhappiness with the stage. He refers to it directly in book 4:

> But held in tenfold bonds the Muses lie,
> Watched both by Envy's and by Flattery's eye:
> There to her heart sad Tragedy addrest
> The dagger wont to pierce the Tyrant's breast;
> But sober History restrained her rage,
> And promised Vengeance on a barbarous age.
> There sunk Thalia, nerveless, cold, and dead,
> Had not her Sister Satire held her head:
> Nor couldst thou, Chesterfield! a tear refuse,
> Thou wepst, and with thee wept each gentle Muse.
> (B 4.35–44)

The image of "sad Tragedy" turning the dagger meant for tyrants to its own breast is moving, but its effect is largely academic since "sad Tragedy" could not really be counted as one of the victims of the Licensing Act. Perhaps Pope is not thinking so much of Attic tragedy as the revivals of Shakespeare, of Dryden's heroic tragedies, Addison's *Cato*, or even domestic tragedies like Lillo's *The London Merchant*. In a plea for drama, however, dramatic language, including the "promised vengeance," can hardly be out of place. A more likely reason for the disappearance of "sad Tragedy" has to do with the nature of tragic drama itself. Classical tragedy always turns on the commission of some fateful error—*hamartia*, as Aristotle named it. In a skeptical age where the boundaries between truth and falsity have become, to say the least, shifty, tragedy can hardly be expected to flourish.[16]

Pope and Fielding held similar views on the connection of error in the period to abuses of the stage. Comedy, Pope tells us, would be dead, if it were not for satire. The image of satire holding her sister's head is appropriate since the Licensing Act all but paralyzed the body of comedy in London theater. Pope's admiration for Fielding was well known and comes out in these lines of support. His 1729 *Dunciad* found echoes in Fielding's *The Author's Farce* (1730), and in return Fielding's piece gave Pope the structure for his *New Dunciad*.[17] Ironically, Fielding was almost single-handedly responsible for provoking Walpole into bringing down the act that Pope protests. Perhaps for this reason, Fielding's own diagnosis of the problem is more local and topical than Pope's. For Fielding a wave of corruption had been sweeping politics and drama down the same muddy stream for some time, and the stream had its fountainhead in St. James. In Fielding's rehearsal play, *The Historical Register for the Year 1736,* Sourwit asks Medley, the author, "[H]ow is your political connected with your theatrical?" Medley replies: "When politics come to a farce, they very naturally lead one to the play-house. There too, there are politicians— there is lying, flattering, dissembling, promising, deceiving, and undermining, as well as in any court in Christendom."[18] Fielding sees a connection: he presents a list of grievances—lying, flattering, dissembling, promising, deceiving, and undermining—all abuses of knowledge that he sees as corrupting national life, but which originate in Westminster; from there, they "lead one to the play-house" where politicians and the politics of deceit replace proper dramatists and proper drama with more lies. Fielding, in other words, is not far from Pope in seeing a connection between a failure of knowledge and abuses of the stage. Pope is alone, however, in wondering whether the malaise is not a far darker curtain of uncertainty and relativism that is falling on the nation as a whole.

It had been falling for a while—certainly long before the 1737 Licensing Act came along—so Pope was not wrong about it. By 1743, for example, the London stage had been barren of new writing for over two generations; play calendars at the two patent houses for the 1742–43 season show only one new play, Fielding's comedy, *The Wedding Day.* The season before had been marked by the debut of Garrick at the Aycliffe Street Theater and a total of 649 performances spread fairly evenly among Drury Lane, Covent Garden, and Goodman's Fields, the last having succeeded in the 1740–41 season in reintroducing plays by squeezing them in between the two parts of concerts so that no one was officially paying to see a play. But of the 649 recorded performances only about half were plays. At Covent Garden, for example, there were 172 performances in the 1741–42 season, but only 68 were plays and these included afterpieces—about half of which were pantomimes. There were hornpipes and minuets, dancing and singing between the acts, masques, acrobatics, and puppetry; there were plenty of revivals, and Italian opera at the King's Theater; but there were no new plays.[19] The sort of stage nonsense Pope complains about was popular before the Licensing Act made it, as it were, the only show in town. An article in the *London Journal* of April 3, 1725, reports an "Attack on degenerate entertainments"; Italian opera in London went back to 1720;

and the riots by footmen at Drury Lane that preceded the act in February and March 1737 had been going on regularly since 1721. They became so serious in the spring of 1737 that soldiers had to be stationed at the theaters. In several instances the unruly footmen had the Riot Act read to them and were carried off to Newgate.[20] The Licensing Act, along with Walpole's generally corrupt and philistine reign, certainly had much to do with the kind of abuses Pope and Fielding complain about, but only Pope seems to have perceived the deeper epistemological crisis of the century.

Because the *Dunciad* is a mock epic it is tempting to see Pope's epic complaints about the failure of knowledge as hyperbole. The ending in particular is an epic indictment of a world where "all is Night" and "Truth" has "fled, / Mountains of Casuistry heap'd o'er her head!"—where "Philosophy . . . is no more"; where "Religion" and "Morality" are expiring; where "CHAOS! is restored"; and where, at the end of the last act, the only one left standing will be the "great Anarch" (B 4. 640–56). The complaints may seem overwrought and even bathetic, or merely rhetorical, but the issue they addressed was real—as Berkeley and many others knew. Pope, in connecting the failure of knowledge to abuses of the stage, makes it clear that he sees knowledge and art as a proper pair—mimetic art in particular (art that *makes* sense) is not, for Pope, a symptom of the encroaching darkness. To the contrary, he characterizes it as a form of enlightenment. The *Dunciad* was certainly not intended as a manifesto for the novel, but the connection here between knowledge and realism could well serve as one.

* * *

Richardson shared Pope's view on the connection, and he both expanded and fictionalized it. The relationship of mimetic art to knowledge was clearly a more pressing concern for Richardson, for a variety of reasons— both religious and secular—where the main one is obviously that he himself was a novelist. For many, the new form of fiction was still a suspect quantity, looked on by its critics as something low, something along the lines of the Smithfield entertainments, a morally dubious affair that had set up camp somewhere between history and romance. In writing fiction that aimed at verisimilitude Richardson was in a sense obliged to represent that suspicion, and he does so by making his Machiavellian artificers blatantly available for the kind of antitheatricalist attacks familiar since Collier. But then, as a practitioner of make-believe himself, he must also in some way defend his own art—a conflict of interests that Pope did not have to deal with.

Another difference lies in Richardson's deeper religious objections to artifice. Defoe had an inward, Puritan understanding of fable—of the essential relationship of God's plot to Man's stories, as Leopold Damrosch puts it; in Richardson's Anglican mind this palimpsest relationship is hopelessly corrupt. Where Defoe always has Providence shadowing the fable so that we are constantly in front of the question of the relationship of the protagonist's quest, whatever it may be, to some form of higher progress, in Richardson this intersection of low and high is fraught with danger. One might say that for Richardson this relationship, or its fraught existence, constituted his principal anxiety—the anguish of not knowing whose stories are indeed benign, whose are not, and which will triumph.

This particular articulation of truth and deceit had a social as well as private importance for Richardson. He shared Pope's critical attitude toward the social, intellectual darkness of bad theater, for example. Like Pope, he strove to fit art into the hard Socratic analogies linking knowledge to virtue and error to vice—art should edify, instruct, and improve, and so on. But while Pope is close to Jeremy Collier in his stage antipathies, Richardson expresses a deeper anxiety over mimetic art, even as he practices it, and undoubtedly because he practices it. The discourse of antitheatricalism with regard to the stage in Richardson's work is thus sharper, louder, and more insistent than it is in Pope.[21]

Mimesis itself, which seems historically to be the offending element for antitheatricalists,[22] was nonetheless part of Richardson's aesthetics from the beginning. His literary impulses were always mimetic in nature, beginning with the imagined situations of what became his *Familiar Letters* and including *Pamela*, which he worked up from a real incident recounted to him by an acquaintance. Even *The Apprentice's Vade Mecum* (1733), which contains his most straightforward attack on theater, is a mimetic formalization, in its second part, of an actual letter he wrote to his nephew, Thomas Verren. His comments in the *Vade Mecum* on abuses of the stage are even more acerbic than Pope's in the *Dunciad*, and, as in Pope, they hinge on the failure of knowledge. Note the familiar recourse to the language of error—just as it appears in Fielding and Pope—in Richardson's scathing (and antimimetic) description of pantomimes as "horrid . . . wicked . . . the infamous Harlequin Mimicry, introduc'd for nothing but to teach how to cozen, cheat, deceive and cuckold."[23] Jonas Barish comments on the contradiction of a writer of mimetic fiction voicing an antimimetic bias by suggesting that the bias is "a prejudice deep enough to blind its exponent to the simplest illogicalities in his own dialectic."[24] In this,

Richardson joins a distinguished company of the blind, including Plato, who expressed a strident antitheatricalism using the dramatic form of the Socratic dialogues, and William Law, whose own antitheatricalism in *The Absolute Unlawfulness of the Stage-Entertainment Fully Demonstrated* (1726) depended on a similar use of imaginary characters engaged in dialogue. Richardson's outrage is directed at pantomimes—at the same kind of stage buffoonery and nonsense Pope and Fielding fulminated about—and his objections often have the stridency of Law's evangelicalism; nonetheless, he does not reject theater wholesale as Law did. There is such a thing as proper theater, which he refers to tellingly as a "rational amusement."[25]

The different political and cultural affiliations Pope and Richardson had also determined their attitudes here. Pope, as we know, was a fierce critic of the Walpole government, while Richardson supported it and published its paper, the *Daily Gazeteer*. And this may partly, at least, explain how the two found themselves on opposite sides in the debate over the Licensing Act.[26] Pope, despite his criticisms of the stage, opposed the act, whereas Richardson supported it, which seems odd on Richardson's part since the act effectively stopped real theater and made the sort of jugglery and trumpery he detested the only thing available. Perhaps his support for the act was cynical and political; but there were other issues involved, not the least of which was Richardson's deep religious feeling. His comments on theater often ring with the religious stridency of his friend, William Law. But to understand more fully Richardson's colliding and conflicting attitudes on theater one must distinguish his purely antimimetic bias from his material concerns with playhouses as a threat to the good business of the nation.

Before Walpole finally took action and brought in the stage Licensing Act in 1737, Parliament had been making noises for several years about regulating playhouses. When Thomas Odell opened Goodman's Fields in 1729, the first reaction of neighborhood merchants in the woolen and silk trades was that the theater would be an irresistible temptation to their apprentices.[27] At first Richardson's objections took the same practical form, and the major portion of his statement in the 1733 *Vade Mecum* centers on practical, business considerations. He opposed the proliferation of theaters, in other words, on material rather than moral grounds: the problem with a playhouse was not so much what went on inside as what went on outside. It was not that apprentices would be corrupted by the plays; rather they would be out late, and this would affect their work.

The woolen and silk merchants in Goodman's Fields also seemed to have a legitimate complaint, and one that had Richardson's sympathy. When Odell's theater opened, for example, bathhouses soon opened nearby; grape clusters appeared over doorways; makers of woolen drawers gave way to the drawers of ale and to the even more alluring whisper of silks. This was clearly more deleterious to the work ethic than time spent with Hamlet, Cato, or Jane Shore. Masters took fright at the prospect of their apprentices—young, impressionable, and easily tempted by a jar— coming home not only late but also inebriated, broke, and possibly with company. They made their case directly before the king and succeeded in procuring a signed order banning performances. George II had nothing to lose by signing such an order, since it was legally nonbinding; and Odell ignored it.

In 1732 John Rich took his patents from Lincoln's Inn Fields to Covent Garden, increasing the number of playhouses to four, and agitation against the spread of theaters increased. Richardson, who lived between the dis- reputable artists' quarters of Whitefriars and Blackfriars, seems to have felt the threat personally and published his *Vade Mecum* pamphlet. The threat to the public weal involved in exposing apprentices to the temptations of the theater was undoubtedly felt as a serious one by many merchants; but still deeper motives were present. When Henry Giffard bought Goodman's Fields from Odell he promptly set about raising subscriptions for yet an- other theater to be opened in St. Martin's Le Grand. The proverbial storm of protest went up, and a stream of merchants paraded their complaints past the chamberlain. Giffard countered by presenting the list of subscrib- ers who had already pledged financial backing for the new theater. To the chamberlain's consternation it was made up predominantly of merchants, shopkeepers, silk-men, weavers, packers, dyers, factors, tradesmen, and even local inhabitants—none of whom seemed to sense the same threat Richard- son did to the good business of the nation. One possible explanation may be that the first thing that happened in a neighborhood when a theater opened was that rents went up. This would benefit those who owned dwellings and places of business there, and a large number of these owners might be expected to support the construction of a theater out of purely material considerations. Many did so. Apprentices, after all, if they were bent on carousing and drinking, never had far to go, wherever they lived; and going to the theater might even be an improvement. Apprentices in fact frequented the theaters just as Richardson had predicted they would —and without doing any apparent damage to the national economy.

Richardson himself was not an owner, but rented his house in Salisbury Court, and as his business expanded—which it did in spite of the proximity of Whitefriars—he rented two more nearby. Like anyone else who rented, he knew that any increase in property values would cost him money.

These were probably all factors in determining someone like Richardson's support for regulation of the playhouses. But regulating the number of playhouses was ultimately not the Licensing Act's purpose. It was specifically designed to blunt the political farces and satire of antigovernment polemicists in the theater, where Fielding was the principal transgressor. Richardson's support of the bill cannot be explained away as the altruistic and patriotic desire to maintain a fit workforce of apprentices, or even as the desire to hold down rents, since neither of these was the final bill's central purpose. His support might be partially justified by the wish to stay in favor with the Walpole clique, as a matter of political expediency, or as a blow against Fielding; but the language of his *Vade Mecum* indicates that his objections had a lot to do with the dangers of collapsing boundaries, discursive as well as social—the "great Anarch" that Pope dramatized. And in this fear he was not alone. A comment in the *Grub Street Journal* of December 2, 1732, emphasizes the class concern: the writer states that "(as all fools are fond of imitation)" apprentices go to the theater dressed as gentlemen; and adds: "but you might still discover the Apprentice, like the ass under the lion's skin."

In the *Vade Mecum* Richardson nonetheless states that he will not, "like some narrow Minds, argue against the Use of any thing, because of the Abuse of it. . . . Under proper Regulations, the Stage may be made subservient to excellent Purposes, and be an useful Second to the Pulpit itself."[28] The attitude here is closer to Collier's in his *Short View* than it is to Law: "If there must be Strumpets, let Bridewell be the Scene. Let them come not to Prate, but to be Punish'd."[29] This is indeed Collier, but it could well be Richardson. There are good reasons why his young readers should avoid playhouses; Richardson is anxious about maintaining the distinctions between high and low. Plays "are calculated for Persons in upper Life." Their "good Instructions," if they have any, "lie much above the common Case and Observation of the Class of Persons to which I am addressing myself." Time, says Richardson, is money; apropos of which he next mentions "lewd Women," and then the fact that plays too often mock the "Man of Business," before getting to the passage on the "horrid Pantomime and wicked Dumb Shew" that cheats and deceives.

Like Pope, Richardson bemoans the domination of the stage by mere entertainments. "There was a Time when publick Spectacles and Shews, Drolls, and Farces (and most of our present Theatrical performances are no better) were exhibited once a Year to very good Purpose. Every Trading Town or populous City had its annual Fair"; apropos of which Richardson mentions that at such fairs "vast Quantities of all Sorts of Manufactures were disposed of." But he quickly returns to his concern with high and low. In previous times "well-regulated Families" did not attend the theater; "But now we are grown much more polite, forsooth; our Young men aspire to the Taste of their Betters." This taste meant going at six in the evening to a play, which might be a reasonable hour for those who finished their daily business around five; but it could hardly do for apprentices who, Richardson writes, ought to work until eight or nine at night.

Only one play escapes Richardson's censure: "I mean, the Play of *George Barnwell,* which has met with the Success that I think it well deserves." The play is to be commended for making itself "useful." It has done so by exposing the "dreadful Example of the Artifices of a lewd Woman." Everything else on the contemporary stage is dross: actors and actresses are "an infamous Troop of wretched Strollers, who by our very laws are deemed Vagabonds, and a collected String of abandon'd Harlots." The principal crime of which they are guilty is "teaching [the lower orders] to despise the Station of Life, to which, or worse, they are inevitably destined." This is a dark view of the stage, and an odd lament for a rigid hierarchical social structure that was crumbling even as Richardson wrote. Indeed, *Pamela* champions and celebrates its disintegration in its story of a lowborn girl's ability to rise, on her own merits, to a higher station in life. One is prompted again to ask how Richardson could condemn with such vehemence the very sort of social mobility that not only Pamela but he himself, along with the rest of his class, sought as well. In any case, antitheatricalism in Richardson's early pamphlet is loud and clear, and mimetic art ("Harlequin Mimicry") comes off looking fallen and corrupt. What is interesting is that the attack on deceit, cozenage, and lies in the theater states the problem again as Pope had—as an abuse and failure of knowledge. In both Pope and Richardson, fusion and failing boundaries represent an epistemological scare as much as a social one. Pope's concerns (and Berkeley's) are thus still very much present in Richardson.

When it came to his own work Richardson took a more nuanced view of mimesis. The novel was not "Harlequin Mimicry." He writes: "Religion never was at so low an Ebb as at present: And if my Work must be supposed of the Novel kind, I was willing to try if a Religious Novel would do good."[30] The begrudging acceptance of what sounds like a necessary indignity sits alongside the quiet assertion that mimetic realism can have a direct relationship to ethics. Johnson still provides us with the best example of how difficult it was to wear both hats. Johnson praises mimesis as he sees it in Shakespeare: "This therefore is the praise of Shakespeare, that his drama is the mirror of life." Shakespeare is great because he "holds up to his readers a faithful mirror of manners and of life." But then this also turns out to be his greatest fault. The presentation of mixed characters in whom good and evil appear, while true to nature, is the Bard's "first defect"; and Johnson begins with it, after prefacing his criticism with the comment that Shakespeare's faults "obscure and overwhelm any other merit." Shakespeare draws his characters after nature, and yet in so doing he "sacrifices virtue to convenience," instruction to pleasure, and "seems to write without any moral purpose."[31] In the famous *Rambler* 4 essay, "On Fiction," in which Johnson mocks romance for its unreality, he begins by granting to mimesis Shakespeare's merits and then takes them away with a similar, perfunctory gesture.[32] Modern "works of fiction," Johnson argues, "exhibit life in its true state" and are born of an "accurate observation of the living world." And yet it turns out that the *is* must be sacrificed to the *ought*. For if fiction is mimetic, Johnson argues, "I cannot see of what use it can be to read the account; or why it may not be as safe to turn the eye immediately upon mankind, as upon a mirror which shows all that presents itself without discrimination." Good art produces good effects by reaffirming the analogies of truth and virtue, error and vice. And vice, Johnson tells us, "begins in mistake."[33]

As Johnson's attitude shows, a novel not only specializes in points of view, it also elicits different "ways of looking" in a single reader. The notion that this sort of Bakhtinian polyphony promotes relativism overlooks the fact that such points of view are always structured, prioritized, and valued in novels. The multivalence of the novel thus makes it an unlikely suspect, on this ground alone, to be charged with relativism. Its ambivalence is better described as the ambivalence of the *pharmakon*, the Greek word meaning both remedy and poison that is used by Plato to describe writing and knowledge.[34] The dialectical quality of the relationship is denied in antitheatricalist attacks on the novel, which must codify terms and isolate them. But the *pharmakon* is not two; and a writer like Richardson is obliged by his choice of the novel form to take the poison for the sake of the remedy. In Lincolnshire, Pamela is up in her closet, not reading the Bible but furiously writing letters. Her narrative is a product of her isolation; and her isolation is a product of her writing. The time she spends on writing is almost in itself a guarantee of her remaining in captivity. And yet it is her letters, and only her letters, that keep her, like Clarissa, in touch with the outside world. This is the ambivalence of the *pharmakon*.

Mimetic fiction exerts an ethical force because it creates a simulacrum of reality in which, among other effects, we can watch characters interact, where intimacy reigns between them as much as between reader and narrator, so that learning takes place. The reason opponents of the novel thought it was dangerous for a woman in her closet to be reading one instead of the Bible was not because novels instilled vicious attitudes instead of pious ones, it was because women learned from these novels about types of interaction that did not necessarily feature submission to biblical and patriarchal authority. "'AUTHORITY,'" says Anna Howe in *Clarissa*, "what a full word is that in the mouth of a narrow- minded person, who happened to be born thirty years before one!"[35] The association of women with novel reading in the century marks Woman as one of the *pharmakon* siblings. Her role is often that of the *pharmakos*, or scapegoat—female *scribblers* were the main producers and consumers of novels. Like Eve, the scapegoat form of knowledge must be expelled, just as the "yelping bitch" of poetry was expelled from Plato's Republic. But throwing out the pharmacy means throwing out the remedy. The bivalence of the *pharmakon* remains not only an ineluctable quality of writing and knowledge, as Plato has it, but of Woman in her close association with them as well.[36] What this equates to for the skepticism/novel dialectic is the necessity, in the novel, of re-presenting antimimetic attitudes to the novel that see it as a kind of poison, while at the same time promoting the discourse of the novel itself as a valid, remedial form of knowing.

This sort of dialectic of knowledge and art is at the heart of the contests in both *Pamela* and *Clarissa*—contests fought over the possession of knowledge and truth. Mr B and Lovelace make their arguments and their claims: this is the situation, this is how you must act, and so on; but Richardson makes it clear from the beginning what we are to think of them: they are wrong. Their stories are corrupt, not part of God's plot, and the artifice they employ is fallen. They represent one part of the old Socratic analogies: vice and error go together, set off against their female counterparts who stand for virtue and truth. These are the simple lines of Richardson's moral fiction making; and his readers recognized them immediately. The male villains are chameleonesque, designers, artificers in the worst sense, plotters, mimics, protonovelists; while the female heroines are singular pillars of rectitude. Richardson thus fulfills his readers' expectations that this indeed is what the moral universe looks like; he re-presents, in other words, conventional attitudes to artifice and knowledge that existed at the time. The theatricalism of Mr B and Lovelace is reprehensible and wrong-headed.

This failure of knowledge in both men is characterized in language familiar as part of the discourse on knowledge in the century. Both are men of experience; their knowledge derives from without, not within, from the world of touch and taste and smell, the world of experience, while the knowledge of the heroines has no visible source and looks innate. Lovelace and Mr B know what they see and try to guess at the rest, but they turn out to be mistaken. Pamela and Clarissa have little experience, in an empirical sense, and are constantly fooled by the villains when they rely on it, but when they do not, when they trust their innate vision, they see more deeply into things than their persecutors. Richardson was hardly sitting down with the intention of saying that knowledge derived from experience was fallacious, while that of his heroines had an innate quality that was not, and yet this is what it comes to. Pamela and Clarissa ultimately distrust knowledge gained from sense experience.[37] Like Kant, they seem to know, to have always known somewhere that while all knowledge may begin with experience, it does not all arise from experience. Knowledge, like education, does not all come from contact with the world, and this is what Mr B and Lovelace are limited to. Clarissa writes Anna Howe that Lovelace is not "so polite as his education, and other advantages, might have made one expect him to be," and that he "has always had too much of his own will to study to accommodate himself to that of others" (3.46). Pamela writes that Mr B's "poor dear Mother spoil'd him," and that "he has not been us'd to be controul'd, and cannot bear the least Thing that crosses his violent Will" (210). The implication is that faulty early education has a lot to do with the subsequent depth blindness and trompe l'oeil approach to life taken by both villains. All they know is what they have learned from their own experience of the outside world. Their story making is destined to be earthbound and in the final analysis benighted.

Richardson, responding to the implication in the query of his Dutch correspondent, Johannes Stinstra, as to where he "acquired such accurate acquaintance of nature, the inborn qualities and manners of mankind," denied that his fiction came from copying what he saw, or from his own personal experience.[38] In the letter in which Richardson writes to Anne Donnellan about Fielding's having "little or no invention," he criticizes

Fielding for dogmatic factualism. He goes caustically through a series of Fielding's characters, from Parson Adams and Tom Jones to Lady Bellaston, Sophia, Booth, and Amelia, identifying them all with their models in real life—often enough Fielding himself and his wife.[39] Visual evidence is unreliable, and a poor source for a writer with a moral purpose. Richardson may not have formulated the position to himself like this, but the failure of knowledge in both his novels is allied to an empiricist epistemology, while the heroines' lack of experience is more than made up for by their inner light.[40]

Mr B and Lovelace are master artificers, but they are working in the dark, while the knowledge they seek is associated with the female body and female writing. The synecdochical alliance of knowledge and female writing in *Pamela* and *Clarissa* is one that Mr B and Lovelace sense but cannot understand. Richardson makes them, along with the Harlowes in *Clarissa*, look like fools when they take one for the other, treating knowledge itself as a commodity, looking for it in the letters, clothes, and closets of the heroines. For Mr B and Lovelace, female writing is both a poison and remedy; even though what the women write will hurt, they lack it, need it, and must have it. Truth is the agon, the consummation they strain to achieve and draw strength from. Mr B, for example, struggles with Pamela for possession of a true account of her character. He wants to convince her that she is not herself when she puts on her homespun clothes, that she is in disguise, a mimic and hypocrite (*Pamela* 61, 62). Pamela answers that he is wrong: "I am Pamela, indeed I am . . . her own self" (61); and that the disguise has really been her previous apparel that placed her above her station. Mr B continues to argue that her "pretended Simplicity and Innocence" is "romantick Invention" (90); that she is a "Mistress of Arts" (160) full of "Tricks and Artifices" (162); and an "artful Creature, . . . [and] speaking Picture" who harbours "perfidious Designs" (145). Readers, however, by this point know the true account of her character, and who holds the "perfidious Designs."

Clarissa is likewise the repository of all that is true. Like Mr B with Pamela, Lovelace does his best to convince Clarissa that she is someone she is not—a woman who will consent to cohabitation. Like Mr B with his charade of the sham marriage, the fake trip to Stamford, and his bedroom disguises, Lovelace has his fire stratagem, his dramatic Hampstead scenario, and his litany of false representations. He is, as Clarissa calls him, a man of obliquity who "delight[s] in crooked ways" (3.293). Mr B was mistaken about Pamela; Lovelace is even more mistaken about Clarissa, and the rape is his final error. He has been so successful in directing his actors and dressing his stage, and is so successful himself as a part of that same scenography—literally a self-composed man in his letters to Belford— that it takes him some time to understand that the rape has been an error worthy of Othello.

The attitude toward artifice in these two novels, in other words, is condemnation on one hand and legitimation on the other. Novel writing is a form of artifice, and Mr B and Lovelace are both heavily invested in artifice. The fact that they are also sadly benighted makes the expected connection, linking artifice to a failure of knowledge. This would satisfy conventional expectations that vice and error go together. But then, it is the women who are the writers in these novels, not the men. Richardson goes even further: Pamela and Clarissa are not only sites of knowledge, they themselves are artificers too. As many readers quickly notice, Pamela can, when necessary, be just as artful and cunning as Mr B. She is no sooner set down at the sister of Mrs. Jewkes, en route to her Lincolnshire captivity, for example, than she begins to employ her own arts to effect her escape. Her "stratagem" (101) to work on her persecutors individually is a good one, and it only fails because Mr B has been so careful in his arrangements. Once at the Lincolnshire estate, Pamela has hopes of "working upon [Mrs. Jewkes] by degrees" to secure her escape (104); she lays a "trap" to get at the old harridan's "Instructions, which she carries in the Bosom of her Stays" (130); and refers to her plan to throw off her pursuers in her planned flight over the garden wall by leaving some of her garments floating on the pond as a "Piece of Cunning" (149). Pamela's arts are to be distinguished from Mr B's. "Alas!" she writes to her father, "your poor Daughter will make an Intriguer by-and-by; but I hope an innocent one!" Neither she nor her creator could have predicted that many would believe she was not. When Mr B refers to Pamela's writings he says: "Nothing . . . pleases me better, than that, in all your Arts, Shifts and Stratagems, you have had a great Regard to Truth; and have, in all your little Pieces of Deceit, told very few wilful Fibs" (202). Could this not stand as Richardson's view of his own practice? Deception, after all, is what fiction is. And yet it seems necessary. Nothing could be more justified and necessary, for example, than the sunflower ruse ("O what Inventions will Necessity be the Parent of!"), and Pamela says that although the intention was "to deceive" Mrs. Jewkes, "my Deceit intended no Hurt to any body" (113).[41] Did astute readers notice that this kind of claim could well stand for fiction writing itself?

Mr B of course tries to contradict Pamela. Even after she is free, he forces her to do a walk-through of the scene of her attempted escape in the garden while he reads her account of it (208); and when Pamela's reversal of fortune takes place, the Darnfords pay a visit and Lady Darnford asks in advance that Pamela appear in the charming country attire she has had described to her. At this point Richardson's readers would have firmly planted in their minds the fact that Mr B himself is the sham, not Pamela. Given that, they could only be alarmed by the notion presented here that the theatricalization of her virtue in itself seems to carry no essential moral danger or sin—quite a statement on theater coming from the author of the *Vade Mecum*. Mr B has Pamela appear from an alcove and approach her spectators along a gravel walk. "Look there, Ladies, comes my charming Rustick!" he effuses (242). Lady Davers in her own vicious visit to a legitimized Pamela tells her she is a fake bride. "Pr'ythee, Child, walk before me to that Glass, survey thyself, and come back to me, that I may see how finely thou canst act the Theatrical Part given thee" (322). At the very least, readers must have been left with the impression that artifice in itself was not linked in any fundamental way to either vice or virtue.

Clarissa, for her part, is relatively artless. Richardson seems determined here to avoid again meriting the criticism that his heroine was a creature of guile. Nonetheless, Clarissa has her own stratagems—attempting to occupy Dorcas with Lovelace while she slips out of the house (5.331), for example; and eventually escaping by exchanging clothes with Mabel (6.90–95). Lovelace refers to her "art" and "cunning villainy" (5.331). But Clarissa is an even more benign artificer than Pamela. Lovelace, when he is not in an uproar, admits: "She is a poor plotter (for plotting is not her talent)" (6.197). Her duplicitous note, when she is in her last stage, informing him that she is "setting out with all diligence for my father's house," and that he "may possibly in time" see her there (7.175–76), gives her some concern. She attempts to mitigate the "stratagem" to Belford, even though its object—keeping Lovelace from her—is completely laudable. She wonders to Belford how she "could be guilty of such an artifice" and tells him she knows it was not right. She makes excuses, saying it was done without thinking and was "an innocent artifice" (7.251). The relationship of Man's stories to God's plot is for Richardson, at best, a dark conceit. Artifice itself appears to carry no essential ethics in either novel; it is available for good as much as for evil. This, Richardson seems to be saying, is the burden and darkness of the age.

In sum, both of the Richardson novels contain their own discourse on the novel, one that bestows a surprising degree of legitimacy on the mimetic art—not by implication, as in Pope, but directly. Pope links a failure of knowledge (universal darkness) to a failure of realism on the stage. Richardson states the positive side of the case by tying up artifice with knowledge and virtue in his heroines. There is indeed bad art—the deceptions, vice, and mistakes of the male villains go together; but there is also good art—the writing and innocent stratagems of the heroines. Readers must have wondered whether Richardson was suggesting that there was really no difference in kind between the two—between the stratagems of Lovelace and those of Clarissa, or between those of Mr B and of Pamela. Indeed, they differ not in kind, but in the purposes to which they are put, and this, even in 1740, even coming from a novelist, is a bold claim to make for a secular and worldly form of artifice. De la Rochefoucauld would have understood, and it is again worth quoting him, this time with Richardson's attitude to artifice in mind: "The shrewdest always pretend to hate it, only in order to use it."[42]

Sterne and Laclos

Atropos or Dissemination

Pope and Richardson both tell us in their own ways that the relationship of knowledge to mimesis is indeed as Aristotle first claimed, a mutually enabling and conducive one. Richardson's antitheatricalism and religious scruples prevented him from making any outright claim for the epistemological nature of his own imitative art, but behind the criticism of artifice he attaches to his male villains is a quiet statement that artifice itself, and make-believe in particular, has its uses. I want to move now to two writers who hold differing opinions on this issue: Choderlos de Laclos follows Richardson and Pope in being a strong believer in the positive epistemological valence of literary realism, while Laurence Sterne gives us our first look at the dissenting view. Sterne's *Tristram Shandy* (1759–67) and *A Sentimental Journey through France and Italy* (1768) participate in the discourse on knowledge and the novel in the century but Sterne is skeptical of both, especially of the notion that the two are mutually enabling. Instead, he proposes sentiment, and this allows us to examine the claim I made in the opening chapter about the language of sensibility in the eighteenth century being part of—one of the languages, if you will—of skepticism. Laclos's *Les Liaisons Dangereuses* [*Dangerous Liaisons*] (1782), by contrast, stresses as Richardson and Rochefoucauld had the epistemological potency of artifice, while dismissing sentiment out of hand as cognitively bankrupt. Laclos goes further, insisting in a way that prefigures Sade, that sentiment is not only cognitively but sexually bankrupt as well, while artifice is potent in both regards.

Sterne's fiction participates even more intensely in the discourse on knowledge in the century than Richardson's: *Tristram Shandy* is all about Locke, and all about knowledge—about how knowledge is constructed, what and who it serves, how it circulates, and how it is expressed. Sterne, following Locke, is more skeptical than Richardson about its possibility, a fact that comes out immediately in *Tristram*'s reference to part of Locke's *Essay* having to do with the collapse of coherence: this is the chapter on the association of ideas, discussed by Locke not as a source of knowledge but as a source of error. "[T]here is another connexion of ideas wholly owing to *chance* or *custom*. Ideas that in themselves are not all of kin, come to be so united in some men's minds, that it is very hard to separate them; they always keep in company, and the one no sooner at any time comes into the understanding, but its associate appears with it; and if they are more than two which are thus united, the whole gang, always inseparable, show themselves together" (1.529).

Uncle Toby personifies this collapse of signification, for whom the bridge of a nose, bed-curtains, and cuckoldom will always signify military bridges and the curtins and horn-works of military fortifications. "Talk of what we will, brother," says Walter Shandy, "—or let the occasion be never so foreign or unfit for the subject,—you are sure to bring it in."[1] In Toby's mind, everything is associated with the famous Battle of Namur, where he received his grievous wound.

And there is the business of Tristram's dispersed "animal spirits," who continues in the passage just cited:

This strong combination of ideas, not allied by nature, the mind makes in itself either voluntarily or by chance; and hence it comes in different men to be very different, according to their different inclinations, education, interest, etc. *Custom* settles habits of thinking in the understanding, as well as of determining in the will, and of motions in the body: all which seems to be but trains of motions in the animal spirits, which once set a going, continue in the same steps they have been used to; which, by often treading, are worn into a smooth path, and the motion in it becomes easy, and as it were natural. (1. 529)

If these "animal spirits" are not "set a going" in a child properly to begin with, his constitution will be damaged. Borrowing Locke's terminology to begin his book and describe the irregularity of his conception, Tristram writes: "Believe me, good folks, this is not so inconsiderable a thing as many of you may think it;—you have all, I dare say, heard of the animal spirits" (1.1.1). And it is these "animal spirits" that are dispersed during his conception by his mother's interruption of Walter Shandy during the performance of his conjugal duties to ask if he has wound the clock, since these two activities always take place on the same night. Taking up Locke's comment on the "combination of ideas, not allied in nature," Tristram describes the problem as "an unhappy association of ideas which have no connection in nature . . . my poor mother could never hear the said clock wound up,—but the thoughts of some other things unavoidably popp'd into her head,—& *vice versa:*—which strange combination of ideas, the sagacious *Locke,* who certainly understood the nature of these things better than most men, affirms to have produced more wry actions than all other sources of prejudice whatsoever" (1.4.7).

Locke's epistemology is ubiquitous in the book; as Ernest Tuveson writes, Sterne "gives concrete reality to what Locke discussed."[2] John Traugott, who first worked on the Locke connection in his 1954 *Tristram Shandy's World,* makes the link to skepticism when he notes that Sterne's "history of the mind is not Locke's history, but it is one informed by the contemporary development of Locke's notion of association-of-ideas madness into an epistemology such as Hume's."[3] Tristram indeed tells his "Critic" that Locke's *Essay* is a history of "what passes in a man's own mind" and that "the cause of obscurity and confusion, in the mind of man" has to do with "Dull organs" of the sense and "transient impressions" (2.2.98–99). Sterne echoes Pope on what Martin Price calls the "breakdown of language."[4] Pope, in his attack on nominalism in the *Dunciad,* wrote of the abuse of words: "Words are Man's province, Words we teach alone . . . on Words is still our whole debate." Sterne answers with this as the explanation of Toby's particular problem; the obscurity Toby labors under does not arise from "Dull organs" or "transient impressions" but from "the unsteady use of words . . . 'Twas not by ideas,—by heaven! His life was put in jeopardy by words" (2.2.101).[5]

When Toby begins to indulge his military hobbyhorse with geometrical calculations of the path of a cannonball through the air, Tristram warns him that knowledge is a "bewitching phantom" and says: "stop! my dear uncle Toby,—stop!—go not one foot further into this thorny and bewildered track,—intricate are the steps! intricate are the mases of this labyrinth! intricate are the troubles which the pursuit of this bewitching phantom, KNOWLEDGE, will bring upon thee" (2.3.103).

And there is the oft-quoted section on "riddles and mysteries . . . which the quickest sight cannot penetrate." We are confounded "in almost every cranny of nature's works . . . we cannot reason upon it" (4.17.350). The discourse on knowledge in *Tristram Shandy* takes this form: a radical Lockian questioning of the nature and possibility of knowledge. Even the epigraph Sterne takes from Epictetus—it is not things that disturb men, but their judgments about things—echoes Berkeley on the unbridgeable duality of *esse* and *percipi*, and Hume's double existence of things.[6]

Critics have responded to the discourse of skepticism in Sterne with a copious commentary that puts it in more modern terms, often enough pointing to the Shandean walking stick having many handles in order to claim Sterne as a Nietzschean perspectivist before his time, relentlessly dissolving the Logos.[7] Benjamin H. Lehman calls *Tristram* "contingency incarnate"; Leopold Damrosch writes of its "radical and unrelenting arbitrariness"; Stephen Werner asserts that Sterne's associationism aims at "denying ultimate meaning"; J. Paul Hunter refers to the book as an "omnivorous maw" that devours whatever it finds; Jonathan Lamb plays on the Shandean walking-stick-of-many-handles trope to assert that "Shandean skepticism is limitless, unbounded by beginning, ends, plots, or reasons"; and Homer O. Brown talks of the book as "nothing more than a series of *mises en abyme*."[8] We do not know exactly why Hume thought it the best book published in thirty years, or why it was Nietzsche's favorite English novel, but one could speculate that it was likely because Sterne's philosophy corresponded to their own.[9] Sterne wrote Dodsley in October 1759 that *Tristram* was a "general satire," and Diderot referred to it the same way as a "universal satire."[10] The words *general* and *universal* (Hunter's "omnivorous"), however, point to the kind of all-devouring skepticism mentioned above by the critics, since satire to be meaningful would require some stable point of reference outside the "general" fray. Tristram does not provide that point of reference. Everything he tells us is suspect, and in this regard Sterne's skepticism is totalizing.

What this does in *Tristram* to the discourse of the novel is apparent, to begin with, in the devastating effect it has on Tristram as a character. Note, for example, how much of Tristram's authority depends on his own constitution through knowledge. In the passage cited above where he refers to Locke's *Essay* as a history "of what passes in a man's own mind," Tristram says that he writes "as a man of erudition . . . I must sustain my character properly . . . else what would become of me? Why, Sir, I should be undone" (2.2.98). Much depends on Tristram being able to "sustain" his "character"; if we lose him and his *authority*, we lose those we get *through* him. If we cannot believe in Tristram, in other words, everything topples over into the "omnivorous maw" as Hunter calls it. What does it mean, then, for Tristram to tell us in the middle of a section in which knowledge itself is placed under erasure that his own existence as a character depends on it?

Tristram strives to ground his existence outside that of his story through the establishment of his own erudition apart from that he parodies, insisting that he is not of the company he describes. He is merely the chronicler of events. Although he may "seem now and then to trifle . . . [or] put on a fool's cap," still, he admonishes his reader, "don't fly off,—but rather courteously give me credit for a little more wisdom than appears upon my outside" (1.6.9–10). In fact, if we divide the learned references in volume 1 into those Tristram parodies and examples of his own erudition, the numbers are remarkably uneven. There are forty-one displays of erudition in volume 1 alone, on Tristram's part, and only eight where erudition is parodied. Examples of the latter would include the treatise on baptism by the Doctors of the Sorbonne, as well as the various offerings of Walter Shandy: on the retrogadation of the planets (1.21.76), the legal status of murder, or the different types of argument (1.21.78–79). But these are outweighed by the numerous displays of Tristram's own erudition. In the introductory chapters of volume 1, for example, in the space of a paragraph, he mentions Bunyan's *Pilgrim's Progress*, tells us what Montaigne's attitude was to his essays, and quotes from Horace (1.4.5). But it is questionable whether Tristram's own erudition survives the general skeptical onslaught enough to "sustain" his character, or whether, as he fears, he himself is also "undone."

Nor does it help that most of Tristram's erudition is borrowed. John Ferriar first catalogued Sterne's borrowings in his *Illustrations of Sterne* (1798), and most of them are intended to establish Tristram as an authority. Learned references aside, Sterne borrowed entire passages from Burton, Montaigne, and Rabelais; English Showalter has pointed out precedents to Sterne's demystifiction of form in the French seventeenth and eighteenth centuries; Wayne Booth has analyzed Tristram's precursors in the world of fallible narrators; Walter Shandy was a Scriblerian before he was a Shandy; and so on.[11] Yorick's sermons (published promptly by Sterne after the success of *Tristram*) came principally from Tillotson and Bishop Hall, while Trim's sermon on "The Abuses of Conscience" comes from Swift.[12] Tristram's reality as a fictional character thus depends to a large degree on borrowed plumage and ebbs away in the direction of the original owners.[13]

The discourse of skepticism in Sterne is often of the first and second orders. With Montaigne and Locke prominent, it is no surprise to find straightforward expressions of both everyday skepticism and fideistic skepticism, where the object is to save knowledge and truth, not dissolve them. Tristram can be as moderate as Montaigne: "For my own part I never wonder at any thing;—and so often has my judgment deceived me in my life, that I always suspect it, right or wrong,—at least I am seldom hot upon cold subjects. For all this, I reverence truth as much as any body; and when it has slipped us, if a man will but take me by the hand, and go quietly and search for it, as for a thing we have both lost, and can neither of us do without,—I'll go to the world's end with him" (5.11.439).

We are wise in our everyday lives to be suspicious, to doubt, to be skeptical; all the better to know the truth when we find it. Tristram continues in the same passage: "But I hate disputes,—and therefore (bating religious points, or such as touch society) I would almost subscribe to anything which does not choak me in the first passage, rather than be drawn into one" (5.11.439). One point of view, says Tristram, is as good as another when splitting hairs. These disputes, however, are set off from important issues having to do with religion and society. Tristram equates skepticism with the curiously misguided notions of his father, which are "as skeptical, and as far out of the high-way of thinking" as they can be (2.19.170).[14] But he wants us to know that when it comes to "religious points" and social questions there is indeed a right and wrong way of thinking about them.

Second-order skepticism takes the form of materialism in Sterne's antinovel, and this is where we move to the question of sentiment. It is this very eighteenth-century, very French form of skepticism that gives Sterne's sentimentalism its unique shape. Materialism is an extreme form of second-order skepticism that, like sensibility, has its roots in the physical world of the senses. It was as familiar in the eighteenth century as Lucretius, after gaining fresh life in Descartes's dissociation of the material from the mental—a separation that tried, like fideism, to preserve Faith and God by placing them in a separate, higher realm called *mind*. Knowledge and reason in the lower material world of pure matter—a world governed by the mechanical laws of cause and effect—have as little power and control as they do in the life of Tristram, whose narrative style and sexual profile are both materially determined—first, through the dispersal of his "animal spirits" at the time of his mis-conception, and second, through his symbolic castration by the falling sash. These two material events, in Tristram's own view, have set the course of his future life as a man of sentiment and of his life as a storyteller: both operate under the sign of Atropos, the cutter of the thread.

This is how sexuality fits into the alignment of epistemological and narrative dispersal in Sterne. A materialist ethic means that the kind of moral sensibility so ostensibly important to Sterne, especially in *Sentimental*

Journey, can never develop out of its material substrate; *cupiditas* cannot transpose into *caritas.* There is a fatal Cartesian abyss between body and mind in Sterne that is never satisfactorily bridged. And yet every good Christian knows that the transposition from eros to spirit must occur—that the corporal must lead up to the spiritual, from the love of kind to the love of God. One could say that making that re-connect is postlapsarian Man's task. As St. Paul reminds us: "[I]t is not the spiritual which is first but the physical, and then the spiritual" (1 Cor. 15.46).

A materialist ethic mitigates against this possibility. Sterne insists quite rightly that there is nothing particularly venal or irreligious about the enjoyment of pleasurable sensations—that "Religion," as he says in the chapter of *Sentimental Journey* called "The Grace," might be "mixing in the dance" his hosts engage in out of doors after their dinner; "that a cheerful and contented mind," as he says, "was the best sort of thanks to heaven that an illiterate peasant could pay—Or a learned prelate either."[15] God, after all, is the "great—great SENSORIUM of the world" (278). The question is—and it was a question posed by readers of Spinoza in the century—is identifying God with the material sensorium not the same as simply eliminating him? In the case of Sterne's "SENSORIUM" his absence means there can be no sharp distinction between innocent and guilty sensations.

Passion, which is Dionysian in its blending of eros and spirit, is taken up in *Sentimental Journey.* Yorick says, "if I ever do a mean action, it must be at some interval betwixt one passion and another" (128–29). Passion of this order is a positive basis for performing noble actions. "The Letter" he borrows from La Fleur has the lines: "L'amour n'est rien sans sentiment. Et le sentiment est encore moins sans amour" [Love is nothing without sentiment. And sentiment is even less without love] (153). Love, like passion, is bivalent, having both erotic and spiritual connotations, and Sterne sees the necessary dialectics of the two as well as St. Paul. Love remains below without the higher feeling of sentiment, which ennobles it, while sentiment itself is empty unless it plays out into the world through love of kind. The end of ethics is not knowledge but action. On this, certainly, moralists from Aristotle, Cicero, and Seneca onward have always agreed. There is a two-way street between low and high: physical love must transpose into its higher form, while sentiment or sensibility, must have some physical consummation in the real world.

This dialectic is deactivated in both *Tristram* and *Journey,* as I said, by their materialism. Sterne was not blind to the proper articulation, since it was a basic tenet of his faith. In the sermon, "Our Conversation in Heaven," he reflects on St. Paul's concern with the dialectic as phrased in the passage from 1 Corinthians cited above. In the case discussed in Sterne's sermon, Paul is writing to the Philippians on the topic, reminding them that the point is to move from the corporal to the spiritual and not make the mistake of letting one stand in for the other, of exchanging the spiritual for the pleasures of the flesh. Sterne knows all about the spiritual risks for those "who mind earthly things" and do not "abstain from fleshly lusts, which war against the soul."[16] And yet pleasure, love, and passion in both *Tristram* and *Journey* are often more fleshly and lustful than benign. In his notes to *Journey*, Stout writes, "Sterne's awareness that, because man's *affections* are radically imperfect, his participation in the virtuous pleasures and joys of the world often becomes excessive and licentious" (30 n. 18). And yet that "awareness" in the texts, if it is there, does not seem to translate into any great concern for the soul, as one might expect it to.

Other explanations have been offered for the lack of transposition in Sterne from eros to spirit. The "man of feeling," as Henry Mackenzie claimed in 1785, was guilty of "*substituting* certain impulses and feelings . . . in the place of real practical duties" (my emphasis).[17] Virginia Woolf attributes the failure to transcend to Sterne's vanity, saying of *Sentimental Journey* that the book's "chief fault" comes from "Sterne's concern for our good opinion of his heart."[18] Knox's statement—"Sentimental affection is but lust in disguise"—often seems borne out in both *Tristram* and *Journey*.[19] Knox's statement speaks not so much to their identity as to the failure of the higher feeling ever really to appear in its own right, ever really to separate itself out from the carnal. It is possible that Sterne does this on purpose, in order to satirize the whole enterprise of sentiment,[20] as some claim Goldsmith is doing in *The Vicar of Wakefield*. But then the satire, as Sterne himself says, is "general," which complicates things. There is no specific target. I would suggest instead that the reason for the failure to transpose from the lower to the higher is simply that sentiment is part of a materialist philosophy.

Materialism in the writings of Diderot and D'Holbach, as mentioned in chapter 1, is a form of second-order skepticism that goes back to the sensationism of Protagoras and Epicurus; it draws on Descartes's cast-off world of *body* and Spinoza's follow-up, monistic, single-substance theory. Knowledge of that substance is possible, but is always pragmatic rather than ultimate, limited by its origins in sense; it is subjective and materially based; our bodies are machines determined in their operations by biology and the way the material world works, from climate to sashes. All this is part of the discourse of skepticism in *Tristram* and *Journey*. Sterne did not need to be instructed in the appetites, sexual or otherwise, by French materialists like Diderot or D'Holbach, whom he met and associated with in Paris in 1762, but their philosophy has much in common with the way the corporal works in his own writings.[21]

Sterne rejected the sort of materialism popular in the D'Holbach circle, since it publicly denied the possibility of anything like the immortal soul. But its sensationist basis nonetheless has a powerful presence in his work; often enough it appears in the raw. In *Journey*, for example, Sterne, sounding almost like Montesquieu, attributes Smollet's crankiness to his health and recommends he see a physician (118). Perhaps Sterne had in mind the same kind of determinism that Tristram voiced on the "animal spirits" when he said that "nine parts in ten of a man's sense or his nonsense, his successes and miscarriages in this world depend upon their motions and activity" (1.1.1–2). There are other examples in *Journey*. In the opening Calais dinner scene, Yorick has an outburst of sentiment in favor of the French king immediately after eating dinner and drinking some Burgundy. His "warm" feelings after eating are a perfect demonstration of materialist philosophy, to the point where Yorick feels he must protest, insisting that his fine feelings are distinct from those produced by the wine: "I felt a suffusion of a finer kind, upon my cheek—more warm and friendly to man, than what Burgundy . . . could have produced" (68). He alludes as well to la Mettrie's *L'Homme machine* (1748), saying of his sudden surge of fine feeling that "'twould have confounded the most *physical precieuse* in France: with all her materialism, she could scarce have called me a machine. . . . I'm confident, said I to myself, I should have overset her creed" (69). He goes on to overset it elsewhere, later telling Madame de Q**** that he is not an *esprit*—not, that is, one of the *Encyclopedia* crowd; and when Madame de V**** tells him "she believed nothing," he takes credit for "unperverting her" to the point where she tells Diderot that Yorick "had said more for revealed religion, than all their *Encyclopedia* had said against it" (263–65). Sterne attempts to deny the affiliation of his thought with the philosophy of his materialist hosts. A key moment in the final scene with Maria of Moulins is when Yorick says that his emotions "could not be accounted for from any combinations of matter and motion. I am positive I have a soul; nor can all the books with which materialists have pestered the world ever convince me of the contrary" (271).

And yet the materialist "creed" accounts very well for the fact that while Yorick's words fly up, his thoughts remain below. He seeks to head off criticism after the ribald tale of toppling the *fille de chambre* ("Ye whose clay-cold heads" etc.) by transposing from *cupiditas* to the higher realm: "Wherever thy providence shall place me for the trials of my virtue . . . let me feel the movements which rise out of it, and which belong to me as a man, and if I govern them as a good one, I will trust the issues to thy justice—" (237–38). Hall-Stevenson may have found all the double entendre on the rising movements of the male and its issues amusing, but rather than raising the low the passage drags down the high, leaving it at the level of a profane jest—the kind of thing the booksellers purged before making the book available to female readers.[22]

Max Byrd writes: "Distresses of poverty or old age . . . might occasionally provoke the complacent ecstasy of the sentimentalist, but more often than not he turns his tearful gaze upon a beautiful young woman in *déshabillé.*"[23] In *Tristram*, the sentimental moment with Maria of Moulins is held at the level of the physical by the exchange of looks Maria gives Tristram and her goat. "Well, *Maria,* said I softly—What resemblance do you find?" Again, the result of the jest is to shackle sentiment to the material and carnal. Tristram's next comment in fact reminds us of what we are getting, and what we should be getting. "[B]elieve me, that it was from the humblest conviction of what a *Beast* man is,—that I ask'd the question" (445). This is indeed what should have been—the realization of our fallenness would imply the better state—rather than the satyr allusion, which Tristram then points to for our appreciation. "I would not have let fallen an unseasonable pleasantry in the venerable presence of Misery, to be entitled to all the wit that ever *Rabelais* scatter'd—" (445–46). Rabelais' wit, however, never comes at the expense of anyone who cannot afford it. "I swore," Tristram tells us, tongue-in-cheek, "I would set up for Wisdom and utter grave sentences the rest of my days—" (446). Regardless of what Sterne intended here by juxtaposing "affection" and "lust" in this way, the result is that sentiment never really takes form as anything apart from the purely earthbound. In turn, eros, without the infusion of true sensibility or spirit from above, is impotent. This is the real wound that has unmanned Uncle Toby.

The articulation of sentiment and skepticism in Sterne takes place under the sign of Atropos, and the book's narrative mode operates under it as well. Tristram ridicules "gravity" because its "essence" is "design," and where there is "design" there is "deceit" (1.11.28). One can imagine

Richardson rising up in protest, since design itself in Nature implies the Designer. A dispersal into moments at the level of narrative has a high cost in terms of ethics, which is only understandable through narrative.[24] It seems quite likely that readers perceived as much, since volumes 1 and 2 of *Tristram*, when they came out, did not gain a wide middle-class readership. They appealed to a limited set, of which Sterne's friend, John Hall-Stevenson, was typical. J.C.T. Oates quotes a line from *Ways To Kill Care* (1761): "'Who is more thought of, heard of, or talked of, by dukes, dutchesses, lords, ladies, earls, marquisses, countesses, and common whores, than Tristram Shandy?'"[25] The middle-class magazines lost interest quickly and the criticisms often had to do with the lack of "design." The first review of volumes 1 and 2 in the *Monthly Review* in January 1760, while being generally optimistic about the book, noted that Sterne "husbands his adventures with great oeconomy," and "sows them . . . extremely thin." And in a prescient comment, Kenrick, the writer of the review, advises the "Author" that "it would not be amiss . . . if, for the future, he paid a little more regard to going straight forward, lest the generality of his Readers, despairing of ever seeing the end of the journey, should tire, and leave him to jog on by himself."[26] This is more or less what happened. Johnson and others dismissed the book as not a literary work; and Burke regretted its failure as a novel. "The story," he writes in the *Annual Register*, "is in reality made nothing more than a vehicle for satire on a great variety of subjects."[27]

The discourse on the novel in *Tristram* is manifested in its narrative antinovelisms. Sometimes these anomalies and interruptions are meant to mock specific novelistic conventions like description. There is the elaborate mock-novel description of Trim's posture, for example, as he prepares to deliver the sermon on Conscience in volume 2; and the detailed description of Walter's collapse on his bed following the disaster of Tristram's misnaming. Occasionally the interruptions are mapped onto the failed dialectic mentioned above. Sentimental set pieces like Yorick's deathbed scene in Tristram, and the story of Maria of Moulins, have a static, picturely quality to them that takes them out of the world of time and out of the action. Visual signals often replace the continuities and narrative of language as a resource, as when Toby despairs of explaining the Battle of Namur and builds a model to do so. John Mullan suggests that gesture in *Tristram* is "a secret . . . aiding to the progress of sociality," where the progress is toward conversation. The conversation, however, only takes place, according to Mullan, between Tristram and the implied reader. This is true, but for it to differ from a sermon it must also take place between the characters. Mullan concludes that, consequently, "the misunderstandings and non-communications shown in *Tristram Shandy* are only apparent."[28] But it is difficult to see how this is the case in many of the abrogated exchanges. There is the one in volume 4, for example, between Walter and Toby, where Walter tries to talk to him "upon MAN . . . that dark side of him," and asks leave to lead him "a little deeper into this mystery." Toby grants him leave to do so—but then the chapter suddenly ends. We are left with the following: "My father instantly changed the attitude he was in, for that in which *Socrates* is so finely painted by *Raffael* in his school of *Athens* . . . [Socrates] holds the fore-finger of his left-hand between the fore-finger and the thumb of his right. . . . So stood my father, holding fast his fore-finger betwixt his finger and his thumb, and reasoning with my uncle *Toby* . . . —O *Garrick*! what a rich scene of this would thy exquisite powers make! and how gladly would I write such another to avail myself of thy immortality, and secure my own behind it" (4.7.332–33).

From potential conversation, to a framed image, to the stage and fame. Sociality here ends abruptly in solipsism.[29] The communication is indeed, as Mullan says, between narrator and implied reader, but exclusively so, and at the expense of the characters, who remain isolated and flat. Robert Alter writes that the reader strives to confer belief on Uncle Toby and his various activities "so that Tristram can be real"; but it might be better to say that we strive to confer belief on Tristram so that we can suspend disbelief about what he tells us.[30]

The best example of the congruence of narrative and materialist discontinuities comes at the end of *Sentimental Journey* when Yorick tells us he stretched out his hand and "caught hold of the Fille de Chambre's END OF VOL II" (291).[31] Coming at the end of Sterne's fictional output, this overlaying of an antinovel discourse and sensationist materialism— the interruption of the narrative with the physical "end" of the chambermaid—dramatizes how the two go together. The discourse of skepticism in *Tristram Shandy* ruptures continuity, eliminates the reality and authority of Tristram as a narrator, and makes impossible the necessary transposition between cupidity and spirit. The result is stasis at all levels: narrative, ethical, and sexual. Indeed, critics have long noted how sexual and semantic dysfunction in *Tristram* proceed together.[32] To have Yorick fall in love and/

or consummate a relationship, for example, just would not fit in this configuration. The philosophy of the configuration itself, operating under the sign of Atropos, is skepticism.

* * *

Dangerous Liaisons offers a different configuration in which sex, knowledge, and narrative flourish together in the intrigues of Laclos's two plotters. Where Tristram operates under the sign of the cutter of the thread, Valmont and the Marquise de Merteuil are spinners and disseminators. And although we are clearly meant by Laclos to see them as bad examples, there is something about Valmont and Merteuil that contradicts the notion that they are ethically bankrupt. In Sterne the discourse of skepticism and sentiment is the governing system of expression, and novelistic discourse is a straw man; in Laclos the articulation is quite different. The discourse of the novel in *Liaisons* is Richardsonian, including an even more forthright reflection on the cognitive power of artifice than we saw in Richardson, while the discourse of skepticism and sentiment is minimal. Sexuality in turn has a different aspect. In Sterne it was a victim of materialism, of the deactivated dialectic of eros and spirit; in Laclos knowledge and narrative realism are sexually enabling, providing a natural discursive home for the couplings of the two protagonists.

Sentiment, to begin with, is associated in Laclos's narrative with the weak and ineffectual, with women like Mme de Tourvel and Cécile Volanges who lack knowledge of the world. Merteuil, in her famous Letter 81 to Valmont, writes of "ces femmes à delire, qui se disent à *sentiment;* dont l'imagination exaltée ferait croire que la nature a placé leurs sens dans leur tête" [those unbalanced women who rave of their *sentiment;* whose excited imagination would make one think nature had placed their senses in their heads].[33] Note how the criticism of sentiment as an idealism is the same one Henry Mackenzie will make in Britain three years later in 1785. Merteuil continues in the same letter on the topic of "ces femmes actives dans leur oisivité, que vous nommez sensibles, et dont l'amour s'empare si facilement et avec tant de puissance; qui sentent le besoin de s'en occuper encore, même lorsque'elles n'en jouissent pas" [those women, active in their idleness, whom you call *tender,* of whom love takes possession so easily and with such power; women who feel the need to occupy themselves with it even when they do not enjoy it].

As for the discourse of skepticism, it is less a discourse in the novel than an attitude—an attitude toward the so-called knowledge of Merteuil and

Valmont that constitutes what might be called the novel's conventional or orthodox moral position. The two libertines may be strong on worldly wisdom and theoretical knowledge (*techne*), but they are far out of the path of truth and moral knowledge (*phronesis*)—which is borne out by the fact that in the end they make a mistake and are cast down. The overall ethical and moral gestalt of the novel looks as orthodox in this respect as that of *Moll Flanders*, with which it has much in common in its guise of cautionary tale. Artifice is deceit. And if it is also, as in Richardson, the marker of fiction, Laclos seems to be condemning it even more unambiguously than Richardson did, since in *Liaisons* it is purely the stock-in-trade of the villains. *Design* in this orthodox reading hides *deceit*, just as Tristram affirmed, and the knowledge of the two libertines looks in the end like mere self-delusion.

The orthodox moral reading of the novel, in other words, rests on a skeptical attitude to the protagonists' knowledge, and to artifice as anything more than deceit. The difficulty with it, however, is more architectural than moral; it does not fit with or seem to provide a place for the novel's ending. For if we are to understand that Merteuil's fateful last decision to *go to war*[34] with Valmont that precipitates disaster for them both is to be accounted for by the fact that her knowledge is as corrupt and flawed as her morals, how do we account for the fact that she has been so strikingly successful up until then?

Other explanations have been offered that are no more satisfactory. For example, perhaps the mistake is not Merteuil's but Laclos's; the author needed a deus ex machina to push his two protagonists into their fatal endgame and chose this rather clumsy way of doing it. After all, there are other implausible events in the story, so this may be just one more.[35] Or perhaps the explanation is psychological. Patrick Byrne argues that the Marquise's only interest is in ruining Cécile Volanges; and that Valmont is merely her tool.[36] But then this does not seem to explain why she seems to care even less about herself than she does about Valmont. Vanity is certainly of near-tragic proportions in Valmont; perhaps it is also the clue to Merteuil.[37] Pride goeth before a fall. Tragedy, at least insofar as it involves such a *fall*, is precipitated, as Aristotle says, by some error or miscalculation (*hamartia*). But there is no evidence that Merteuil makes the kind of mistake Lear, or Oedipus did; to the contrary, she seems quite aware of what the consequences of her action will be.[38] Laclos even makes Valmont himself doubt Merteuil's knowledge. He wonders at the end whether she knows what she is doing when she returns to Paris from the country and takes up with Danceny. He discovers the two of them together and lectures her using the language of the schoolroom: she should train her novice better since she is in the business of education; she should teach her pupils not to blush and embarrass their schoolmistress; and most importantly, she should not treat him, Valmont, like a schoolboy (151).[39]

Valmont is certainly no schoolboy; he is almost as intelligent and artful as she is. His claim that no virtuous woman can complain of him underlines the fact that he manages his affairs with tact. Richardson's Lovelace, with his kidnapping and imprisonment, looks like a rustic by comparison. One thing both Lovelace and Valmont know, however, is that involving a woman in an exchange of letters is the first step toward seducing her (76). And Valmont has other tidbits of professional wisdom, such as his astounding statement that a man can get a woman to lose respect for herself by getting her first to lose respect for her mother. His conquests, especially of Tourvel, speak for his skills. Nonetheless, if Merteuil treats him like a beginner it is because, compared to her, he is one. What matters is that *she* is not.

We seem then to be left without an explanation for her mistake—what Aram Vartanian calls "the colossal blunder" of her famous and fateful, "Hé bien! la Guerre" [Very well! War.] (153).[40] Valmont himself has erred—in his judgment of Mme de Tourvel, finally; in his overestimation of himself; in his underestimation of Merteuil—but it is the Marquise who is the resident professional, so to speak, in charge of planning, so for her to make this kind of mistake seems, as Vartanian again says, "completely senseless." Nor does Laclos offer any help. "The *dénouement*," as Vartanian writes, "does not, in fact, untie this particular knot; if anything, Laclos's conclusion may be said only to perpetuate it by surrounding it with a permanent silence."[41]

I would suggest, however, that if we begin with the assumption that Merteuil makes no mistake—that is, if we do not give the text's skeptical discourse the position needed for an orthodox reading—we can account for the ending without any difficulty. This leads us away from the discourse of skepticism to a consideration of how knowledge and artifice are configured in the novel. When we take a closer look at this we can see how the picture easily accommodates the ending.

Again, Merteuil's Letter 81 provides the clue. Merteuil tells Valmont that artifice and knowledge are at the very basis of her character. Her survival, she tells him, has depended on deception and playing a part. She learned to dissimulate at a young age, practiced control of her facial expressions, and discovered that the hardest thing about sincerity, as Wilde said, was how to fake it. Her description of her *education* as a libertine combines knowledge and art directly. "Je ne désirais pas de jouir" [I did not desire to enjoy], the Marquise writes, "je voulais savoir" [I wanted to know].[42] And her knowledge facilitated her art. "Cette utile curiosité, en servant à m'instuire m'apprit encore à dissimuler; forcée souvent de cacher les objets de mon attention aux yeux de ceux qui m'entouraient; j'essayai de guider les miens à mon gré; j'obtins dès lors de prendre à volonté ce regard distrait . . . je tâchai de régler de même les divers mouvements de ma figure. Ressentais-je quelque chagrin, je m'étudiais à prendre l'air de la sérénité" [That useful curiosity which served to instruct me also taught me to dissimulate; I was often forced to conceal the objects of my attention from the eyes of those about me and I tried to direct my own eyes at will; from this I gained that ability to simulate . . . I tried to govern the different expressions of my face in the same way. Did I experience some grief, I studied to show an air of serenity].

Before she was fifteen, she tells us, she already possessed the skills to which most politicians owe their reputations. She read—studying manners in novels, opinions in philosophers, and behavior in the moralists. She became a story. As for love, her goal was only "l'inspirer et le feindre" [to inspire and to feign it]. And to feign it, "il suffisait de joindre à l'esprit d'un auteur, le talent d'un comédien" [one had only to join the talent of an (actor) to the mind of an author].[43] In putting her talents to use she did not seek "les vains applaudissements du Théâtre" [the vain applause of the theater] but "à déployer sur le grand théâtre les talents que je m'étais donnés" [to display on the great stage the talents I had procured myself]. Dissimulation, imitation, deceit, fiction, and above all, knowledge— Merteuil is a self-written artifact that Rochefoucauld would admire, a simulacrum of a person who is her own finest performance. "Je suis mon ouvrage" [I am my own work], she says.

Letter 81 is justly remarked upon, since it is the one place in the novel where we get a privileged, even sympathetic look into Merteuil's character—a look at what made her what she is. She studied her survival. Rochefoucauld would have agreed with her that she was not wrong in judging her society to be one where design combined with a first-rate mind would be prerequisites for success. As a woman, she refused to be held in a traditional female stereotype, especially the one called the "woman of sentiment." Her statement that she was "née pour venger mon sexe" [born to avenge my sex] is difficult not to sympathize with; and the fact is that the one man she *ruins* in the novel, Prévan, has been responsible for destroying the reputations of three women in one night.[44]

Merteuil ends her career, appropriately and literally, in the theater. Following the scandal set off by Valmont's death, as rumors begin to fly, she leaves Paris for the country. On returning two days later she goes to the Comédie Italienne. After the performance she is publicly humiliated in the drawing room, presented with the spectacle of a re-instated Prévan, and shown in no uncertain terms that her private reputation as a libertine is now her public one (173). Like a bad performance, she is booed. But by this time it is a little late to pass anything but a belated moral judgment on it. She has demonstrated her superiority—a superiority based on her intelligence and talents as an actress—so glee at her downfall in these circumstances only rings the change on the moral of the story. Despite her exposure and disfigurement, after all, Merteuil does live to fight another day, and when she escapes to Holland she manages to take enough ready money and jewels with her so that she will fight in style.

There is still another way in which the discourse of knowledge in the novel is articulated and bound up with artifice, and this in an even more writerly fashion. Consider the letters themselves. Knowledge is the main commodity for Valmont and Merteuil as they attempt to control events; and their letters are integrally involved in producing and controlling it. We are drawn into the process.[45] The phrase of J. Paul Hunter that "most novels seem to begin in epistemology," is doubly true for an epistolary novel like *Liaisons* where the letters are not mere reports, as they are in Richardson, but actants involved in motivating the action, in hiding and persuading.[46] Peter Brooks writes on *Liaisons* that "we, as readers, are involved in an essentially epistemological problem—how to know, how, from fragmentary and slanted accounts of character and events, to put together a total and objective view."[47] In *Liaisons*, as Seylaz writes, epistolarity is "a project we participate in."[48] The project is a hermeneutic one, and ultimately not that different from what we do in reading any novel. In this case, tying the hermeneutic challenge to documents that are slanted—that are obviously documents of deception rather than reports—reminds us of that. The discourse of the novel in *Liaisons* thus contains an even stronger self-reflection on the cognitive nature of artifice than we saw in Richardson. Only a very narrow definition of *phronesis* would disqualify what happens in such deciphering from the title of moral knowledge.

But if we credit rather than discredit Merteuil's knowledge in the novel in this regard, we must grant the two protagonists self-awareness rather than self-delusion. And this immediately determines what we do with the discourse of love in the novel, which is indeed abundant. An orthodox moral reading tells us to discount it; that the two libertines know no more about love than about truth. And this seems to rule out one very attractive possible explanation of the ending: jealousy. Vartanian says that "the Marquise is not, in the first place, sufficiently in love with Valmont to become uncontrollably jealous."[49] Laclos seems to agree; he writes in a letter to Mme Riccoboni that the Marquise had "un coeur incapable d'amour" [a heart incapable of love].[50] Martin Turnell asserts that the aim of Laclos's libertines is "to eliminate the emotional factor altogether. Love comes to mean the intellectual satisfaction they get from the pursuit and defeat of the *enemy*, and the sensual pleasure which accompanies it."[51] And there are Merteuil's comments in Letter 81 on love mentioned above where she tells Valmont that her interest in love during her *formation* was not to feel it, but to learn how to fake it. Love, at least as far as the sentimental kind goes, is for Valmont nothing but disorder and nonsense (70).

But there are other kinds of love, and both Valmont and Merteuil use the language of love with one another as much as they disparage it. For Valmont the turning point of the story is his falling in love with Tourvel, almost as if showing him capable of it was the point of the novel. Love comes in more than one variety and Laclos seems untroubled with the idea that someone like Valmont can feel its arrows. To claim that he really feels nothing for Tourvel cannot be supported in the text. Merteuil too knows that there are different kinds of love.[52] She has no qualms about using the word to describe the innocent Danceny's feelings for Cécile, or the Chevalier's altruistic feelings for her own person; while at the same time mocking sentiment. Merteuil and Valmont were once in love, and in the conventional way. Again in Letter 81 she tells him that he was the only man "qui ait jamais pris un moment d'empire sur moi" [who ever for a moment conquered me]. And near the end, as she fences verbally with him, she suddenly interjects: "Savez-vous que je regrette quelquefois que nous en soyons réduits à ces ressources! Dans le temps où nous nous aimions, car je crois que c'était de l'amour, j'étais heureuse; et vous, Vicomte!" [Do you know, I sometimes regret that we are reduced to these resources. In the time when we loved each other, for I think it was love, I was happy; and you too, Vicomte!] (131)

Merteuil's outburst could be read as nostalgia for a properly female role that she traded in for that of the male libertine.[53] Her travestied desire, in this view, comes out in her attraction to Cécile, whom she speaks of as "un rival dangereux" that Belleroche must contend with for her affections: "Je raffole de cet enfant: c'est une vraie passion" [I am passionately fond of the child; it is a real passion] (20); and even more explicitly later: "Elle est vraiment délicieuse! . . . naturellement très caressante, et je m'en amuse quelquefois: sa petite tête se monte avec une facilité incroyable" [she is really delicious! . . . naturally very caressing, and I sometimes amuse myself with her; she grows excited with incredible facility] (38).[54] But a simpler explanation would be that Merteuil does indeed regret that she and Valmont are no longer as they once were, and wishes they could be; that this is really what is motivating her; that her actions are those of a woman trying to bind a particular man to her. At this point she is trying to convince Valmont to seduce Cécile, and puts herself, figuratively speaking, in the same bed with the girl.

The discourse of love between Valmont and Merteuil is often conducted in the language of chivalric romance. Merteuil is the heroine and Valmont her knight. Her scheme with Cécile at first seems like an excuse to get him back from the country. "Partez sur-le-champ, j'ai besoin de vous . . . vous devriez venir, avec empressement, prendre mes ordres à genoux . . . jurez-moi qu'en fidèle chevalier, vous ne courrez aucune aventure que vous n'ayez mis celle-ci à fin" [Come at once, I need you . . . you should come eagerly to take my orders on your knees . . . swear to me like a faithful knight that you will engage yourself in no other adventure until you have accomplished this] (2).

When Valmont informs her that he has just embarked on such an adventure with Tourvel, the Marquise reacts with a jealous, disparaging attack on her rival (5). Tourvel has no expression or grace; she is "encroutée" [encrusted] after two years of marriage; is "une espèce" [a poor creature]; dresses ridiculously and is a prude. As such, says Merteuil, she will be incapable of pleasure. At best she will manage "des demi-jouissances" [half-enjoyments], but never that complete self-abandon, that delirious "volupté" [delight] in which pleasure is purified in the very furnaces of its excess; "ces biens de l'amour" [those treasures of love], she says, will not be for Tourvel. Or for Valmont, one presumes, should he get involved with her. The Marquise thus reminds Valmont of what she herself is capable of and can give him. Given this language it is pointless to say that the Marquise is not really in love with Valmont.

She reminds him again of what she can give him by telling him of the delights she is experiencing with the Chevalier Belleroche, and Valmont now replies in the way she might wish, with appropriate jealous reproaches of his own. Take me back, he tells her, or at least take another lover to prove that Belleroche is not special. The tone of Valmont's letter is one of semiserious bantering, and he uses their pet language of knights and their ladies, of lovers enslaved and unendurable slights. Then he abruptly changes registers, as if to be serious, and speaks of Mme de Tourvel: "C'est bien assez, sans doute, que j'aie à me plaindre de l'amour . . . En effet, si c'est être amoureux que de ne pouvoir vivre sans posséder ce qu'on désire, d'y sacrifier son temps, ses plaisirs, sa vie, je suis bien réellement amoureux" [No doubt it is quite enough that I should have to complain of love. You see that I agree with your ideas and admit my faults. Indeed, if to be in love is not to be able to live without possessing that person one desires, to sacrifice to her one's time, one's pleasures, one's life, then I am really in love] (15).

This is the Marquise's nightmare: that Valmont can switch so easily from easy avowals of his love for her to a passionate account of his love for another. He has been so taken in by her callous manner he does not realize the pain this causes her. He is essentially faithless. He tells Merteuil that he often thinks of coming back to her and giving the world an example of constancy, "mais de plus grands intérêts nous appellent; conquérir est notre destin" [but more important interests must occupy us; to conquer is our fate] (4). No doubt he loves Merteuil in his way, but she will not be part of a harem, as she says, and that is what being with Valmont would mean. The Marquise, we should note, takes her own lovers one at a time: we see her with Belleroche, until he loses his place in her affections, and at the end briefly with Danceny; but never running between partners as Valmont does from Tourvel to Emilie to the Vicomtesse de M. In Letter 131 where she reminds Valmont that they were once in love, she tells him in so many words that all she asks from him is his fidelity; they cannot reanimate their love, she says, because it would mean that he, Valmont, would have to sacrifice too much; "et puis," she adds, "comment vous fixer?" [and then, how is one to retain you?]. She loves him and is doing what she can to bind him to her, but the advent of Tourvel on the scene spells disaster. She realizes for the first time that she is in danger of losing what little of Valmont she *has* managed to hold onto.

After Valmont writes her about being in love with Tourvel and being willing to sacrifice to her his time, his pleasures, and his life (15), she lets a week go by, then writes him back as if he had been pressing her to take him back. She warns him that she could again make him her slave, but instead will give herself to him if he conquers Tourvel. This of course begs the question and both presumes and hopes that Valmont accepts what she wishes—that she herself is the desired object. Again, she puts herself, figuratively speaking, in the bed Valmont will come to. This way, she tells him, "je deviendrai une récompense au lieu d'être une consolation" [I shall become a recompense instead of being a consolation] (20). The fact that she is so frank testifies to how well she thinks she knows him.

From here, as the seduction proceeds and Valmont begins to fall more and more under Tourvel's spell, events from Merteuil's perspective begin to take on a heavy inevitability. After the final seduction Valmont writes her that his ecstasy outlasted physical pleasure, that he left Tourvel's arms only to "tomber à ses genoux" [fall at her knees]—a cruel phrase for Merteuil to hear, using their own private language of chivalric romance for a rival. But it does again emphasize that these creatures are involved in love of a both carnal and spiritual nature. Valmont tells Merteuil that he swore to Tourvel "un amour éternel; et, il faut tout avouer, je pensais ce que je disais" [an eternal love, and, I must admit it, I believed what I said] (125). But Merteuil does indeed seem to know her man, well enough at least to force him to break with Tourvel in spite of everything. Valmont does so and writes the famous "Ce n'est pas ma faute" [It's not my fault] letter dictated by Merteuil (141), which she requires as part of the condition for readmitting him to her favor. But when Tourvel retires to the convent on receiving it, Valmont tells Merteuil the letter was meaningless and he hopes for a reconciliation. Naturally, she is outraged by his notion that he might claim his prize without giving up Tourvel. But worse yet, this is the moment when she seems fully to realize that she has lost him. "Oui, Vicomte, vous aimiez beaucoup madame de Tourvel, et même vous l'aimez encore; vous l'aimez comme un fou" [Yes, Vicomte, you loved Madame de Tourvel very much and you still love her; you love her like a madman] (145). The orthodox moral reading of the novel may encourage a view of Valmont and Merteuil as irremediably fallen creatures, incapable of any feeling higher than earthbound, fleshly lust, but the text, in its explicit transpositions from sex to ecstasy, says something else. Sentiment has no role here.

When Merteuil refuses Valmont his prize, it is he, ironically, who accuses her of misunderstanding. "[J]e tâcherai d'être clair; ce qui n'est pas facile avec vous, quand une fois vous avez pris le parti de ne pas entendre" [I shall try to make myself clear; which is not easy with you when once you have made up your mind to misunderstand] (153). He asks her if she has forgotten that they have the power of destroying one another. But bullying only shows that it is he who does not understand. In the dark about what is happening, Valmont puts himself beyond explanations. But Merteuil at this point is long past giving them. What follows is Laclos's fine variation on a crime of passion ending in which Merteuil destroys them both.

Such an ending only looks anomalous if we think the Marquise is not capable of love, but there is too much evidence to the contrary. Nor is it possible to believe she does not know what she is doing, or know her own heart; or know Valmont. The history of her success speaks eloquently against these possibilities. So her declaration of war at the end with Valmont is no mistake.

The articulation and cooperation of knowledge and artifice in Laclos's novel thus provides a space for sex and love that is qualitatively different from what we saw in Sterne, where the dialectic governing transpositions between the corporal and spiritual is problematized by a materialist and skeptical ethic. No such ethic is in play in Liaisons, where the knowledge of the two protagonists is proudly displayed on almost every page. Sterne attempts to promote sensibility as independent of both knowledge and novelistic continuities, but in so doing he isolates and sterilizes it. Laclos, by contrast, ignores sentiment while he vaunts and connects knowledge and mimetic art. Where sexuality in Sterne falls under the skeptical abrogations of Atropos, in Laclos it is relentlessly consummated, linked to the configuration of knowledge and mimesis in the protagonists, and juxtaposed dialectically to its higher form. Laclos makes no explicit causal connections in Liaisons linking the protagonists' knowledge, their full sexual and amatory lives, and the skills of illusionism they specialize in; but the fact that the three parts fit together as well as they do, in a discursive atmosphere free of skepticism and sentiment, adds something new to our examination of the antithetical configuration of skepticism and the novel. In Sterne and Laclos we see for the first time how eros behaves when brought into the configuration. What we find is that skepticism abrogates the kind of transposition between lower and higher that St. Paul insists on, producing discontinuity rather than consummation.

4

Skepticism, Diderot, and the Novel

Until now we have been looking at different articulations of the skeptical and novel language systems in a more or less static state. The work of Denis Diderot gives us a chance to look at them in process as they develop alongside one another. Diderot's materialist philosophy and the discourse of and on the novel in his writings have each been well-documented, but the relationship between the two has been poorly understood. The latter usually vanishes into the larger and more general category of the *literary* where the relationship then studied is that of materialism to Diderot's literary writings in general. At this level the connection could be described as complementary. Wilda Anderson, for example, makes some acute observations on how Diderot's materialism is reflected in *Le Rêve de d'Alembert* [D'Alembert's dream] (1769).[1] I want to be a little more specific, however, and examine the relationship in terms of one particular aspect of the literary—the discourse of the novel—in order to show that its own unique relationship to skepticism and materialism in Diderot's work is not complementary but antithetical.

Materialism, as I noted above, in its prioritization of the physical, is an extreme form of second-order skepticism. Over time it grows in Diderot's work, while the discourse of the novel is gradually forced into a conforming and compromised posture. Diderot regretted both events at different times, but he did not appear to think there was any connection. He occasionally referred to his philosophy as a burden—there is the famous comment to Sophie Volland, for example: "J'enrage d'être empêtré d'une diable de philosophie que mon esprit ne peut s'empêcher d'approuver et mon coeur de démentir" [It makes me fume to be hobbled by a devil of a philosophy that my mind can't help approving and my heart denying].[2] And he likewise regretted the demise of the discourse of the novel in his work, most famously, and with something close to despair, at the end of the famous *Éloge de Richardson* [*Eulogy of Richardson*] (1762). But he did not think one had anything to do with the other, and perhaps he was right. It is one thing to say that the two systems are incompatible, another to prove a causal relationship. Diderot's idiosyncratic understanding of realism, for example, in which, as Goethe put it, he confuses nature and Art, seems as much to blame for the demise of mimesis in his estimation as anything else.

Diderot's own view of the relationship, however, comes close to expressing a causal link. Diderot judged his inability to write like Richardson to be a result of his thwarted genius, or even lack of genius. The diagnosis occurs in the *Eulogy*, but also in *Jacques le fataliste* [*Jack the Fatalist*], begun in 1762, the same year he wrote the *Eulogy*. In *Jack* the narrator says: "S'il faut être vraie, c'est comme Molière, Regnard, Richardson, Sedaine; la vérité a ses cotés piquantes, qu'on saisit quand on a du génie; mais quand on en manqué?—Quand on en manque, il ne faut pas écrire" [If truth is the object, it's got to be in the manner of Molière, Regnard, Richardson, Sedaine; truth has interesting sides, which a writer will grasp if he has genius; but what if he hasn't any? Without genius, one shouldn't write].[3]

A lack of genius is one way of putting the fact that Diderot's mental habits were not of the sort to make for good fiction writing—something he himself occasionally admitted. Those habits—disorder, formlessness, a lack of control and design, errancy, chance, free association, digression, mystification and even confusion—are also qualities of the materialist universe Diderot and his friends imported from Spinoza and Lucretius. There is no concept, no system. A good example is the way knowledge is arranged in the *Encyclopedia* (see chap. 1, pp. 11–12). Diderot's view in the *Prospectus* was indeed that the arrangement itself was what it was all about, that its contribution lay in the *way* the knowledge was presented rather than its actual content. The lack of any discernible system in moving through the articles was what irritated Voltaire and made him call the whole thing a Tower of Babel. But the word *system* connoted metaphysics for the philosophes; in their view it was a positive virtue to be without one. It is in this sense that one might argue that Diderot had that positive virtue—that he was a natural skeptic in his unsystematic thinking, a man whose own habits of mind corresponded perfectly to the chance-driven, arbitrary nature of the materialist paradigm. These same habits, however, are clearly antithetical to the writing of successful fiction.

The most dramatic rearrangement of the two discursive systems occurs in the 1760s, around the time Diderot reads Sterne; but to get a proper picture of what leads up to it we have to begin in the 1740s, a time that might be called Diderot's British period since it was when he learned English and read Hobbes and Locke.[4] He also read Shaftesbury; and the three dialogues Diderot wrote in the decade attempt to combine philosophy and art in Shaftesbury's manner. The first was a translation of Shaftesbury's *An Inquiry Concerning Virtue, or Merit* (1699), which appeared in 1745 as an *Essai sur le merite et la vertu* [*Essay on Merit and Virtue*]. Diderot's name was not attached; nor was Shaftesbury's, which is fitting since the piece effaces, to say the least, Shaftesbury's ideas without replacing them with Diderot's. Shaftesbury's aesthetic solution to the dilemma of skepticism was to turn ethics into a kind of theater of virtue where God was replaced by Beauty.[5] It would be nice to think that Diderot's attraction to Shaftesbury lay in a perception of this sort of pre-Kantianism since it is what Shirley Brice Heath's respondents voice as reasons for reading novels; that is, that one way of justifying the ways of novelists to Man is to point to the ethical valence of form-giving itself; but this was not what Diderot had in mind. His main concern was getting Shaftesbury's own skepticism with regard to religion past the censors, which he tried to do by disguising Shaftesbury's deism.

This had interesting results, both philosophically and aesthetically. In the Preliminary Discourse he becomes a kind of ghost writer inside Shaftesbury's text, shaping it to his own ends, and claims that Shaftesbury's purpose in writing the *Inquiry* had been, first, to show that virtue was part of "la connaissance de Dieu" [the knowledge of God], and second, to prove that virtue meant happiness—a commonplace from the *Nicomachean Ethics* that Shaftesbury does not address. "Point de vertu," writes Diderot-as-Shaftesbury, "sans croire en Dieu" [no virtue without believing in God].[6] Shaftesbury's targets, Diderot tells us, are atheists, "sans probité" [without integrity], who claim not only to be virtuous but to be happy too. Shaftesbury, however, had said there was no necessary link between virtue and God and that atheists could be as virtuous as anyone else. He did not distinguish between deism and theism—between a belief in God but not in Revelation and a belief in both; but Diderot insists that he does, attributing to him a distinction that Diderot in fact took from La Chambre's 1727 *Traité de la véritable religion* [*Treatise on True Religion*].

The idea, in other words, is to disguise the radical nature of Shaftesbury's thought, and Diderot's creative rewriting succeeds in doing so. At the same time he displays a cavalier disregard for the formal qualities of Shaftesbury's text, bowdlerizing it, attributing to Shaftesbury beliefs he never had, and interpellating into it large sections from Shaftesbury's *Characteristics* (1711) and *The Moralists* (1709). Where *The Moralists*, however, had presented a balanced argument between its two interlocutors, Diderot's translation mercilessly hammers home one point of view with unrelenting didacticism, sacrificing the aesthetic quality of the text to make the point; and in the process, Diderot claims Shaftesbury's thoughts as his own.[7]

Much is thus lost in the translation. The discourse of skepticism, however, insofar as we get it in the deistic writing of Shaftesbury, translates across the Channel quite successfully. The key passage on moral relativism in Shaftesbury's *Inquiry* comes at the end of a discussion defining levels of life as systems and subsystems: "So that we cannot say of any Being, that it is *wholly* and *absolutely* ill, unless we can positively shew and ascertain, that *what* we call ILL is no where GOOD besides, in any other System, or with respect to any other Order or Oeconomy whatsoever."[8] In the secularization of virtue, the *good* is first stripped of its metaphysical grounding and made part of a clockwork universe; then it is turned inward and attached to a value-free biological field in the guise of the moral sense—a physicalist and materialist base that henceforth leaves ethical judgments as a matter of taste. Diderot picks up on the mechanist vocabulary and translates Shaftesbury's "Order," "Oeconomy," and earlier (in section 28) "Animal-Order or Oeconomy" as "lois mécaniques" [mechanical laws] (*DPV* 1.312), but holds onto Shaftesbury's larger sense of the unity—"le tout" as Diderot repeatedly calls it in his writing—that eighteenth-century machine metaphors always presuppose. He takes it for granted that a tendency toward harmony is an active principle in such a model. So we can see the early glimmer of Diderot's future materialist universe here, wedded to an odd disregard for the aesthetic qualities of Shaftesbury's polished and graceful prose.

This first experiment with skepticism and what might at best be called a few formal literary concerns is followed by a more engaged structuring the following year in the *Pensées Philosophiques* [*Philosophical Thoughts*] (1746), which again shows the influence of Shaftesbury, repeating many of the ideas from his *A Letter Concerning Enthusiasm* (1707), *The Moralists*, and *Characteristics*. It is also a dialogue, one that presents an exchange of thoughts among an atheist, a *superstitieux*, and a skeptic; and although its ideas are commonplace it shows some style and originality in the way it handles the interchange among the three interlocutors. The ideas are presented in short sections almost like aphorisms, but they are not disguised—with the unfortunate result that the book was judged heretical by the Paris Parliament and ordered burned by the public hangman.[9] The piece is important as the earliest clear example of the fluctuating balance of skepticism and art in Diderot's writing. His skepticism at this point is still a mitigated combination of first- and second-order skepticism that is not inimical to truth claims. Diderot in fact calls it the "premier pas vers la vérité" [the first step toward the truth] (*Pensée* 21, *DPV* 2.35), much the way Philo in Hume's, *Dialogues Concerning Natural Religion*, calls skepticism "the first and most essential step towards being a sound, believing Christian" (139). Diderot sets it apart from Pyrrhonism in *Pensée* 30: "Qu'est-ce qu'un sceptique? c'est un philosophe qui a douté de tout ce qu'il croit, et qui croit ce qu'un usage légitime de sa raison et de ses sens lui a démontré vrai: voulez-vous quelque chose plus précis? rendez sincère le pyrrhonien, et vous aurez le sceptique" [What is a skeptic? it is a philosopher who has doubted everything he believes, and who believes what a legitimate use of his reason and senses has shown him to be true: do you want something more precise? Force a pyrrhonist to be sincere and you will have a skeptic] (*DPV* 2.35).

A skeptic, in other words, is first of all a philosopher, which here is not much different from a Baconian and man of science. Second, the philosopher-skeptic does not doubt now, at the present moment: he doubted in the past; now he believes. And what he believes is that both his mind and his body can be relied upon to furnish him with true knowledge. The resemblance to Descartes's reliance on the "cogito" was also present in Shaftesbury's *Inquiry:* "For let us carry *Scepticism* ever so far; let us doubt, if we can, of everything about us; we cannot doubt of what passes *within ourselves, Our Passions and Affections are known to us. They* are certain, whatever the *Objects* may be, on which they are employ'd."[10]

Diderot's construction of Pyrrhonism in the *Pensées* is rhetorical, designed to create space for the more acceptable first- and second-order skepticism he expresses. At the same time we can see the seeds of his materialist philosophy. He claims, for example, that the fine points of metaphysics— what he calls, "les subtilités de l'ontologie" [the subtleties of ontology]— have created skeptics, and that one of their concerns is the nature of movement in matter: whether "le mouvement soit essentiel ou accidentel à la matière" [movement is essential to matter or accidental] (*DPV* 2.25). Diderot says no more. But if movement is *accidental* it must come initially from God; if it is *essential* we have the conditions for a godless, materialist universe.

Beginning in *Pensée* 22 deism starts sliding toward Montaigne's skepticism. The deist believes in God but not in church dogma. An atheist, by contrast, as Shaftesbury also claimed, is anyone who does not believe in God, including those who only doubt. Diderot straddles both positions with a second-order skepticism like Montaigne's that allows one to doubt without being an atheist. In *Pensée* 24 he cites with approval a passage from Montaigne's *Essais* on the need to soften and moderate the boldness of one's assertions, without giving them up. "Le vrai sceptique," Diderot writes, "a compté et pesé les raisons" [the true skeptic has counted and weighed his reasons] (*DPV* 2.31).

In Diderot's next piece, however, *La Promenade du Sceptique* [*The Promenade of the Skeptic*] (1747), Montaigne is categorized as a Pyrrhonist (*DPV* 2.116) without the shift being commented on. The *Promenade* is another dialogue, and we now get some real awkwardness in the effort to put together a pointedly skeptical debate with a formal concern for credibility and realistic dialogue. The inconsistency on Montaigne and Pyrrhonism carries over into a wider confusion among the positions presented: deism, atheism, skepticism, and Spinozism are presented, but the positions are jumbled and inconsistent, and the argument is impossible to follow.[11] The thread of skeptical thought linking the positions is lost, as is any formal consistency of characterization for the speakers. This time, however, rather than simply using the characters as mouthpieces, Diderot tries to *novelize* the scene; he adopts the device of the found manuscript, choosing as his narrator a "militaire philosophe" [soldier-philosopher] whose manuscript, dating from around 1710, has been recently rediscovered and recirculated. But when his two interlocutors come into the "allées," where the argument is to be dramatized, the realistic elements disappear and the piece falls into a heavy-handed didacticism. Conversation all but disappears, and the philosophical positions become incoherent. Herbert Dieckmann suggests that one might explain it by saying that Diderot intended the work as a satire of *all* the positions, but even that would seem to require a degree of coherence that the piece does not possess.[12]

Reading these early dialogues, one is reminded of the fact that the dialogue itself, when it employs the conversational rather than the catechetical method, is itself a skeptical form. As Hume noted, it is ideally suited for questions to which there are no clear answers: "Any question of philosophy . . . which is so *obscure* and *uncertain,* that human reason can reach no fixed determination with regard to it; if it should be treated at all; seems to lead us naturally into the style of dialogue and conversation."[13]

Diderot flirts with an awareness of this as a problem, but it never really takes hold. He nurtured a lifelong self-identification with Socrates and believed his whole life that the Socratic dialogue was the best vehicle to get his ideas across.[14] For what he wanted to do, he might have done better to consider Cicero. Like the Church fathers who followed him in the Middle Ages, Cicero emptied the Greek dialogue of its Socratic irony and turned it into a lesson, presenting long, alternating speeches that always ended with the triumph of one side; St. Augustine, St. Anselm, and Scotus Eriugena also used master-disciple dialogues of a similarly catechetical nature. The distinction between the two, however, was blurred by the eighteenth century, so that Diderot might be excused for not making it. Descartes and Berkeley also thought of the dialogue in general terms as a good way to both present and popularize their ideas, so Diderot's view was common.[15] "Le dialogue," he writes, "est la vraie manière instructive: car que font le maître et le disciple? Ils dialoguent sans cesse" [The dialogue is the true way to instruct: because what do the master and disciple do? They ceaselessly engage in dialogue]. He realized it was a skeptical form but thought it was a matter of first-order skepticism: the dialogue is "la manière sceptique de procéder" [the skeptical way of proceeding], but "en doutant on s'assure de tout" [by doubting one makes sure of things].[16]

The Socratic form, however, was as inimical to his attempts at realism as it was to his ideas. Aristotle was right to be cautious about classifying it as one of the imitative arts. Diderot seems to have valued its literary component for two purposes. First, it allowed him to disguise his identity. In the opening comment in the *Promenade* he says that his intricate style will fool those trying to guess the identity of the author—"les prétendus connaisseurs en fait de style chercheront vainement à me déchiffrer" [the so-called experts in matters of style will seek in vain to make me out] (*DPV* 2.73).[17] However, this did not happen; often enough it was the ideas that ended up disguised, while readers generally had no trouble guessing who the author was. The *Promenade* in fact was partly responsible for getting Diderot thrown in the dungeon at Vincennes two years later. Second, the novelistic elements were intended, as I said, to popularize his argument— to gild the pill and make the message accessible. In a letter to Sophie Volland on the literary style of *D'Alembert's Dream* he writes: "Il faut souvent donner à la sagesse l'air de la folie, afin de lui procurer ses entrées"

[It is often necessary to give wisdom the air of folly, in order to gain it admission].[18] But again, this had mixed results; readers often had trouble sifting out the *sagesse* from the *folie*. In short, the dialogue style Diderot employs seems as inhospitable to the discourse of the novel in his writing as it is to his argument.

In 1749 he tried a different format, putting his first full expression of philosophical materialism in letter form in the *Lettre sur les aveugles* [*Letter on the Blind*] (1749). Like the previous dialogues the piece also contains novelistic elements, including a narrated deathbed conversion scene, but Diderot's attention is as always on the argument. In this case it contains a refutation of Condillac's dualistic world of percipient and perceived in favor of a kind of Leibnizian monism. We get a good sense here of materialism as a form of second-order skepticism grounded in the physical senses. Knowledge is a matter of synapses and impulses, of vibrations traveling down nerve fibers.[19] If we accept that the senses are the sole source of knowledge, Diderot asks, what happens when one of them is absent? Are the blind somehow less knowledgeable? Diderot points to Nicholas Saunderson, the former mathematician at Cambridge who had been blind, and whose specialty, nonetheless, had been optics. If one sense is lacking, the others—touch and hearing in this case—become more acute. The key is in the way things connect. Truth is biology, a matter of the collision of atoms. In the imaginary deathbed conversion scene, the clergyman, Holmes, asks Saunderson if he is not convinced of the existence of God by the irrefutable deistic argument from design, and Saunderson replies that he only believes what he can touch (*DPV* 4.48). The *Letter* is the first indepth expression of materialism in Diderot's work and was the main reason he was arrested. For the moment, it appears as a radical expression of second-order skepticism whose sensationist basis renders knowledge relative and ethical judgments a matter of feeling.

Interestingly, the piece has many of the same formal flaws that were in evidence in the earlier dialogues: thoughts and ideas flow about pell-mell as if produced by free association until the narrator excuses his digressions to his correspondent by citing the form of their exchange: "Et toujours des écarts, me direz-vous: Oui, Madame, c'est la condition de notre traité" [And always the digressions, you will say to me: Yes, Madame, it is the condition of our agreement] (*DPV* 4.66).[20]

His *Lettre sur les Sourds et Muets* [*Letter on the Deaf and Dumb*] written the next year and published in 1751, is both more polemical than the *Letter on the Blind* and more formally disjointed. Its title seems unrelated to its subject, which turns around Diderot's differences with l'Abbé Batteux on the question of the natural word order in sentences. Batteux had just been awarded the Chair of Greek and Latin philosophy at the Collège de France, and Diderot clearly feels the recognition was undeserved. Unfortunately, as his attack proceeds he unwittingly adopts Batteux's own positions, becomes entangled, and although he sticks to his attack, ends up reaffirming Batteux's thesis. Jacques Chouillet writes: "It's hard to make out his point" (*DPV* 2.111; my translation).[21]

By 1750, then, Diderot had experimented with a couple of different forms as vehicles for his philosophical arguments and had given the discourse of skepticism in his work a shape that would henceforth remain constant. At the same time, he had introduced into his writings novelistic elements in character portrayal, setting, and dialogue to try to popularize his argument. A fuller expression of the discourse of the novel in its own right came in 1748 with the publication of Diderot's first piece of extended fiction, *Les Bijoux Indiscrets* [*The Indiscreet Jewels*]. It was a strange undertaking, insofar as it was unexpected that a man who saw himself as a scholar and philosophe and was beginning the project of the *Encyclopedia* should suddenly decide to write a "dirty" book. But such books were in vogue since 1742, and according to his daughter, Diderot wrote it on a bet. The action takes place in the Congo and features the Sultan Mangogul who has a ring that when turned toward any woman has the power to make that part of her anatomy talk, which, as Arthur Wilson puts it, "if it ordinarily had the power of speech would be most qualified to answer a Kinsey questionnaire."[22] The book is an extended satire on the politics, manners, and fashions of the day, written in the spirit of Montesquieu's *Lettres Persanes* [*Persian Letters*], and is of interest for the way it gives a first distinctive shape to the discourse of and on the novel in Diderot's writing. As a work *of* mimesis *The Indiscreet Jewels* has no pretensions to originality, borrowing freely from its predecessors in the field of erotic literature, but its comments *on* mimesis are revealing.

I mentioned at the beginning of this chapter that Diderot's idiosyncratic understanding, or misunderstanding, of realism had much to do with the demise of the novel in his estimation. We begin to see what this means here in the way the word *vrai* shifts unsteadily between the universal and the particular, from true to human nature to representational accuracy. Neoclassicisms on the former heading abound: the only rule in drama is the proper imitation of nature; Greek drama was impressive because it was true to Nature; and so on.[23] But the word *vrai* also regularly slips into its second, more quotidian use, as in the following: "Il n'y a que le vrai qui plaise et qui touche . . . La perfection d'un spectacle consiste dans l'imitation si exacte d'une action, que le spectateur, trompé sans interruption, s'imagine assister à l'action même" [Only the true pleases and touches us . . . perfection in dramatic art consists in so exact an imitation of an action that the spectator, fooled repeatedly, thinks he is looking at the action itself].[24]

Naturally, Richardson would never have said his object was the reproduction of reality. The two types of truth—the Truth of Human Nature and verisimilitude in detail—are of different kinds, and Diderot's preference for the second, but inability to give up the first, would eventually force a reckoning. At this stage, though, his discourse of and on the novel is still developing. He lists some of the sins against *vraisemblance* on the contemporary French stage and suggests that classical drama, by contrast, never destroyed the play's illusion—a realist aesthetic that, interestingly, he does not apply to his own metafictional *Jewels*, with its flaunted fantasy and digressive asides to the reader.

Eight years went by before Diderot tried his hand again at a piece of fiction, this time a play, *Le Fils Naturel* [*The Natural Son*] (1756). Here he goes back to the cut-and-paste borrowing techniques he used in *Jewels*, only more so, since in this case he borrows outright the plot and characters of Goldoni's *Il Vero amico* [*The True Friend*], the story of a man who falls in love with his friend's fiancée and then gives her up out of moral compunction.[25] The action is somewhat preposterous, even by the standards of Greek drama, and Diderot sought help in revising it from Grimm and some of his friends. What they did, rather than try for a more credible treatment of the action and characters, was come up with a framing device for the play that, like the found manuscript gambit, aims at establishing the work's historicity. Writing in his own name, Diderot provides an introduction that recounts a brief trip to the country he recently took during which he met "Dorval," the lead character in the love-triangle story. For its time, this was ingenious enough, conferring historicity on the piece by bringing its lead character out into the real world as the play's author. Dorval tells Diderot that his father wanted the play as a commemorative piece to be performed yearly using the actual people involved, acted by them and then re-enacted by their descendants in the same house where the sad events had taken place—an idea brilliant on its own to imagine— and that he, Dorval, had in fact written this play. Unfortunately, everything had been upset by his father's untimely death. But that Sunday the protagonists in the real-life drama plan to perform it, and Diderot is invited to watch clandestinely. He does so, and what he witnesses is *The Natural Son*, minus the final scene. The text of the play then follows. At the end, Diderot explains that the final scene had been interrupted when the actor portraying Dorval's father entered. Everyone was so overcome that they broke into tears and could not continue! All in all, a brilliant hoax, and one that was judged so by its readers, although how much of it was Diderot's own invention is impossible to say.[26]

What matters, however, in terms of the developing discourse of and on the novel in Diderot, are the three long conversations—the *Entretiens avec Dorval* [*Conversations with Dorval*]—that follow the play, in which Diderot and Dorval discuss the nature of realist theater, Diderot's now-familiar theory of domestic tragedy, and the theatrical tableau in which characters behave and speak to one another in a natural way. And here we find the same kind of semantic slippage on the notion of Truth that occurs in *Jewels*: a shift again between a straightforward neoclassicism and something closer to a naïve reflection-theory mimeticism. The *Conversations* voice their fair share of neoclassical commonplaces: art must always prefer the *ought* over the *is*; and the object of drama is "d'inspirer aux hommes l'amour de la vertu, l'horreur du vice" [to inspire in men the love of virtue, an abhorrence of vice].[27] Dorval says: "Je vois la vérité et la vertu comme deux grands statues élevées sur la surface de la terre, et immobiles au milieu du ravage et des ruines de tout ce qui les environne" [I see truth and virtue as two grand statues towering over the surface of the earth, motionless in the middle of the destruction and ruin of everything that surrounds them] (122).

But Diderot is equally, if not more, concerned with the *is*. Drama should "rendre les choses comme elles s'étaient passées" [portray things as they happened]. The object is "vraisemblance" (88) and the avoidance of the "incroyable" (85). There are "les actions de la vie" [the actions of life] and "l'imitation qu'on en fait au théâtre" [their imitation in the theater] (128–29). Things on the current French stage are "ni vraisemblable, ni vrai" [neither lifelike nor true] (88); and Diderot comes down hard on the "coup de théâtre," which he defines as "un incident imprévu qui se passe en action, et qui change subitement l'état des personnages" [an unforeseen incident that suddenly changes the relationship of the characters] (92). Such things, they both agree, always depend on improbabilities of plot. Drama should rely instead on "tableaux" or groupings of characters where emotion is integrated into the actors' positions and gestures. What is important is "la vérité des tableaux" [the truth of the tableaux] (117).

There is plenty of evidence that Goethe was right in saying Diderot confused nature and art, but there are nonetheless moments when he knows the difference. In "De la Manière" ["On Mannerisms"], he says, "l'artiste est abandonné à sa propre imagination. Il reste sans aucun modèle précis" [the artist is left to his own imagination. He remains without any precise model] (DPV 16.534). Art, in other words, is not the reflection of an exterior reality. In the first of the Salons he writes that representational art is "un tissu de faussetés qui se couvrent les unes les autres" [a tissue of lies, one covering the other] (DPV 13.373). In Jack the Fatalist Jacques makes the following rejoinder when his Master insists that, in his storytelling, he just tell it like it is: "Cela n'est pas aisé. N'a-t-on pas son caractère, son intérêt, son goût, ses passions, d'après quoi l'on exagère ou l'on atténue? Dis la chose comme elle est!" [That's not easy. Isn't it the case that everyone has his own personality, interests, taste, passions, that determine whether one exaggerates or attenuates? Just tell it like it is indeed!] (67). But in the Conversations what Goethe remarks seems borne out. Theater is "un art d'imitation" [an art of imitation], and the definition of "la beauté d'imitation" [the beauty of imitation] is "la conformité de l'image avec la chose" [the conformity of the image with the thing] (150). The majority of Diderot's comments in the Conversations champion realism in this way. "Rapprochez-vous de la vie réelle" [Get close to real life], says Dorval (140). The notion of the fourth wall that appears two years later in the Discours de la Poésie Dramatique [Discourse on Dramatic Poetry] (1758) attached to Diderot's next and last play, Le Père de Famille [The Father of the Family], is also designed to accentuate illusionism. Actors must sink themselves in their parts rather than play to the audience. Spectators become "les témoins ignorés de la chose" [the ignored witnesses of the thing] (DPV 10.368). Romance plays no part in the realist paradigm. Dorval dismisses the "monde enchanté" [enchanted world] of lyric theater as a thing for children (110); and says that "les dieux de la fable, les oracles, les héros invulnérables, les aventures romanesques, ne sont plus de saison" [fairy-tale gods, oracles, invulnerable heroes, and romance adventures are no longer in season] (147).

At this stage, then, it might be said that while Diderot's materialist philosophy has matured, the discourse of the novel has waxed and waned in his writing like a flickering lamp. In the 1760s, however, it went through a different and remarkable transformation. In the art Salons of 1761–67 Diderot continued to advocate a realist aesthetic, but in his own work things took a new shape. The change coincided roughly with his discovery of Sterne in 1762 but existed alongside a renewed moralism and a dissatisfaction with his own inability to master realist techniques. These were the years of *La Religieuse* [*The Nun*] (1760), Diderot's most successful piece of sustained realism; *Le Neveu de Rameau* [*Rameau's Nephew*] (1761); the famous *Eulogy of Richardson* (1762); and *Jack the Fatalist*, begun in 1762 and finished in the late 1770s. *The Nun*, although tendentious in its politics and morality, is far from a failure as a piece of literary realism. As brilliant in its way as *The Natural Son*, the elaborate scheme at the bottom of it was also cooked up by Diderot and his friends, this time to convince one of their company, the Marquis de Croismare, to return to Paris by forging a series of letters to him from a young nun he had once befriended. Diderot decided to enlarge on one of the letters in which the nun, Suzanne Simonin, tells the Marquis the story of her life, and over the rest of the year developed the novel around it. It is successful on several levels, especially in creating a strong sense of the principal character (voice and ventriloquizing his characters was one of Diderot's strengths), and it holds onto the integrity of setting and tone. As Robert Mauzi says, it succeeds "in creating a coherent universe" in spite of containing "irruptions of the author's garrulity, broken pieces of anecdotes and a dizzying settling of accounts."[28]

But Diderot was not happy with it, and after working on it for the better part of the year he put it away. Despite its strengths, the story is hurt by the "irruptions," and by temporal and narrative troubles that have to do with the double narrative point of view of the memoir-novel.[29] Even twenty years later when he revised it Diderot was unable to straighten these out, and indeed added more. Mauzi puts it rather harshly: "Diderot does not have the necessary authorial detachment to tell a ready-made story."[30] Diderot was aware of his difficulties. In November he writes to Mme d'Épinay: "Je ne m'en donne pas le temps. Je laisse aller ma tête; aussi bien ne pourrais-je guère la maîtriser" [I don't take the time. I let my mind go, which I might as well do since I absolutely can't control it].[31]

After struggling with the novel, Diderot sat down in April 1761 and wrote *Rameau's Nephew*, returning to the dialogue form which, for him, meant returning to argument. The argument in this case consists of a sudden new critique of mimetic art per se, and is made, ironically, using a character who has become one of French literature's most vivid literary creations. Rameau *le fou* has several purposes in the dialogue, serving as a mouthpiece for Diderot's ripostes to his critics and for some sad reflections on his own lack of genius; but his main function is to act as a lightning rod for an in-depth critique of mimetic fiction. Rameau is a replica of Jean-François Rameau, nephew of the famous composer,[32] and his own principal characteristic is his ability to imitate. He performs nineteen pantomimes in the dialogue, six in which he imitates musical instruments or song, and thirteen in which he imitates people and events. A duplicate himself, his unique talent is duplicating others. He is the embodiment of mimesis, and as such comes in for some surprisingly harsh criticism.

The piece, despite its polemical intent, surpasses its precursors in the 1740s in its novelistic content. It begins in the story mode with the Narrator providing exposition, establishing himself as a character and a voice. He is a man governed by chance, who follows his whims. It is his custom, he says, to take a stroll in the Palais-Royal at the end of the afternoon; and he compares his solitary ruminations there to the activities of "nos jeunes dissolus" [our dissolute youth] who flit from woman to woman. "J'abandonne mon esprit à tout son libertinage" [I give my mind over to all its promiscuity], he says, and he calls his thoughts his whores or "catins."[33] The Narrator then brings us into the *café de la Régence*, where he tells us he goes to watch the chess players when the weather is bad, and then focuses quickly on Rameau, whose description goes on for over two pages. It is the longest sustained description of a character in Diderot's fiction, surpassing by far anything in the earlier novels or plays, and succeeds in thoroughly establishing the character. In terms of the discourse of the novel in Diderot, it is his best work.

Once we are established inside the café the piece goes about its business, which is the moral indictment of mimesis in the person of Rameau. Rameau is a talented storyteller and he tells two tales that serve as targets for the argument. The first is about the procuration of a young girl, in which Rameau mimics the procurer who sells her for two thousand ecus. It is well-told, with convincing details of everyday life and realistic dialogue between the girl and Rameau. The Narrator's reaction, however, is what matters. He is both amused and appalled and does not know whether to admire the performance as art or deplore it as nature. Finally he notices that his moral reaction is being stifled by his aesthetic one: "Vingt fois un éclat de rire empêcha ma colère d'éclater; vingt fois la colère qui s'élevait au fond de mon coeur se termina par un éclat de rire" [Twenty times a burst of laughter prevented my anger from breaking forth; twenty times the anger rising from the bottom of my heart ended in a burst of laughter] (50). This alarms him and decides the matter against Rameau: "Ah, malheureux," he says, "dans quel état d'abjection, vous êtes né ou tombé" [Ah, you wretch, what a state of abjection you were either born or fell into] (51). But of course Rameau has done nothing but tell a story. This is what Goethe means by Diderot's confusion of nature and art. Art is not differentiated from reality. Of course, even if there were no confusion, the Narrator could still find Rameau morally culpable as an artist through the invocation of a neoclassical aesthetic (based on the separation of art, artists, and nature); and that will happen, but not until much later in *Paradoxe sur le comédien* [*Paradox of the Actor*], where Diderot finally gets the confusion straightened out.

Rameau next tells a story about a rogue who pretends to befriend a Jew by telling him they have both been denounced to the Inquisition, only to trick the Jew out of his money and leave him behind to be burned. Again, the Narrator does not know whether he should react to what he has just heard as invention or reality; "rester ou fuir, rire ou m'indigner" [stay or flee, laugh or be outraged] (99). And again it is the second alternative that wins out. He cannot help but admire Rameau, but he also pities and despises him. What the dialogue shows, in other words, is suddenly a lot of uncertainty on Diderot's part about the morality of showing the *is* rather than the *ought*, since showing the *is* is what he thinks realist art does. His neoclassicism tells him that art should tell the truth about human nature—that it should instruct and delight; but what should he do about the perverse pleasure he takes, as the Narrator, in verisimilitude all on its own? In the *Nephew* the discourse of the novel shows some remarkable accomplishments in terms of both setting and character portrayal that mark an advance in Diderot's fiction; it is ironic that they should take place in a piece that suddenly doubts the very basis of that fiction.

At a conscious level for Diderot the doubts spring from what is essentially a misprision of mimesis, what could be described as an inconsistent combination of neoclassicism and a reflection theory of art. The former will eventually triumph. It is constantly reminding him to seek the higher moral and universal truth in the particular, while the latter is content to celebrate the particular alone. There is an excitement in Diderot's love for verisimilitude, perhaps most evident in the art criticism of the Salons, but at the same time a moral concern with the propriety of showing life as it is—the sort of thing that bothered Johnson about Shakespeare. And it is the moral concern that is eventually going to win out. Diderot discusses realist art as if it were reality itself. But this kind of reflection or mirror theory of art effaces the artwork, turning it into a mirror or transparency.

Here Diderot's doubts are put in moral terms. He was surely sincere in voicing them; but they coincide neatly with others that have more to do with his mental habits.

These surface the following year in the *Eulogy on Richardson* (1762).[34] In this piece, Diderot recognizes with something like regret that literary realism involves the illusion of a "multitude de petites choses" [multitude of small things] that an author like Richardson summons into his work—things so hard to imagine that, from the reader's standpoint, they must be true (*DPV* 13.198).[35] In one way, his praise, like his condemnation of Rameau, is the highest one can give a realist: that is to say, he again takes Richardson's characters as if they were real. In the *Nephew* this worked against Rameau; here it works in Richardson's favor as Diderot likens himself, reading *Clarissa*, to a child witnessing his first play and shouting to the actress, "Don't believe him, he's tricking you . . . if you go with him you are lost!" The reader, he says, actually plays a role in Richardson's fictions: "on se mêle à la conversation, on approuve, on blâme, on admire, on s'irrite, on s'indigne" [one joins the conversation, one approves, blames, becomes irritated, indignant] (*DPV* 13.193). Nor is he alone: "J'ai entendu disputer sur la conduite de ses personnages," he writes, "comme sur des événements réels; blâmer Pamela, Clarice, Grandison, comme des personnages vivants" [I have heard people argue over the conduct of his characters as they would over real events; blaming Pamela, Clarissa, Grandison as if they were living beings] (200).

But while Diderot is full of this kind of praise for Richardson's art, the fact remains that he misunderstands it, as he misunderstood Rameau, and perhaps as a result he has little to say about it. His own attempts in the realist mode had not been completely successful, and he was disheartened. His two plays had been failures, his one novel remained in manuscript form, and the literary aspects of his published dialogues had only succeeded in mystifying readers. He had written nothing purely literary so far that had been hailed as a masterpiece, while Rousseau's *Nouvelle Héloïse*, published in February 1761, had been acclaimed as one instantly. His labors with the *Encyclopedia* had been praised, but he is worried here about whether he is a genius or a failure, and how he will be rated by posterity. The ratings, unfortunately, were already out, and they were not that good. The *Année Littéraire* of July 18, 1761, for example, had called his plays pompous, disorderly, obscure, and pedantic. The framing devices, prefaces, and caveats he inserted to direct reader response and rationalize the fragmented and disorderly appearance of his work had not taken. In the *Eulogy* he talks about "ces lignes que j'ai tracées sans liaison, sans dessein et sans ordre, à mesure qu'elles m'étaient inspirées dans le tumulte de mon coeur" [those lines I traced without connection, without design and without order, as they were borne up to me out of the tumult of my heart] (208). Today, we may well decide to follow Diderot, along with our postmodern fancies, and make a virtue of that lack of design, but readers of his day did not take to it. They appreciated his tumultuous and generous heart, but appeared to agree with the *Année Littéraire* in wondering whether work that mirrored the messy state of the world instead of making something of it was really what realist art was about. In this respect they were more sophisticated on the topic of mimesis than Diderot himself.

Diderot ends his praise of Richardson with the above comment on his own lack of self-discipline and goes on to muse on his other troubles. The genius of Richardson, he writes, has extinguished his own. Richardson's characters wander about incessantly in his imagination. When he wants to write they distract him and the pen falls from his hand. He concludes on a note of bitterness. In conversation with Richardson's heroines, he writes, years have passed that might have been productive and brought him recognition. Instead, he is heading down the last mile without anything to recommend him to posterity (208).

That Diderot should think this way just when he was writing the kind of work that perhaps more than anything else was going to carry that recommendation down to posterity is one of the many ironies in his life. If not *Rameau's Nephew*, then certainly the piece he began early in 1762, after meeting Sterne and reading the first six volumes of *Tristram Shandy*, was going to carry it. *Jack the Fatalist* is a kind of picaresque dialogue in which Diderot's principal purpose again is polemical rather than creative, but which once more contains a significant novelistic component. The work is a watershed in Diderot's career in the way it articulates the two, the polemical and the creative, in a starkly antithetical manner, juxtaposing in an aggressive manner the two discursive systems we are examining.

The discourse of skepticism in the piece is patent in Jacques's deterministic materialism—where the determinist aspect that was only latent in *Letter on the Blind* is manifest in Jacques's fatalism—the Great Scroll upon which he insists all has been pre-scribed. Purely mechanical laws determine every effect. The ghosts in this machine are clearly no longer Bayle or Montaigne, but Lucretius, La Mettrie, Hobbes, and now especially Spinoza. No effect is without a discoverable cause in the grid, no action is without a reaction, motion is essential and eternal, not imposed. Knowledge is possible but it too is a material effect—as we saw in the *Letter on the Blind,* a result of physical sensation. Thought itself, as Wilda Anderson notes, is spatial and material: motion imparted to one molecule carries its effect through the whole body, which reacts like a struck clavichord, a musical instrument that is "attuned to certain harmonies" but not others.[36] Everything we know and feel is linked through the nerve fibers and is part of a causal chain.

Jacques can thus connect his falling in love to the past action of an innkeeper who sold him the wine upon which he got drunk, which made him forget to water the horses, causing his father to get angry and beat him, which resulted in his joining the army and being shot in the knee, which brought him with his limp to his *love.* "Elles se tiennent," he says, "ni plus ni moins que les chaînons d'une gourmette" [They all hang together just like the links of a chain] (13–14). Jacques and his Master are two "vraies machines vivantes et pensantes" [true living and thinking machines]. There is no free will; even desire is mechanical. Jacques insists that wanting is not volitional—"Il n'y a dans les deux machines qu'un resort de plus en jeu" [It's only a matter of another cog moving in the two machines] (291)—and later proves it by cutting the girth on his Master's saddle, causing him to fall, fly into a rage, and chase Jacques fiercely around and around the horse. Says Jacques: "N'est-il évidemment démontré que nous agissons la plupart de temps sans vouloir?" [Isn't it obvious that most of the time we act without volition?] (309).

The structure of the machine makes reason irrelevant. All we know is what we feel; and necessity is the link that binds in the chain of events. Diderot and the philosophes took their lead from the *Ethics,* changing Spinoza to suit them. Diderot was not against accepting the idea that Spinoza's "single Substance" could be called God; but he and his friends preferred a model that removed God *ex machina* altogether, leaving only the *machina.* The narrator tells us Jacques got all his ideas from his Captain, who in turn got them from Spinoza (200). The body, like the universe, is a machine, tending toward harmony, even unity, but not as a result of any higher laws. Systems and subsystems organize themselves into discursive bodies into which we may gain insight, which may be harmonious or dissonant in the manner in which they are articulated at any given moment, but which cannot be understood as products of the human will. Their laws are immanent and a-hermeneutic, and yet they determine what we can know and feel. Ceci n'est pas un roman [this is not a novel].

In conjunction with this, the discourse *of* the novel in the piece is parodic in the manner of Sterne. Along with *Rameau's Nephew*, it is one of the most vivid of all Diderot's efforts; but it is also more troubled than the simpler *Rameau's Nephew*. It consists of a tale of a master and servant who, like Don Quixote and Sancho Panza, travel together, talk, display irritation with and attachment to one another, and fall into a series of adventures as they go. Handling this presents more difficulties than the *Nephew*, and Diderot makes a multitude of mistakes that are reminiscent of his troubles with *The Nun*. Jacques's past history with his Captain is chronologically incoherent; at one point a so-called widow dies, but then, curiously, is mourned by her husband; and in the two interpellated tales of the Machiavellian Père Hudson and the conniving Mme de la Pommeraye there are a plethora of implausibilities in the plot that Diderot either did not notice or think worthwhile to attend to.[37]

All this could be explained without going further than saying that the errors are a product of Diderot's errant mental habits, but the errors can also be seen as typical of a skeptical rejection of form and design. *Jack*, as J. Robert Loy puts it, tries "to deny the need to impose form on reality," and this fits nicely with a materialist philosophy where such an imposition is futile.[38] In the end, it is this, more than Diderot's confusion of nature and art, or his neoclassical leanings in aesthetics, that shapes the discourse of and on realism in is work—not just suddenly in 1762, but over the long term.

In *Jack*, under the influence of Sterne, that shaping takes on a slightly programmatic quality. Diderot even surpasses Sterne in flaunting the antinovel aspect of the work by taking his narrator out of the action; unlike Tristram his voice is authorial, removed, and omniscient as he interrupts the story at every turn to discuss it with the reader, objectifying it as a fiction in such a way that the suspension of disbelief in its novelistic discourse becomes impossible. Novels are something only the landlady of the tavern reads, the one who tells the Rameau-like tale of Mme de la Pommeraye. She has come down in the world, and it is hinted that her descent from convent to tavern was at least partly brought about by reading novels instead of the Gospels, although Diderot does not distinguish by "romans" novels from romances (147).

Sterne has now replaced Richardson as the model. Diderot borrows for Jacques's own story the device of the infinitely postponed tales of Uncle Toby's amours in *Tristram Shandy*, as well as the tale of Trim's knee, which he read when volume 8 appeared in 1765 and promptly built into *Jack*, even making the borrowing explicit when he tells of Denise coming in to dress Jacques's wound: "Voici le second paragraphe, copié de la vie de *Tristram Shandy*" [Here is the second paragraph, copied from the life of *Tristram Shandy* (*sic*)] (313). After the charges of plagiarism involved in his borrowing from Goldoni for *The Natural Son*, his repetition of the exploit here can only mean that he looked on the work's literary aspect, as vivid as it is, as once more beside the point. The narrator, however, says, "Je n'aime pas à me faire honneur de l'esprit d'autrui" [I don't like taking credit for someone else's ideas] (200).

Whether the Sternian surface was all under Diderot's control or not, its irregularity and intertextuality has made it, with *Tristram*, a favorite with modern critics. Thomas Kavanagh's *The Vacant Mirror* treats it brilliantly as language philosophy, rather than a novel or dialogue, while Jack Undank and Stephen Werner, following Diderot's own theory of realism as a mirror held up to the world, see its Shandean quality as a reflection of reality. Its aim, says Undank, is to reproduce "the effect of an environing world as it leaned upon human perception." And Werner uses Derridean terms like *rature* and *self-erasure* to claim it as a "roman réaliste" that "shows as a consequence a jumble of forms and shapes." That the work "has no dramatic pulse" is, from this perspective, a positive virtue.[39] This celebration of the blatant downturn in the discourse of realism in Diderot in the 1760s under what has been a steadily expanding skepticism thus finds its latest sanction in postmodernism.

After *Jack*, although Diderot continues to mix the literary and philosophical, their relative position in the overall map of his expression is fixed. I want to conclude with a look at a couple of important pieces that make this plain. In *D'Alembert's Dream*, written at the end of the decade in 1769, the discourse of skepticism attains even fuller expression than it had in *Jack*, while the discourse of the novel shrinks back to the sort of liminal presence it had in the early dialogues of the 1740s. There is no narrator as there was in *Rameau's Nephew* and *Jack* to introduce or describe the characters, and no real action to speak of. Wilda Anderson notes how the formal features of the work (which must include the absence of evident design or direction, its disorderly and restless quality, and the inconclusive ending) are all grounded in Diderot's materialism. Motion is essential to matter, so it makes sense that the text should be restless; everything is the effect of some cause, so "the text must induce in the reader the active-and-reactive state." The dialogue form complements the content. As Anderson says, "a standard treatise format would not be appropriate for . . . the multifaceted experience" of the *Dream*.[40] Form at this level mirrors or complements function, which is similar to the approach taken by many critics toward *Jack*. This is a unifying approach that stresses consonance and makes welcome sense of Diderot, but as I have suggested, one can also understand the disorderly quality of Diderot's novelistic discourse as dissonance, not as somehow mirroring the dissonance of the world as many of his critics would have it, but as a dissonance between form-giving and his materialist philosophy.

The principal interest in *D'Alembert's Dream* is the way it characterizes sensibility, again as in Sterne, as a purely material phenomenon. In the *Encyclopedia*, *sensibilité* has a double definition, one by a natural scientist stressing its material, physical substrate, another by a moral philosopher stressing its abstracted meaning as sentiment. We saw in Sterne how sentiment remained mired in the physical; in the *Dream* Diderot makes sensibility a purely material affair of *"molecules sensibles"* (182). The one-substance model means the universe is monistic and infinitely divisible, each atom connected to the next, so that an impulse anywhere is carried through the entire being. These molecules are in constant motion, just as reality was for Heraclitus with his flux theory, rendering verbs of stasis and statements of being, including statements of fact (truth and knowledge) obsolete the moment they are made. D'Alembert in his dream asks Mlle de l'Espinasse to imagine a swarm of bees, all "accrochés les uns aux autres par les pattes" [attached to one another at the feet], where if one feels a pinch it will be passed on to the next, and so on through the whole body (183). We are a bundle of nerve fibers, a network, "un système purement sensible" [a purely sensible system] (201) where everything is based on the physical sense of touch and where the affinity between human beings is best understood as chemical.[41] Human reason and free will do not play a part.

Skepticism also marks several of the short pieces written around the same time. *Ceci n'est pas un conte* [*This Is Not a Story*] announces its Sternian negation in its title and adds a turn to the diminished profile of mimesis in Diderot's work. A real story, says Diderot, always has a listener; and a listener always interrupts. Hence, what follows will not be a story (an unreal one, apparently) because there are going to be a number of such interruptions (*DPV* 12.521). An example of how difficult it is to really "make" sense of Diderot's conscious attitudes to aesthetics or find any pattern to the promiscuous "catins" he called his *thoughts* is that in *The Two Friends of Bourbonne* he even reasserts his faith in novelistic illusionism. There are three kinds of stories, he tells us: the sort typified by Homer,

Virgil, and Tasso, where nature is exaggerated; the tales of La Fontaine and Ariosto, which are "invraisemblable"; and the "conte historique" [historical story] as practiced by Scarron and Cervantes. The object of the conte historique is illusionism, which involves a strict verisimilitude (*DPV* 12.454–55). With regard to Cervantes, Diderot surely had in mind once more the attention to detail, to the multitude of small circumstances that realist writers specialized in. There is no question, in any case, about which of the three types of story he favors. As usual, however, the discourse of the novel itself in the piece shows all the flaws of his early forays into fiction, lacking, ironically, the very attention to detail Diderot claimed was so necessary. In a letter to Grimm he begs him to correct in his copy an instance where, as with Sister Ursula in *The Nun*, he forgot that a character had died and had her suddenly turn up again in the story. And there are numerous other examples of a lack of discipline that recall the earlier novel.[42]

The work, however, that rings the final change on the new configuration of the two discursive systems in Diderot's work is *Paradoxe sur le comédien* [*Paradox of the Actor*] (1773). In this theoretical piece, Diderot purges his aesthetics completely of the reflection theory that had grounded his pleasure in realism, leaving a moral neoclassicism in possession of the field. The result is a level of antitheatricalist language reminiscent of earlier decades. The "paradox" in the piece is that a good actor must not feel the emotions he portrays. The First Interlocutor asserts that an actor who does so, and through a strong act of sympathetic identification feels what his character would feel if he were real, cannot be a good actor since his rational and technical powers will necessarily be subsumed in the passion of the moment. A truly great actor is a conscious technician, not a mere copy of an original, and his work is a careful construction. He is a student rather than a participant, "un spectateur froid et tranquille" [a cool and calm observer].[43]

Almost as if he had heard Goethe's remark about confusing nature and art, Diderot explodes in a barrage of language that insists he had always known the difference: "Et comment la nature sans l'art formerait-elle un grand comédien, puisque rien ne se passe exactement sur la scène comme en nature?" [And how would nature without art make a great actor, since nothing happens on the stage exactly as in real life?] (126); "Réflechissez un moment sur ce qu'on appelle au théâtre *être vrai*. Est-ce montrer les choses comme elles sont en nature? Aucunement" [Think for a moment about what is called *truth* in drama. Is it showing things as they are in real life? Not at all] (137); "Vous me parlez d'un instant fugitif de la nature, et moi je vous parle d'un ouvrage de l'art" [You talk to me about a fugitive moment of real life, and I'm talking to you about a work of art] (139). The good actor is never hurried out of himself by his emotions; he sits calmly above them, calculating and in control. To say he believed in nothing would be untrue, he believes in himself; at his center is a hard, focused singularity, a formidably strong sense of self and identity that allows him to put on and off the personal traits of his models at will. Such is "Le Premier's" portrait of a great actor.

But this new type of mimetic artist is just as morally culpable as Rameau. This is because, for Diderot, the common ground between a reflection theory of art and the neoclassical model of agency he promotes here, remains the essential morality or amorality of what is represented. Rameau was "une glace toujours disposée à montrer les objets" [a mirror always ready to reflect objects], so the moral quality of the representation was congruent with that of the original. He was blamed as if there were no difference. But in this model the artist is just as guilty, in fact more so since here the act is premeditated and calculating. And Le Premier is as severe a tribunal as the Narrator in *Rameau's Nephew*. The cool technician has a strictly mechanical interest in his character—and none in its morality. He knows no shame. He will portray Iago with the same conviction as Othello, and the spectator will be drawn to both. Diderot's record of praise for realism makes it hard to accept that when he says that the actor's ability is "rendre si scrupuleusement les signes extérieurs du sentiment, que vous vous y trompiez" [to so scrupulously render the external indicators of feeling that you are deceived] (132), he has in mind the cunning and deception of the consummate pretender. "Il sait le moment précis où il tirera son mouchoir et où les larmes couleront" [He knows the precise moment when he will pull out his handkerchief and the tears will flow] (133). That could be praise, but it is not wrong to hear in it the critical tones of the moralist.

The First Interlocutor in the *Paradox* is Diderot. The Second takes the First's comments on the actor as praise, since he understands Le Premier to be a man of the theater. But he gradually becomes puzzled. If an actor does not base his role on any real-life model (which would entail identification, sympathy, and sensibility), but instead merely collects specimens to put together later as he constructs his character, that character would appear to be, strictly speaking, devoid of reality, an ideal. This is where Diderot's materialist philosophy comes in to settle the question. The Second Interlocutor is obliged to come to the only possible conclusion: if the actor's construction is purely ideal in this way, then his art is devoid of knowledge; this must be true, "or, il n'y a rien dans l'entendement qui n'ait été dans la sensation" [because there is no knowledge that was not first in the senses] (154). Thus, in a rather straightforward way we see how skepticism, in limiting knowledge to a material, sense-knowledge, must insist that realism on stage is an epistemologically illegitimate form.

In the *Paradox* this conclusion leads to the question of whether there can then be something that might be called "une sensibilité artificielle" [an artificial sensibility] (157), as distinct from the strictly physical as the stage imitation is from reality. Le Premier, who has posed the question rhetorically, answers it with a yes, describing it as something that does not lead to art, but rather is a product of art. The fact that Mme de la Merteuil would agree should warn us that this type of sensibility is not one Diderot the moralist, in the guise of Le Premier, is going to approve of. Sensibility on stage is reduced to an actor's "facilité de connaître et de copier toutes les natures" [ability to know and copy all natures] (157). The moral judgment comes when Le Premier suddenly, and somewhat illogically, turns the definition back to the material body; or more specifically, to its weaknesses. Sensibility is "cette disposition compagne de la faiblesse des organes, suite de la mobilité du diaphragm, de la vivacité de l'imagination, de la délicatesse des nerfs, qui incline à compatir, à frissoner, à s'évanouir, à secourir, à fuir, à crier" [that disposition accompanied by a weakness of the organs coming from the mobility of the diaphragm, from the liveliness of the imagination, the sensitivity of the nerves, that moves one to sympathize, to shiver, to faint, to help, to flee, to cry out].

But while this does not sound all that bad, the continuance does. Le Premier goes on: "à perdre la raison, à exagérer, à mépriser, à dédaigner ... à n'avoir aucune idée précise du vrai, du bon et du beau, à être injuste, à être fou" [to lose one's reason, to exaggerate, to despise, to disdain ... to have absolutely no precise idea of the true, the good, the beautiful, to be unjust, to be mad] (158).

What began as an assertion that there was an artificial sensibility ends in collapsing it back into the material, where it is condemned as nothing but a physical weakness in a way reminiscent of Laclos. From this point on, Le Premier's criticism is part of the same discourse of orthodox antitheatricalism that Laclos invoked against Merteuil. Actors are notorious libertines, poor and uneducated. None ever choose acting as a profession but are forced into it by circumstance. It is not the love of virtue that motivates them, or the desire to be useful to society, or to serve their country or family that leads them into the profession. They are not motivated "par aucun des motifs honnêtes qui pourraient entraîner un esprit droit, un coeur chaud, une âme sensible vers une aussi belle profession" [by any honest motive that might lead a spirit of rectitude, a warm heart, a sensitive soul to such a beautiful profession] (163), but because they have no character, because in acting they can put aside what character they have. Actors suffer from "une vanité qu'on pourrait appeler insolence" [a vanity that could be called insolence]. Acting is a profession that like no other sacrifices "l'intérêt commun de tous et celui du public . . . à de misérables petites prétentions" [the common interest of all and that of the public . . . to miserable small pretensions]. Actors are the "petits et bas dans la société" [the small and low in society] who rarely have any merit: "un comédien galant homme, une actrice honnête femme soient les phénomènes si rares" [an actor who is a gallant man, an actress who is an honest woman are rare enough phenomena] (164). This sounds strangely like Collier or William Law; but it is Diderot.

It could be argued that the character delivering these hard accusations is himself a fiction. But like Philo at the end of Hume's *Dialogues*, the position of Le Premier is never contradicted; and he is openly identified in the work as Diderot. Or it could be said that the criticisms are made against actors not acting, and certainly not against realism in drama. But the tones really are those of William Law, fulminating against theater as a form of deception. Le Premier finally wonders openly about the influence of the stage on public morals, and notes, as Collier had in his 1698 pamphlet *A Short View of the Immorality and Profaneness of the English Stage*, whether one should applaud sentiments on the stage that one would not countenance in everyday life. He asks: "Où est le poète qui osât proposer . . . à des femmes . . . de débiter effrontément devant une multitude d'auditeurs des propos qu'elles rougiraient d'entendre dans le secret de leurs foyers?" [Where is the poet who would dare suggest . . . to women . . . that they retail things unabashedly before a crowd of listeners that they would blush to hear in the privacy of their own living rooms?] (165–66).

Compare this to Collier's similar question at the turn of the century: "Obscenity in any company is rustic uncreditable talent; but among women 'tis particularly rude. Such talk would be very affrontive in conversation, and not endured by any lady of reputation. Whence comes it to pass that those liberties which disoblige so much in conversation should entertain upon the stage?"[44]

Like Collier, Le Premier does not want to dismiss theater as a whole, but reproducing on the stage what one would not countenance in real life is now a vice. Diderot's *Père de Famille* [*A Father and His Family*] was undergoing a revival at the time and Le Premier does not hesitate to cite this fact as a kind of authorization of his views. Suddenly, views on realism that were put forth years before in the conversations with Dorval in *Le Fils Naturel* [*The Natural Son*] are discarded in favor of the superiority of the "comédie larmoyante." The irony argument—that Diderot is setting his new antitheatricalist views up for a fall—is contradicted by the fact that they never take one; and by the fact that Le Premier voices other attitudes that are clearly Diderot's.

The strain of antitheatricalism is jarring and "Le Second" is still confused. Le Premier continues to put himself forward as an advocate of theater. In a statement that could apply equally to dramatists like Diderot he says: "Le théâtre n'est méprisé que par ceux d'entre les acteurs que les sifflets en ont chassés" [Theater is only despised by actors who have been booed off the stage]. But this and similar comments on the praiseworthy nature of theater are contradicted by others advising neophyte actors, for example, that they are wasting their time and should give up this dissolute way of life for an apprenticeship with a painter or sculptor.

Perhaps Diderot was just bitter over the failure of his own plays, but the negative moral discourse on dramatic realism in the *Paradox* is jarring, especially since the criticisms are fundamental and apply equally to realist fiction. It is impossible to know if Diderot himself realized it. After all, the writer too must remain detached, and the emotions of characters like Clarissa, sensibility included, have no more exact model in reality (as Richardson himself admitted) than the simulated and artificial emotions of the actor. Whether Diderot would agree or not, the shape of his argument on the immateriality of the creator's model is such that mimetic art can no longer be considered a form of cognition or knowledge.

In a letter to his daughter in 1781 Diderot makes the surprising admission that he had always looked on novels as essentially frivolous productions.[45] One recalls small hints early on, such as the critical attack in 1748 in *The Jewels* on the novels of Marivaux, Duclos, and Crebillon *fils* as uninteresting (*DPV* 3.216–17). Jean Catrysse catalogues a host of such comments across Diderot's writing that characterize romances, novels, and stories as variously useless, full of commonplaces, made up of interchangeable elements, ridiculous, and dangerous for the morals of young women, including the remark of Mirzoza in *The Jewels* that such writing belongs to "la classe de ceux en qui l'âme ne visite la tête que comme une maison de campagne où son séjour n'est pas long" [the class of those in whom the heart only visits the head like a kind of summer house where it doesn't stay long].[46] The remark is poignant in that it describes only too well Diderot's own troubles.

The articulation of the discourse of skepticism in conjunction with that of the novel in Diderot goes through interesting changes over the course of his career, but takes a particularly definitive shape, as I have tried to show, in the 1760s, when Diderot discovers Sterne. In that decade his materialist philosophy begins to develop serious strengths and shape its surroundings. The discourse of the novel, as part of those surroundings, does not thrive, and in the end is reduced to a minimal presence. In 1772, writing again on the attention to observed detail in realist fiction, Diderot refers to "ce petit espionnage journalière des mots, des actions et des mines . . . que je comparerais volontiers à l'art de faire passer des grains de millet par le trou d'une aiguille, c'est une misérable petite étude" [this little daily spying out of words, actions, and looks . . . that I would gladly compare to the art of dropping grains of millet through the eye of a needle, is a miserable little study].[47]

And looking back in 1781 Diderot was able to revise his whole attitude to the genre, saying: "J'avais toujours traité les romans comme des productions assez frivoles" [I had always treated novels as frivolous enough productions].[48] In the end the "devil of a philosophy," that his mind could not help approving and his heart denying, carried the day.

The Realization of Romance

Radcliffe, Godwin, and Goethe

The language of sentiment in the eighteenth century is a subset of the larger system of skeptical discourse affiliated with antirealist and antirational forms like romance, the gothic, and the sublime. Descartes's mindbody paradigm left behind a materialist universe for Enlightenment skeptics to inhabit, one whose secular mechanism was elaborated in different ways by Spinoza and Diderot. The delegitimation of mind as a controlling guide in the literature of sentiment in this new universe goes hand in hand with a redefinition of *judgment* in sensationist terms: the *good* is what feels good, what looks good, what tastes good. Ethics becomes, as in Shaftesbury, a matter of *taste*.

We know that in literature this had a long vogue, beginning indeed with Shaftesbury, and with sentimental drama circa 1700, and leading all the way through the "cult of sensibility" and rage for sentimental novels in the second half of the century. It also progressed as a taste. The senses get jaded, and when Louis Bredvold talks about the "culmination" of sensibility in "horror," he is referring to the increasingly stronger doses of sensation that were gradually required to produce an effect. We see them in the taste for Ossian and Graveyard Poetry, for Wertherism, Piranesi, Rosa, and the sublime, in the lubricious terrors of the gothic, and finally in a return to a frighteningly physical re-materializing of feeling in Sade.[1] In this chapter I want to focus briefly on sensibility, romance, and the sublime in three writers whose work sets these literary manifestations of skepticism in direct opposition to the discourse of realism and knowledge.

Radcliffe's *The Mysteries of Udolpho* and Godwin's *Things As They Are; or, The Adventures of Caleb Williams* both appeared in 1794. Radcliffe treats sensibility, superstition, and the sublime, while Godwin deals directly with romance. In romance, sentiment and sensibility are not always prominent, but what they have in common is a downgrading of rationality in favor of feeling. The tenacity of romance and sentiment in the century is remarkable, and has been well-documented. By 1794 the vogue for sentiment, for example, had been under severe review for well over a decade, but still held a powerful popular appeal. Chatterton's suicide in 1770, however, had shocked people, and the critical reception of Goethe's *The Sorrows of Young Werther* when it appeared in translation in 1779 showed that readers were becoming more aware of the dangers of a feeling heart. Henry Mackenzie's comments on the dangers of sensibility appeared in 1785, the same year Clara Reeve published *The Progress of Romance,* in which she dated the demise of romance back to the time of Defoe.[2] But sensibility and romance were still very much in the air in the 1790s, and in the bookshops. Imitations of *Werther* that stressed his sentiment over his suicide appeared through the end of the century, despite attempts by writers like Burke to lay the bloodbath of the Reign of Terror at the feet of sentimentalists. Mary Wollstonecroft's *Vindication of the Rights of Woman* appeared in 1792 and kept the issue of sensibility alive by offering a scathing attack on the "susceptibility of heart" that she claimed kept women enslaved; but Wertherism and a taste for the gothic lived on through the turn of the century.[3]

Radcliffe's *Udolpho* nonetheless casts a powerful vote on behalf of the countervailing Richardsonian tradition. It is important for the way it articulates and juxtaposes skepticism and novelistic discourse. The *supernatural expliqué* that is Radcliffe's trademark entails the steady movement of textual meaning from one system to the other. In particular, it entails a steady rationalization and realization of elements native to the discourse of skepticism—moving out of the dark, so to speak, toward knowledge and verisimilitude. At the end of the story, a realist aesthetic is left in tentative possession of the field; tentative only because so much of the unreal has preceded it that its complete effacement is impossible. Radcliffe, after all, was undoubtedly aware that the sensational was what made the book popular.[4] The story she tells, however, brings forth the unreal in order to purge it.

Radcliffe's ambivalence on the topic has its analogue in St. Aubert, whose advice to Emily is to beware of sentiment, but also to hold onto it.[5] Radcliffe uses the standard language of feeling. Emily has, in her father's opinion, a "delicacy of mind, warm affections, and ready benevolence." But St. Aubert knows this is a charm, not a virtue; and that it puts her at risk. He wants "to strengthen her mind; to enure her to habits of self-command;

to teach her to reject the first impulse of her feelings." She must learn to make a "cool examination" of facts and troubles, "to resist first impressions, and to acquire that steady dignity of mind, that can alone counterbalance the passions."[6] Her effort to "restrain her sensibility" on the death of her mother is a "triumph" (19); and St. Aubert talks to her about the "duty of self-command" and tells her that she must "let reason . . . restrain sorrow" (20). Radcliffe's duplicitous text will not exactly practice what it preaches, giving it a curiously stereophonic effect.

St. Aubert, in his warnings, is in fact the apostle of the *via media* and is far from recommending anything like the hardened moral realism that a Rochefoucauld or Laclos might have thought helpful for a young woman in Emily's circumstances about to launch out into the world. "I would not annihilate your feelings, my child," he says, "I would only teach you to command them." Whatever dangers a too susceptible heart may present, St. Aubert says, "nothing can be hoped from an insensible one" (20). But later when he is dying he returns to his warning with more urgency: "Above all, my dear Emily, said he, do not indulge in the pride of fine feeling, the romantic error of amiable minds. Those, who really possess sensibility, ought early to be taught, that it is a dangerous quality, which is continually extracting the excess of misery, or delight, from every surrounding circumstance" (79–80).

St. Aubert speaks as if he had just read *Werther*, or as if Radcliffe had. He tells Emily that he is not "an advocate for apathy," only control, and concludes on the keynote of all ethics: that sentiment is a "disgrace" unless it translates into an active "practical virtue." Otherwise it is "abstract" and dangerous (81). By the 1790s this was a familiar criticism. Sensibility, as I mentioned in relation to Sterne, must transpose from high to low, from spirit to real action, if it is ever to be more than self-indulgence. As Samuel Johnson put it, the love of virtue should not stand in for virtue itself. Radcliffe, however, allows St. Aubert to indulge in a little fine feeling himself that turns out to be the result, not the motivator, of a good action. Having distributed stipends to his pensioners, he walks home through the woods feeling intense pleasure at "having done a beneficent action." It spurs him to indulge the sentiment completely, and we are suddenly transported, in his account, out of the moment into the land of faery: "I remember that in my youth this gloom used to call forth to my fancy a thousand fairy visions, and romantic images; and I own, I am not yet wholly insensible of that high enthusiasm, which wakes the poet's dream: I can linger, with solemn steps under the deep shades, send forward a transforming eye into the distant obscurity, and listen with thrilling delight to the mystic murmuring of the woods" (15).

The ideal is to be able to hold onto such susceptibilities, which would strike a familiar and powerful chord with many sentimental readers, without having them become a weakness. But the sentiment here is really gratuitous, just the sort of thing St. Aubert himself warns against. The need to keep the book's stock-in-trade before the reader occasionally leads Radcliffe to the edge of bathos. She tells us, for example, that St. Aubert did not fish because "he never could find amusement in torturing or destroying" (8). One recalls Uncle Toby's refusal in *Tristram Shandy* to kill a fly.

The journey into Languedoc introduces the sublime, which is also slowly brought into juxtaposition with the discourse of realism. Emily and St. Aubert are going into Provence for the air on the advice of St. Aubert's physician, and instead of taking the direct route along the base of the Pyrenees they choose the mountain way for its "more extensive views and greater variety of romantic scenery" (27). What follows is a deluge of such scenery. They are surrounded by dizzying crags and sublime vistas. Pastoral valleys, however, spring up at every turn to counterbalance them. St. Aubert looks back with melancholy at their home receding behind them in the haze, and when he turns his eyes back to the front is faced with the "grandeur" of the scene, with "stupendous" walls of rock, "lofty" cliffs, and a heavy dose of "magnificence." But Radcliffe wants this sublimity refunctioned and quickly moves our eyes from the cliffs down into a valley that has suddenly appeared, carrying us away from the sublime to the pastoral, to "vast plains" instead of vast mountains, to "woods, towns, blushing vines, and plantations of almonds, palms and olives" (27–28). Contemplation and high feeling are replaced with an inhabited landscape overflowing with the suggestion of Man's industry. The fruits of one's own labor, as Werther failed to learn, can be a good antidote for what ails the sensitive at heart.

Radcliffe repeats the lesson a number of times. At one moment Michael, their driver, has them rattling along the edge of a precipice "which made the eye dizzy to look down." St. Aubert is helpless, and Emily "terrified almost to fainting." Then suddenly they are at the bottom and resting by a "rivulet." They continue and within a few lines again are plunging into a landscape "scorch'd by lightnings," passing a "torrent," and lost in a "gloom" where no living creature but the lizard dares go. Radcliffe writes: "This was such a scene as Salvator would have chosen, had he then existed, for his canvas; St. Aubert, impressed by the romantic character of the place, almost expected to see banditti start from behind some projecting rock, and he kept his hand on the arms with which he always travelled."

But then the valley once again opens, "its savage features gradually softened," and by evening they are in a Lorrain canvas, listening to sheep bells and the "voice of the shepherd calling his wandering flocks" (30). The transitions are reassuring—the sort of resolution of unpredictability and uncertainty that, according to Shirley Brice Heath, gives pleasure in reading novels. Struck by the "grandeur of the scenes" as they amble along precipices so desolate that even the mules must proceed with caution, Emily and her father "linger" over the solitude and indulge in "sublime reflections." The last oxymoron is indicative of Radcliffe's determination to bridge two heterogeneous ideas, since the sublime can only be recollected and reflected upon, like Wordsworth's spontaneous feelings, in later tranquility. Such "reflections," Radcliffe tells us, "soften, while they elevate the heart, and fill it with the certainty of a present God" (28). The natural sublime was close to religious exaltation; but Radcliffe is far from that here.[7] The point is really to bring the discourse of the sublime steadily along the road to a more domestic habitation.

That habitation is the beautiful and the picturesque. The rationalization of the sublime involves first transposing away from it to the beautiful and the picturesque and then associating this different visual aesthetic with the discourse of reason. The sublime is nondiscursive, something one experiences, even suffers; but the beautiful can be discussed and interpreted. Climbing up to the convent in the moonlight, St. Aubert, Emily, and Valancourt stop to appreciate the "deep repose" and "silence" of the pastoral landscape and forest they are passing through. They sit down and become "wrapt in the complacency" that the still night scene inspires. Valancourt says such scenes "soften the heart, like the notes of sweet music." They "inspire delicious melancholy" and "awaken our best and purest feelings, disposing us to benevolence, pity, and friendship." Here the language of sentiment is conscripted to convey the idea, but it is the landscape that creates the disposition toward good works. St. Aubert holds Emily's hand as his thoughts turn to his late wife. Emily feels a warm tear fall on her hand and knows what her father is thinking. The memory of those we love, he says, "steals upon the mind" in such moments, "all tender and harmonious." But then, somewhat surprisingly he suddenly comes out with: "I have always fancied, that I thought with more clearness, and precision, at such an hour than at any other" (45–46). It may indeed be the hour, but his acuity seems rather to be a function of where they are. St.

Aubert, after all, never associates mental acuity with sentiment—it is quite the opposite. And one does not think at all in front of sublime vistas.

The character of Montoni, when he appears, furthers the novelization and realization process. Montoni is not much of a romantic villain, but more importantly for his purpose, no sentimentalist. To the contrary, he is a Machiavellian and a lover of "dissimulation" (143). As in Laclos, the quality has sex appeal. Montoni is "an uncommonly handsome person, with features manly and expressive"; he shows a "haughtiness of command," but also a "quickness of discernment" (23). Compared to the insufferable Quesnels, who introduce him, he appears to advantage as a man both more substantial and more interesting than those around him. We are told it was seldom that he met in company a man of more address or understanding than himself. And although he is cast to play the villain he is like Valmont in *Dangerous Liaisons*, unafraid "to measure his talents of dissimulation with those of any other competitor for distinction and plunder" (143). Being heartless is right for his role as persecutor, but it also clears him away from the language of sentiment that the text is slowly bracketing. In fact Montoni has the same attitude to sentiment as Emily's father. He tells Emily: "When you are older you will look back with gratitude to the friends who assisted in rescuing you from the romantic illusions of sentiment, and will perceive that they are only the snares of childhood, and should be vanquished the moment you escape from the nursery (196)."

The terrors that beset Emily in the castle are a result of such "illusions" and "snares." Montoni, however, encourages her not to imagine things, "to endeavour to adopt a more rational conduct than that of yielding to fancies, and to a sensibility, which, to call it by the gentlest name, is only a weakness" (23). His job as villain obviously fills only one of his purposes in the novel. Up against his plea, Radcliffe piles all the stock props of the gothic, all of which rely on the terror of the unknown. Any outdoor scene around twilight will likely include a shadow moving suspiciously through the shrubberies, and once we are in the castle it is only a matter of time before Annette will scream "Holy Virgin!" or "Holy St. Peter!" and ask Emily if she did not hear some footsteps or see a figure sliding through a doorway. One might say that the gothic takes sentiment's link to skepticism and dramatizes it. Everyone is literally in the dark. Emily, for example, is in the dark either literally or figuratively almost all of the time. She wonders, for example, what Madame Cheron's fate will be, given what appears to have happened to Signora Laurentini. In addition to what she knows, there is much she does not know; and this is the real source of her anguish—the "thousand nameless terrors, which exist only in active imaginations, and which set reason and examination equally at defiance" (240).

F. W. Murneau realized in making *Dracula* that showing a closed door was to show the unknown. The closed door was its objective correlative, so to speak. Doing so could inspire more fear than revealing what was behind it. There is a door like that in Emily's room in the castle as well, locked from the other side, and although Count Dracula is not behind it, it makes rough going for susceptible hearts. After her first experience with it Emily has breakfast with Montoni and says: "Oh could I know . . . what passes in that mind; could I know the thoughts, that are known there, I should no longer be condemned to this torturing suspense!" Montoni tells her again: "release yourself from the slavery of these fears . . . conquer such whims, and endeavour to strengthen your mind" (244). Again, good advice. In the end, he will prove to be right. The veil will be lifted and everything will be *realized;* events, that is to say, will be purged of the supernatural.

Montoni's own dissembling turns out to have a very un-romantic purpose—one familiar in realist fiction since Defoe: he wants money. In particular he wants Emily to sign over the estates she has inherited from Madame Cheron. She might as well, since if she does not he can keep her there until she does; and for him there is no other way to get them. But she refuses. He tricks her into signing. When she protests he tells her: "It was necessary to deceive you—there was no other way of making you act reasonably" (436). Clarissa, at the end, might have said as much to Lovelace. When Radcliffe sends Montoni off to prison at the end, one imagines less a fearsome hulking brute dragged away in chains than a kind of cynical aristocrat, slouching off with a shrug and a half-smile, his hands in his suit-jacket pockets. Montoni's exit has some of the bathos of Merteuil's in *Dangerous Liaisons.* He is gone, but not forgotten.

The shift to events in and around Chateau-le-Blanc once Emily is back in France allows Radcliffe to close out the movement of her *supernatural expliqué* with a last episode involving superstition. Neighbors believe the chateau is haunted, but we learn that smugglers are merely creating that impression to keep people away so they can use the vaults of the castle as a cache for their spoils. Knowledge ends the superstition, reinscribing events firmly within a realist aesthetic. *Udolpho,* in short, displays a new awareness of the dangers and ultimate epistemological bankruptcy of its own sensibility by placing it squarely in the company of its irrational affiliates, gothic horror and the sublime. Radcliffe's *supernatural expliqué* should be understood in this sense as an attempt to rationalize such skeptical manifestations and bring them within the confines of the discourse of realism.

* * *

William Godwin's *Things As They Are; or, The Adventures of Caleb Williams* effects the same transposition and realization, but does so in a more programmatic way. Godwin had politics rather than aesthetics in view when he wrote the novel, but the story is nonetheless a kind of allegory of genre that dramatizes the dissolution of romance in a realist aesthetic, which is not dissimilar to what happens in Radcliffe. Godwin's novel is also important for the way it introduces the concept of justice to the configuration we have been examining. In skeptical times, it is justice as much as ethics that suffers from the delegitimation of reason; so Godwin's attempt to eliminate a particularly unreasonable genre of skeptical discourse (romance) in favor of the novel is an aesthetic way of articulating justice. His Jacobin agenda fits in well with the formal aspect of the novel.

We can see the programmatic nature of the configuration in the binarism of the title where "things as they are" defines the real, and "adventures" signals romance. The duality is also present in the two endings Godwin wrote: the original manuscript ending stresses *things as they are* by having the institutional forces that surround Falkland triumph, while the published *happy* ending is a wishful romance ending where Caleb's greatness of heart elicits a change of heart in Falkland and the two all but fall on one another's necks in tears of remorse and shared understanding. Similarly, Godwin's original 1794 preface stresses the first ending, while in the later 1832 preface to *Fleetwood* he recasts the novel in retrospect as a psychological thriller. Indeed, in the 1831 Bentley edition Godwin changed its primary title to *The Adventures of Caleb Williams*. The different political climate of 1830 makes the revisionism understandable, but the novel is nonetheless beset by a heavily overdetermined set of polar opposites that in turn shape the way the genre conflict is presented.[8]

Godwin's comments on aesthetics in his writing are scattered, and there is no point trying to read into them a coherent theory of genre, but we do know he was a fan of Richardson rather than Fielding or Sterne, and it is likely that he preferred his original true-to-life ending as more politically honest than the commercial, romance one he decided to publish.[9] He was reading Richardson as he wrote *Caleb Williams*—we can see Grandison, for example, in Falkland, in the latter's trip to Italy, his character as a paragon of male virtue, his duel and so on. And Godwin's criticism of Holcroft's *Anna St. Ives* shows the same preference for realism. Godwin criticized Holcroft for his busy authorial intrusions and claimed they shattered the story's illusion.[10] There is also the remark in the *Enquiry Concerning Political Justice* (1793) to the effect that "literature has reconciled the whole thinking world respecting the great principles of the system of the universe, and extirpated upon this subject the dreams of romance and the dogmas of superstition."[11] Godwin has in mind Newton and Locke but his position vis-à-vis "romance" and "superstition" is clear.

It is equally clear in his attitude to Burke and Rousseau.[12] In a letter he wrote Burke in 1785 Godwin accuses him of having his principles deformed by a misguided sense of chivalry that has led to his wrong-headed views on the French Revolution. Burke has "a refined and exquisite sensibility" that must unfortunately rank him, somewhat literally, among the odorous and dewy followers of Rousseau—a man of "weakness and imbecility" who has "created to himself a new world, which impressed him on every occasion, instead of that which really existed, and ascribed to men a variety of motives, extremely different from those by which they were actuated."[13] The associations are definitive and illuminating: sensibility and romance; sensibility, Rousseau, and a failure of mind, where Rousseau's world is not the world "which really existed."

These are the associations attached to Falkland in his battle with Caleb. Hume's line that Reason is a slave of the Passions explains him quite well.[14] He is a man who has "imbibed the love of chivalry," who "had too much good sense," Collins says, "to regret the times of Charlemagne and Arthur," but still felt there was "something to imitate" in the "manners depicted by these celebrated poets." As we quickly discover, Falkland goes far in this direction. His "opinions" turn out to be "illustrated in his conduct," which in turn "assiduously conformed to the model of heroism that his fancy suggested."[15] Falkland's chivalric code and ruling passion—his concern for reputation—are what bring him to grief.

His characterization takes an important turn when we learn about his qualities as a "philosopher" and a "poet" (30). Tyrrel complains that he is a man who would rather scratch his head for a rhyme and count his fingers for a verse than do an honest day's work—that he is a man of "learning." He wants nothing to do with Falkland's "rhymes and rebusses," his "quirks and conundrums," and looks on his nemesis as "sophisticated and artificial" (20, 30, 46). Clare, the poet, sees Falkland's good points and even approves of his poem, ominously titled "Ode to the Genius of Chivalry"

(26). But Clare puts his finger on Falkland's weakness: on his deathbed Clare warns Falkland to beware of a "weakness" for "impetuosity and an impatience of imagined dishonour." This, Clare tells him, can "make you as eminently mischievous, as you will otherwise be useful." Think seriously, he tells him, "of exterminating this error" (34). Romance in the person of Falkland is allied to a failure of reason. Caleb calls Falkland's concern with reputation his ruling passion, but Clare describes it as a failure of mind, an "error." Clare thus serves to introduce the issue of knowledge, suggesting that romance is an instance of its failure.

And Clare's fears are borne out. Following the public beating Falkland takes at the hands of Tyrrel, his course of action is determined by his reading. "He was too deeply pervaded with the idle and groundless romances of chivalry," Collins says, "ever to forget the situation, humiliating and dishonourable according to his ideas, in which he had been placed upon this occasion." Collins underlines Falkland's quixotism: "There is a mysterious sort of divinity annexed to the person of a true knight, that makes any species of brute violence committed upon it indelible and immortal. To be knocked down, cuffed, kicked, dragged along the floor! sacred heaven, the memory of such a treatment was not to be endured" (97).

Like Clare, Collins sees the problem as a failure of knowledge: "If Mr. Falkland had reflected with perfect accuracy upon the case, he would probably have been able to look down with indifference upon a wound which, as it was, pierced to his very vitals" (98).

And later, when Caleb toys with Falkland on the topic of the license great men may or may not take with the lives of others, Falkland's reply reminds us of Don Quixote's tendency to take sheep for armies: "The death of a hundred thousand men is at first sight very shocking; but what in reality are a hundred thousand such men more than a hundred thousand sheep?" (111). This is a failure of understanding in a mind ruled by passion. The political allegory and the literary come together in Falkland like a key in a lock.

Caleb's case, by contrast, is not quite so neatly defined. Although he cannot escape his place in the overdetermined landscape of the novel as the politically correct foil to Falkland, he has enough frayed edges to indicate that Godwin was not consciously using him to make as clear a statement about literary realism as he was about romance. Caleb begins with the sort of hunting-and-gathering instinct that Diderot thought was the key attribute of the little spying mind of the novelist and ends—also a bit as Diderot did—with some hard thoughts about the practice. In the beginning Caleb makes no distinction between novels and romances, although knowledge once again is his theme: "I could not rest till I had acquainted myself with the solutions that had been invented for the phenomena of the universe. In fine, this produced in me an invincible attachment to books of narrative and romance. I panted for the unravelling of an adventure . . . I read, I devoured compositions of this sort. They took possession of my soul; and the effects they produced, were frequently discernible in my external appearance and my health . . . my imagination must be excited; and, when that was not done, my curiosity was dormant" (4).

Caleb is a reader, and although at this stage what he says applies to both romances and novels, the common factor is his thirst for knowledge. For readers at this point in the century that would probably prompt the idea of the novel more than romance, since the qualities of logic, deducibility, and narrative Caleb values are more aspects of the first. Falkland's actions are "pregnant with meaning" (5) and have a rational explanation that Caleb will attempt to bring into narrative form. In a sense he will try to do what Radcliffe did in *Udolpho:* realize the enemy. Late in the novel he says that when he was young "he beheld the world as a scene in which to hide or to appear" (277). He is already a man of disguises with an imaginative bent.

"Design" is Caleb's principal strategy as he begins to investigate the meaning of Falkland's "great wound." After Collins's narrative, which takes up all of volume 1, Godwin wastes no time in putting Caleb to work on the crime at the beginning of volume 2. Sounding a bit like D'Alembert on the *Encyclopedia,* Caleb tells us he strove for complete knowledge, to "comprehend" Falkland's mystery in "its full import." To do so he "turned it a thousand ways, and examined it in every point of view" (107). Volume 2 then begins with a burst of questions that Caleb has to answer with regard to the events Collins has just recounted to him. What about Hawkins? Did it make sense that a man "so firm, so sturdily honest and just" could "all at once . . . become a murderer"? Was it possible Falkland was the killer? And if he wasn't, how did one explain all his "agonies and terrors" (107)? Caleb only hears Collins's story, which strongly exonerates Falkland, after he has had personal experience of Falkland's puzzling "terrors"—terrors that are those of a guilty man. What Collins says merely brings back his suspicions. He tries to put things together, to concretize a picture of events that makes sense. As facets of Falkland's behavior are revealed to him, he narrativizes them, looking for the design, the *figure in the carpet.*

Artifice becomes his best resource in pursuing fuller knowledge. When he decides to play detective, he says, "I found a strange sort of pleasure in it" (107). The task, he says, is "to guard my designs." He plans his artful probing of Falkland's conscience to proceed by way of offhand remarks, "at one time implying extreme ignorance, and at another some portion of acuteness, but at all times having an air of innocence, frankness and courage." He strives like a Jamesian to create the impression of artlessness: "There was still an apparent want of design in the manner," he says of his investigations, and this pleases him. Falkland is falling into his net. He had his suspicions, Caleb says, "of my knowing more than I expressed" and constantly wondered "what was the degree of information I possessed" (108–9). Falkland knows he is being written into the pages of Caleb's narrative and asks Caleb if he thinks that he, the master of the house, is "an instrument to be played on." He calls Caleb an "artful wretch" (118).

Godwin takes care not to allow us to think too poorly of Caleb for his obsessive novelization; he has him recognize, as Collins had, Falkland's good qualities, and voice his love and admiration. Caleb insists on the God-like quality of this most admirable and amiable of masters. But driven by his curiosity he cannot abandon his design. Godwin is equally careful to withhold any real evidence upon which Caleb might base his conviction: in a variation on the story of the veil in *Udolpho*, which hid nothing, Falkland's mysterious trunk, which seems to hold some damning evidence, is never examined; during the fire Caleb is so obsessed with the trunk that he loses his head and is in the process of breaking into it when Falkland sweeps in upon him. The issue of evidence is important and will remain one of the touchstones throughout the novel. At this point Caleb has no factual proof of Falkland's guilt, only his own fiction. Indeed things seem to point away from Falkland; there is the failure of the trunk, for instance, to release its secrets. But "in spite of inclination, in spite of persuasion and in spite of evidence" (125), Caleb knows Falkland is guilty. On one hand, this seems to make Caleb look unfair; he ought to doubt, after all, until there is some empirical evidence for belief. On the other hand, fictional knowledge here is going to prove real in spite of the desire on the part of the allegorical figure of romance to suppress it. Caleb's knowledge, with its inner, intuitive sense of right, has much in common with that of Richardson's heroines.

Hamlet uses *The Mousetrap* to "hold as 'twere the mirror up to nature";[16] Caleb uses the trial in which Falkland sits in judgment on the boxer accused of murder—a case whose circumstances closely resemble those surrounding his murder of Tyrrel—as his own mousetrap. When

Falkland reacts to the play by rushing out of the room, Caleb knows he is guilty. "What had occurred amounted to no evidence that was admissible in a court of justice," he says; but he knows the truth nonetheless: "He is guilty! I see it! I feel it! I am sure of it!" (130). A mimetic re-presentation of the crime produces belief in *Hamlet*, and, finally, justice; and it works toward the same end for Caleb.[17]

Evidence returns as an issue when Caleb is charged with the robbery of his master. As part of the empirical world, physical evidence has a limited value when truth is at stake; and Caleb tries to convince his accusers of as much. Arguing like a Kantian, Caleb tries to get them to admit that while all knowledge may, as they believe, begin with the senses, it does not all arise from the senses. Forester and Caleb's fellow servants, however, are positivists. The evidence speaks more loudly than Caleb. Thomas tells him he can talk all he wants, "but it will not do; you will never be able to persuade people that black is white" (176).

But when Caleb goes on the lam this is just what he does persuade people of. He goes from being the writer of a crime narrative to being a kind of literary product himself. If survival, as Rochefoucauld said, calls for finesse, Caleb's skills as a novelist come to his aid now in his new life as a man of disguises. "From my youth," Caleb says, "I had possessed a considerable facility in the art of imitation" (238). Now is the time to use it. He appears first as a beggar, puts on a "peculiar slouching and clownish gait," and adopts an Irish brogue accent. He becomes a carman, a Jew, a hunchback; and when he gets to London he takes up the occupation of fiction writer for a magazine. Appropriately, he writes rogue biographies, composing, as it were, stories of his own life that he does not agree with. He has, he says, "a counterfeit character to support" (256). Gines, the sleuth and bounty hunter, has also written Caleb's story—"the most wonderful and surprising history, and miraculous adventures of Caleb Williams." Caleb reads it and discovers that he is indeed as much a literary product as a producer. Gines has in fact reduced him to a pamphlet that sells in the street "for the price of one halfpenny" (268–69).

Had Godwin's intention been to write a book extolling literary realism in this kind of allegorical economy, the novel would probably not contain the harsh comments that accompany Caleb's mimicry. But Godwin wants it to be clear that Caleb's "studied artifice," as Caleb himself calls it, is a "miserable expedient"; a purely defensive response to the "inexorable animosity and unfeeling tyranny of his fellow man" (238). When he is hiding out, and writing rogue biographies, his talent for artifice and mimetic fictionalizing not only saves him, it provides him with an income also. But Caleb looks on himself as a poor player and marionette whose strings are being pulled by others. He tires of impersonation, and when he is recaptured, then freed when Falkland fails to appear in court, the idea of "personating a fictitious character" gives him a feeling of "disgust." At this point in the story, and in his mind, "artifice" is associated not with freedom and material advantage but with "sadness, and terror" (288).

The sudden change of attitude is understandable as a function of the book's politics. In a just society Caleb would never be forced into such a necessity, but since he is he can only regret the playacting. Moreover, painting things as they are means people like Caleb have to be portrayed as out of tune with their world. Not only do Caleb's efforts have to be denied, what he stands for has to be denied as well—even if, in the work's aesthetic allegory, that is realism itself. The turnaround comes once more in a discussion about evidence, this time in the Welsh village. Caleb has been hiding there, working as a tutor to Laura's children, and doing well at it, until Gines turns up again with the pamphlet of his "Wonderful and Surprising History" to expose him. The question becomes: what is "history" and what is fiction? Godwin's language continues to trope the question in literary language. Until the arrival of Gines, Caleb had felt safe: "In the theatre upon which I was now placed," he writes, "I had no rival" (290). But suddenly he is accused of being a fake. Laura considers the facts and like Thomas, tells Caleb that the evidence against him speaks for itself. However, this time there is no evidence beyond the pamphlet. Caleb is now in a variation of the position he was in when he was accused of robbery. Now it is his accuser, Laura, who is relying on fictional knowledge, while he wants facts and complains that there are none to support her opinion. "Can you have no anxiety for my justification," he asks, "whatever may be the unfavourable impression you may have received against me?" Laura is unmoved. "That tale," she tells him, referring to the pamphlet, "which in its plain and unadorned state, is destructive of the character of him to whom it relates, no colouring can make an honest one." Caleb asks if she can condemn a man without a hearing. Answers the blithe Laura: "Indeed I can." So this time Caleb is forced to take his own medicine. After all, he can hardly ask her to let the facts speak for themselves when he denied them that ability in his trial for robbery, or when he did so well without them in his conviction of Falkland.

It would be a mistake to think that Godwin has lost his way here. The message is that Caleb is destined to lose, whichever side he plays on: that is life. Laura refuses to explain what has changed her mind about him and delivers the following speech: "I stand still and hear you: because virtue disdains to appear abashed and confounded in the presence of vice . . . true virtue refuses the drudgery of explanation and apology. True virtue shines by its own light and needs no art to set it off" (299).

This sounds good—noble, exalted, above dispute. And artless. But there is something familiar about these lines, and if we think back we can find their counterpart in Falkland's speech at Caleb's trial. After saying that his noble mind would not allow him to persecute his victim, Falkland says to Forester: "I care not for consequences . . . I will obey the dictates of my own mind. I will never lend my assistance to the reforming mankind by axes and gibbets; I am sure things will never be as they ought, till honour and not law be the dictator of mankind, till vice is taught to shrink before the resistless might of inborn dignity, and not before the cold formality of statutes" (175).

This also sounds good—noble and exalted. But these are the words of a murderer. They are also, Forester reminds Falkland, a form of romance. "The language you now hold, said Mr. Forester, is that of romance, and not of reason" (175). Knowledge is once again the object and the site of contention. Caleb asks Laura if "the most upright conduct, is always superior to the danger of ambiguity." Laura replies on cue: "Exactly so." Things with Laura are either off or on. She continues: "The good man and the bad man are characters precisely opposite, not characters distinguished from each other by imperceptible shades" (299). Laura and Falkland speak the same language.

The ambivalence in the text, as in *Udolpho*, might be read as a matter of Godwin simply hedging his bet: Caleb is the mimic, but pretense and artifice, even at this stage in the century, cannot be openly or directly praised. On deciding to return and confront Falkland, Caleb says that "artifice and evasion" are things "I shall no longer be reduced to" (316). And on the ambivalence toward Falkland, Godwin himself writes: "It was necessary to make him, so to speak, the tenant of an atmosphere of romance, so that every reader should feel prompted almost to worship him for his high qualities" (337). Like the published ending—along with the second half of the title and the second Preface,—the backpedaling on Caleb and Falkland could be understood as a matter of expediency. But the overall configuration of skepticism and the novel that we find in *Caleb Williams* still has Falkland heavily inscribed under the sign of the first, while Caleb's hunger for knowledge, and his exposure of the truth, makes him the realist hero of the piece. Despite the programmatic quality of this allegory of genre, or perhaps because of it, Godwin's novel offers one of the most polemical examples in the century of the oppositional relationship of a failure of knowledge not only to the discourse of the novel but also to what its man in this novel represents: justice.

* * *

Goethe's *The Sorrows of Young Werther* (1774) is usually discussed as a beginning—the beginning of the Sturm und Drang movement, or of German romanticism—but I want to consider it here briefly as part of an ending, as part of the "culmination in horror" that Louis Bredvold mentions in tracking the eighteenth-century cult of sensibility. Bredvold, Carol Ann Howells, and others have gothic horror in mind when they think of this culmination, and we have just considered two texts that are both more gothic than *Werther*. But Goethe's novel must be mentioned for its importance as a transitional moment in the development of the literature of sentiment, and hence of the discourse of skepticism in the century. Werther is a Janus-like figure who looks back at all that seemed right with the sentimental hero of the past, but also ahead to all that will be wrong with him in the near future, and what goes wrong has a particularly violent turn. He is part Grandison, part Falkland, both the finest and most extreme embodiment of the cult of sensibility in the century, and one of its most horrid little monsters, as Auden put it.[18] It is the relational quality of these two aspects of Werther's character that I want to stress here, since the relation is between sensibility and romance on one hand, and the social and ethical dangers of a materialist philosophy on the other, which in Werther's case are articulated together as one function. This is worth noting since it is slightly different from what Godwin shows us in Falkland. Falkland, as we have seen, also demonstrates the culmination of sensibility and romance in violence and social injustice, but Godwin does not make the connection to philosophical materialism.

The discourse of sentiment in Goethe's novel is obvious, and for many eighteenth-century readers it was all they heard. It appears that Goethe himself was under its spell at first, and a vast readership followed suit all the way into the next century. We may find this puzzling, or suspect Goethe of being ironic—of giving us something Popean in the vein of a mock-*Empfindsamkeit* [sentimental] tale—since Werther today seems less like a sentimental hero than a dangerous parody of one. The damage he causes is serious, and the criticisms directed at him are severe. The advice he is given on the dangers of sentiment by his mother, by his friend Wilhelm, and by Lotte herself, is the same kind of advice St. Aubert, and even Montoni, will give Emily twenty years later in Radcliffe's *Udolpho*. Lotte, for example, begs him to be reasonable and abandon what she calls "dieser Heftigkeit, dieser unbezwinglich haftenden Leidenschaft für alles, das Sie einmal anfassen" [this violent temper, this uncontrollable clinging passion for everything you touch]. "Seyn Sie ein Mann!" [Be a man!] she tells him,[19] gender-marking sensibility as a feminine weakness in the same way that Laclos, Sade, and others will do. But Werther has all the faith in passion of his romantic followers. Reason is a cold and specious repast and a check on his feelings.

Werther's passion made readers swoon, but it shatters the happiness of Lotte and Albert. In the appended "Der Herausgeber an den Leser" [The Editor to the Reader], we are told frankly of Werther: "er glaubte, das schöne Verhältnis zwischen Albert und seiner Gattinn gestört zu haben" [he believed he had destroyed the harmonious relationship between Albert and his wife] (94, 127). This is a compelling statement on the debilitating power of sentiment and the ruling passion, since a man of Werther's intellectual mettle has so little control over it. If Goethe had wanted to condemn outright the whole tradition of the sentimental hero as cognitively and ethically bankrupt, he could not have chosen a better way. In the same vein, it is difficult to think that he did not know what he was about, especially when he inserted the story of the ex-servant who killed his rival for the affections of the widow, with whom he is as madly in love as Werther is with Lotte. According to the Editor, Werther thinks: "Liebe und Treue, die schönsten menschlichen Empfindungen hatten sich in Gewalt und Mord verwandelt" [Love and loyalty, the most beautiful of human emotions, had turned into violence and murder] (95, 129). Werther cannot see the irony of his own words, but it is difficult to think that Goethe could not, or that at the end of the novel, readers did not see it and wonder about the author's motives. In any case, by the time of the French Revolution, critics of sentiment like Burke must have looked back at a line like this as a perfect epigraph to the history of the ethics of feeling in the century as a whole.

Goethe himself did not see what British critics called the "pernicious tendency" of the novel until much later, at which time he too advised maturity for his young male readers.[20] Until then he looked on his protagonist, modeled on himself and his similar affair with Lotte Buff, as another Rousseau, a man of feeling in the line of Goldsmith's Primrose and Sterne's Yorick.[21] Goldsmith and Sterne were two of Goethe's favorite authors, and he took *The Vicar of Wakefield* so seriously that he fell in love with the daughter of a country parson from a family that was so much like the Primroses that he swore he felt when he was with them that he was playing the part of Burchell in Goldsmith's novel.[22]

The fact that *Werther* is part of the culmination of sensibility in the century, while also marking the beginning of romanticism, tells us that this ostensible transition in literary history is more heuristic than historical; the eighteenth-century discourse of sensibility in fact feeds directly and seamlessly into romantic subjectivism. Both operate under the sign of Spinoza's single substance theory, which undergirds romantic pantheism just as it had Diderot's and D'Holbach's materialism; in both cases a skeptical attitude to reason prevails which limits, circumscribes, and discredits it in favor of feeling, genius, and passion. The mad but happy Heinrich moves Werther to ask: "Gott im Himmel! Hast du das zum Schiksaal der Menschen gemacht, daß sie nicht glüklich sind, als eh sie zu ihrem Verstande kommen, und wenn sie ihn wieder verliehren!" [God in Heaven! Did you make it men's destiny only to be happy before they come to reason and after they have lost it again?]. Werther is not foolish enough to wish that he were in an asylum, as Heinrich had been, but he exclaims, "Elender und auch wie beneide ich deinen Trübsinn, die Verwirrung deiner Sinne, in der du verschmachtest" [Poor fellow!—and yet how I envy you your melancholy mind and the confusion of your senses in which you wander] (90, 121).

Heinrich has lost his reason and does not see that he has no hope with his love, so Werther envies him. But again, the connection between sensibility and a skeptical delegitimation of mind comes to the fore. Lotte and Albert keep trying to call Werther back from this abyss but he only sinks further and further into it. His progress is marked from the beginning by a change in reading preferences from Homer to Ossian. Homer is the poet of moderation who writes "Wiegengesang" [cradlesongs] that lull his "empörtes Blut" [rebellious blood] and restless heart, but this is no longer what he wants. His restless heart is moving "vom Krummer zur Ausschweifung, und von süßer Melancholie zur verderblichen Leidenschaft" [from grief to excessive joy, from sweet melancholy to fatal passion], and he is going to indulge it as one would a "krankes Kind" [sick child] (7–8, 10). The ethics of feeling, divested of reason, will lead to death.

Goethe places this sensibility-violence connection under the sign of philosophical materialism, the second-order skepticism associated by the philosophes with Spinoza. Spinoza's single-substance theory presented a materialist universe where God could be either conspicuous by His absence, as he was for the philosophes, or inserted anywhere and everywhere, as he was by the later pantheists and romantics. In *Werther* there are clear links to the older materialist philosophy. No one likes to admit, Werther says, "[d]aß [aber] auch Erwachsene gleich Kindern auf diesem Erdboden herumtaumeln und wie jene nicht wissen, woher sie kommen und wohin sie gehen, ebensowenig nach wahren Zwecken handeln, ebenso durch Biskuit und Kuchen und Birkenreiser regiert werden" [that grownups too stumble like children on this earth, not knowing whence they come or whither they go, acting as little according to true purposes, being ruled like them by cakes and birch rods] (12, 13). This is Goethe but it could well be Diderot in *Jack the Fatalist* or *D'Alembert's Dream*.

Motion imparted to one molecule, be it through cakes or rods, carries its effect through the whole body, which reacts like a struck clavichord, or in the romantic paradigm, an Aeolian harp. Everything is linked through the nerve fibers and is part of a causal chain. This is a "Kerker" [prison] (13, 14) that only death can free us from. Yorick, in Sterne's *Sentimental Journey*, has an attack of fine feeling toward the French king after eating dinner and drinking some Burgundy, and suggests that Smelfungus's bad humor is also a function of diet. In *Werther*, the pastor's wife explains foul humor the same way: "Wir haben aber unserer Gemüt nicht in unserer Gewalt ... wie viel hängt vom Körper ab! Wenn einem nicht wohl ist, ist's einem überall nicht recht" [We cannot command our dispositions ... How much depends on the body! If one does not feel well, everything seems wrong]. Werther agrees and says: "Wir wollen es also . . . als eine Krankheit ansehen und fragen, ob dafür kein Mittel ist?" [Then . . . we'll look at moodiness as a disease and see if there is a remedy for it] (33, 38). The discourse of sensibility here is expressed in the familiar language of materialism that in the Enlightenment was germane to second-order skepticism.

Even suicide is explained in materialist terms. "Die menschliche Natur . . . hat ihre Grenzen; sie kann Freude, Leid, Schmerzen, bis auf einen gewissen Grad ertragen und geht zugrunde, sobald der überstiegen ist" [Human nature . . . has its limits; it can bear joy, suffering, and pain to a certain degree, but it collapses as soon as that degree is exceeded]. The economy of pain here is the same as the chemistry of human reactions in *D'Alembert's Dream*. Werther goes on: "Hier ist also nicht die Frage, ob einer schwach oder stark ist, sondern ob er das Maß seines Leidens ausdauren kann; es mag nun moralisch oder körperlich sein" [The question, therefore . . . is not whether someone is weak or strong, but what degree of suffering he can actually endure, be it moral or physical]. Once the limit is reached the machine reacts predictably. Psychology plays no part. Werther continues: "und ich finde es ebenso wunderbar zu sagen, der Mensch ist feige, der sich das Leben nimmt, als es ungehörig wäre, den einen Feigen zu nennen, der an einem bösartigen Fieber stirbt" [and I find it just as strange to call a man who takes his own life a coward as it would be improper to call a coward a man who is dying of a malignant fever]. Albert is as outraged with this as earlier readers had been with similar explanations by Spinoza. "Paradox! sehr paradox!" [Paradoxical! Very paradoxical!] he protests (48, 60).

Werther asks Albert to understand the mind in strictly materialist terms:

> Du gibst mir zu, wir nennen das eine Krankheit zum Tod, wodurch die Natur so angegriffen wird, daß teils ihre Kräfte verzehrt, teils so außer Wirkung gesezt werden, daß sie sich nicht wieder aufzuhelfen, durch keine glükliche Revolution den gewöhnlichen Umlauf des Lebens wieder herzustellen fähig ist.
>
> Nun, mein Lieber, laß uns das auf den Geist anwenden. Sieh den Menschen an in seiner Eingeschränktheit, wie Eindrücke auf ihn wirken, Ideen sich bei ihm festsetzen, bis endlich eine wachsende Leidenschaft ihn aller ruhigen Sinneskraft beraubt und ihn zugrunde richtet.

> [You admit that we call a disease fatal which attacks nature so violently that her forces are partly consumed or so largely put out of action that they cannot recover and restore the ordinary course of life by some lucky turn. Now, my friend, let us apply this same sort of reasoning to the mind. Let us watch man in his limited sphere and see how impressions affect him, how he is obsessed by ideas, until finally a growing passion robs him of any possible calmness of mind and becomes his ruin.] (48, 60)

This is the same sort of physicalist understanding of sensibility that reigned in Sterne and in *Jack the Fatalist*. Our thoughts are as determined as our actions when impulses flow in on our senses from the outside. Against this, reason is powerless. "Vergebens, daß der gelassene, vernünftige Mensch den Zustand des Unglücklichen übersieht, vergebens, daß er ihm zuredet! ebenso wie ein Gesunder, der am Bette des Kranken steht, ihm von seinen Kräften nicht das geringste einflößen kann" [A composed, sensible person who has a clear view of the condition of the unfortunate man tries in vain to give advice; just as the healthy man, standing at the bedside of the sick, is unable to transfer to the latter the smallest fraction of his own strength] (ibid.).

Knowledge in this economy is close to meaningless. Sounding like Heraclitus on the impossibility of making true statements, Werther asks: "Kannst du sagen: *Das ist!* da alles vorübergeht? da alles mit der Wetterschnelle vorüberrollt" [Can you say: *This is!* when everything passes, everything rolls past with the speed of lightning]. Nature is incomprehensible, ungraspable—a system that functions according to its own laws, not Man's. "Da ist kein Augenblick, der nicht dich verzehrte und die Deinigen um dich her, kein Augenblick, da du nicht ein Zerstöhrer bist, sein mußt" [There is not one moment . . . which does not consume you and yours, and not one moment when you yourself are not inevitably destructive]. His heart, he says, is worn out by "die verzehrende Kraft, die in dem All der Natur verborgen liegt; die nichts gebildet hat, das nicht seinen Nachbar, nicht sich selbst zerstörte" [the consuming power latent in the whole of Nature which has formed nothing that will not destroy its neighbor and itself]. The view of Nature here is ominously close to the one Sade will put forth. Like Sade, Werther sees Nature as "ein ewig verschlingendes, ewig wiederkäuendes Ungeheuer" [an eternally devouring and ruminating monster] (52–53, 66).

But *Werther* would not have been perceived as something new if it had adhered only to this older materialist aesthetic. The romantics reacted to Spinoza by infusing their own spirit into his lifeless world and Werther does the same, making over Nature in the image of his mind. When he is happy, Nature is a "Paradiese" [Paradise] that displays an "innere glühende, heilige Leben" [inner, glowing, sacred life]; when he is unhappy, "der Schauplatz des unendlichen Lebens verwandelt sich vor mir in den Abgrund des ewig offenen Grabes" [the scene of unending life is transformed before my eyes into the pit of the forever-open grave] (51–52, 65–66). This is how Werther constructs the world when he is respectively happy and unhappy; but Goethe has already made it clear that such feelings are themselves materially based, a product of physical conditions. Again: "wie viel hängt vom Körper ab!" [How much depends on the body!], says the pastor's wife (33, 38). Nature—material causes and conditions—takes precedence. The romantic re-projection of these feelings back into the landscape then follows. Romantic subjectivism from this perspective, rather than being a radical break with the past that suddenly makes Mind generate Nature, appears as a continuance of the Cartesian elimination of Mind from that natural world—a continuance, that is, of the Spinozist and materialist delegitimation of mind germane to the earlier cult of sensibility.[23]

In sum, the skeptical failure of mind in *Werther* is more philosophical than gothic, but it is still an important part of the culmination of sensibility in the century. The turn to violence it foregrounds points ahead, through Godwin's Falkland, to the radical representations of skepticism and mimesis that I want to examine in the final chapter.

Sensibility and the Moral Divide

Charles Brockden Brown and D.A.F. Sade

In this chapter I look at two writers who offer fin de siècle views of the relationship of literary realism to skepticism in the eighteenth century. Charles Brockden Brown follows in the footsteps of Godwin and Richardson in promoting an epistemological realism, while Sade takes the irrational quality of sensibility and romance beyond Wertherism into the farthest reaches of violence. Brown was a disciple of Godwin, and in his American Gothic *Wieland; or, The Transformation: An American Tale* (1798) he presents the same configuration of skepticism and mimetic art that Godwin did in *Caleb Williams*. In Godwin's novel, Falkland was the dangerous and irrational Quixote; Caleb was the reasoner and master of disguise. Brown gives us a similar configuration. Like Godwin, Brown associates the failure of knowledge with his villain; Wieland is in the grip of an irrational religious enthusiasm and comes within a hair's breadth of taking the heroine's life. Standing opposite him, and ultimately saving Clara's life, is Francis Carwin, the mimic. At first Carwin's imitative arts are demonized, but in the end a surprising settling of accounts occurs that places Carwin in a rather different light.

Sade, for his part, pushes *sensibilité* and the irrational further down the line of dissolution established by Goethe. It took Sade to show what the culmination of the cult of sensibility in the century looked like, and he does so by associating it with violence, as Goethe had. Sade moves completely free of the discourse of the novel into a netherworld of romance and fantasy while painting a vivid picture of the collapse of reason under the weight of a materialist understanding of sensibility of the sort put forth earlier in the century by the philosophes.

In *Wieland*, we begin with another figure of the artist, one who is cut from the same cloth as Caleb Williams. Carwin the Biloquist is a variation on Caleb, another practitioner of the mimetic arts, a man of design, theatricalism, and artifice. And through him Brown asks some of the same questions Godwin had—questions, in particular, about the relationship of the discourse of the novel to knowledge. For much of *Wieland* this relationship is portrayed in a negative light, implying that novelistic discourse itself is an expression of skepticism. Carwin's fictions sow doubt, not truth. But this association changes, allowing a somewhat different understanding of the word *transformation* in the title from the literal one referring to the transformation of Wieland into a murderous religious fanatic. By calling his novel *An American Tale*, Brown tells us that there is something uniquely American about the latter, literal "transformation"—one that throws a family into the turmoil of barbarism and mindlessness; but one can also read the transformation as referring to a shift in attitude toward genre.

As a novelist Brown might be expected to do as Godwin and Richardson had done before him and underwrite that shift, affirming if only obliquely the ethics of his own aesthetic choice of the novel form, and this is indeed what happens as we watch the transformation of Carwin from a cardboard gothic villain into a character who, at the end, appears as a kind of misunderstood master of mimesis. Until then Brown also follows his past masters in leaving pro forma regrets in the book that this kind of deception is a form of survival. In Godwin, Caleb uses, but also very much regrets the mimetic skills he is forced to employ; and Richardson's heroines voice the same regrets, but nonetheless employ the same form of artifice to survive.[1] In Brown things are much the same.

It is tempting to read the case biographically. To be a man of letters in the 1790s in Philadelphia was to be, like Carwin, without a vocation. F. L. Pattee writes that fiction at the time was "a literary form almost untried in America, and one attacked by prejudice, denounced in every pulpit, and thundered against by all the moralists."[2] The title, *An American Tale*, thus takes on even more significance: characters like Caleb and Carwin can expect to meet prejudice in a culture that at this point in its history took a much more severe view of the art they practiced than had ever been taken in England or France. Brown himself could not hold out against the current, eventually giving up writing and returning to the family business while voicing antitheatricalist sentiments with regard to the novel that had been used by its critics in England for a hundred years. Novel-writing, for instance, was the practice of "fashioning falsehood."[3] Paul Allen goes so far as to claim that Brown never took his fiction seriously, quoting Brown's comment that his work "was not worth a perusal."[4] The same language appears in Brown's letter to Jefferson, to whom he sent a copy of *Wieland:* "To request your perusal of a work which at the same time is confessed to be unworthy of perusal will be an uncommon proof of absurdity."[5] To be absurd in Brown's case, however, was merely to be a writer of fiction in Philadelphia. The artistic impulse was suppressed. William Dunlap writes that the passionate and poetic side of Brown's character was nonetheless real, and in Philadelphia a source of anguish to him. Brown had to be sober and circumspect, but Dunlap paints him as a man of feverish passions and wild imagination.[6] So survival through the deceptions of fiction has a particular significance in Brown's own life.

Wieland was written in a hurry and Brown did not revise it, so it is possible that his conscious intentions with regard to the attitude he wanted the reader to take to this question, or to Carwin himself, simply developed without any premeditated plan. But in the later *Memoirs of Carwin the Biloquist,* which Brown began in order to clarify Carwin's character, the connection to Godwin's Caleb is clear and rests on the relationship of art to knowledge. In Godwin's novel Caleb tells us: "I could not rest till I had acquainted myself with the solutions that had been invented for the phenomena of the universe. In fine, this produced in me an invincible attachment to books of narrative and romance. I panted for the unravelling of an adventure . . . I read, I devoured compositions of this sort. They took possession of my soul; and the effects they produced, were frequently discernible in my external appearance and my health . . . my imagination must be excited; and, when that was not done, my curiosity was dormant."[7] In his memoirs, Carwin tells us: "My thirst of knowledge was augmented in proportion as it was supplied with gratification. The more I heard or read, the more restless and unconquerable my curiosity became. My senses were perpetually alive to novelty, my fancy teemed with visions of the future, and my attention fastened upon every thing mysterious or unknown" (281).

Carwin's memoir reads like an apology for the novelist. His father is a tyrant and beats him; to avoid this, Carwin says—sounding like Pamela or Clarissa—"I was incessantly employed in the invention of stratagems and the execution of expedients" (282). What he calls his "perverse and pernicious curiosity" (286) is merely the desire to read, which he does late at night, when the family is asleep, by taking his book out into the moonlight. His discovery and practice of ventriloquism takes place during these outings, so that Brown connects Carwin's experiments in throwing his voice to his reading and education: "There remained but one thing to render this instrument as powerful in my hands as it was capable of being. From my childhood, I was remarkably skilful at imitation. There were few voices whether of men or birds or beasts which I could not imitate with success. To add my ancient, to my newly acquired skill, to talk from a distance, and at the same time, in the accents of another, was the object of my endeavors" (288).

The first use Carwin has for his new combination of talents is to help him escape from his brutal father. But this involves deception and Carwin is repelled. He thinks of going up beside his sleeping father some night and imitating his dead mother's voice, encouraging the man to let the boy go to his aunt's, but he cannot go through with it. The boy eventually succeeds in joining his aunt, where he says he stayed for three years, during which time he "reflected deeply on the use to which [his biloquism] might be applied." He says, "I was not destitute of pure intentions; I delighted not in evil; I was incapable of knowingly contributing to another's misery" (295).

Francis, however, is young and wants to show off. He admits to having ambition, and he has not forgotten that his aunt is planning to leave him her fortune. When she dies, however, it is discovered that she has left all her money to her servant, Dorothy. Francis is sure that Dorothy is guilty of a more heinous type of imposture here than merely throwing her voice, that she has in fact suppressed the aunt's later will and allowed an old one to be discovered and stand, in which she is named as legatee. Dorothy is superstitious, and Francis asks himself enthusiastically: "Could not her conscience be awakened by a voice from the grave! Lonely and at midnight, my aunt might be introduced, upbraiding her for her injustice, and commanding her to attone [sic] for it by acknowledging the claim of the rightful proprietor" (302). But again this plan is never carried out, as if Brown wants to keep his protagonist morally irreproachable. Brown never really gets anywhere in this sequel and the plot peters out and stops, but not before certain admirable aspects of Carwin's character are established.

Wieland itself begins in a quite different tenor with Carwin and the discourse of the novel associated with deception, error, and danger. However, the discourse of skepticism in the novel is not associated per se with Carwin but, rather, with religious enthusiasm, which has led to the deaths of two previous members of the Wieland clan, and does so again with Clara's brother. Their grandfather jumped from a cliff, supposedly on a command from God; and the father was a religious fanatic who came to believe he had disobeyed God and was going to be punished, dying finally from spontaneous combustion—an explanation Brown promotes in a footnote. And now Theodore goes mad and kills his family in the story Clara tells of her own misery.

Brown wants uncertainty to cloud these events. Clara's uncle, who was with the father in his last moments, found the explanation of his death "an imperfect tale" and believed "that half the truth had been suppressed" (20). The language of doubt then proceeds to infect the entire story, to the point where one wonders whether Clara herself is not mad.[8] Much of what is left unexplained, it must be admitted, may have to do with Brown's hasty writing habits. All five of his novels were quickly written and contain numerous dangling references to absent events, misspellings and variations, pointless interpellations, and changing intentions. One particular problem in *Wieland*, for example, is that while Wieland's mental degeneration and eventual murderous frenzy should be the center of attention, Brown only visits him intermittently in the narrative, so that his story, when it occasionally reappears, seems tangential, and his eventual actions unmotivated. Nina Baym suggests that Brown may simply have become interested in the tale of Carwin's voices and let it displace Wieland's story.[9] Be that as it may, the fact remains that doubt is a powerful element of the story.

Once unleashed, uncertainty and doubt spread finally to the key question of whether Carwin is responsible for the voice and vision that direct Wieland to murder his family. Although the answer is clearly no— Wieland is quite specific at his trial, telling the court that he saw "the lineaments of that being" who spoke, "whose veil was now lifted, and whose visage beamed upon my sight," and that this being then spoke and gave him the order (190)—Carwin is nonetheless difficult, even for critics, to separate from the crime.[10] The mystery spreads to whether Wieland actually takes his own life, even though the description of the event is unambiguous.[11] In the defining scene, for example, the penknife Clara has been holding has fallen to the floor. "His eye now lighted upon it, he seized it with the quickness of thought. I shrieked aloud, but it was too late. He plunged it to the hilt in his neck" (264). This seems clear enough, unless we are to believe Clara is lying to us, or has gone mad. But it is a testimony to the power of "Universal Darkness," as Pope might call it, that these uncertainties exist.

Another example of the dark conceits at work occurs during the same scene, when Wieland is about to murder Clara, even though she has the penknife in her hand ready to strike him. Her arm in fact "was lifted to strike" when a voice suddenly "burst from the ceiling, and commanded him—*to hold*" (261). Clara recognizes Carwin's "agency," although it is not clear from where Carwin can be observing them, unless through the keyhole. But the real difficulty is with what the voice says next. It tells Wieland that he has made a mistake, that he is a "Man of errors" suffering under a "delusion"; that it is "not heaven or hell, but thy senses have misled thee to commit these acts" (262). This presents certain logical difficulties, since it is unclear why this voice should be any more credible to Wieland than the others, if what it says is true. But it also brings us back to the issue of enthusiasm.

The language of error in the novel is tied to religious enthusiasm, which is the principal expression of skepticism and the failure of knowledge in Brown's novel. Enthusiasm had been identified as a danger to religion as far back as the mid-seventeenth century and was attacked by Locke in his chapter "Of Enthusiasm" appended to the *Essay Concerning Human Understanding*. Locke discusses it as a matter of enthusiastic sentiment, or the substitution of sensuous feeling for reason. He refers to it as "rising from the conceits of a warmed or overweening brain"; and as "freed from all restraint of reason and check of reflection."[12] It is a form of sensibility (sensuous emotion) and stands over and against the discourse of reason: Wieland's senses have misled him. In *Wieland* it is almost exclusively associated with hearing voices, and hence with Carwin who is supposedly their source. His mimetic ability is thus linked early on with this failure of knowledge.

What the voices say is often untrue: a voice tells Pleyel, for example, that his fiancé in Saxony is dead, which is confirmed soon after, but at the end turns out to be false. And sometimes his deceptions have worse effects, sowing discord between Clara and Pleyel, and driving Clara close to madness. But even in the worst of his performances—where he appears out of her closet—Brown is unable to paint him unambiguously in the colors of a villain. What happens in this particular scene is difficult to understand. Clara is about to open the door of her closet when a voice (obviously Carwin's) warns her to stop. She now fears that her mad brother is in the closet and that her life is in danger; she nonetheless opens the door and Carwin appears. He tells her he planned to rape her but that the voice warning her has saved her. "Whoever he was," says Carwin, "he hast done you an important service." Then he says: "The knowledge that enabled him to tell you who was in the closet, was obtained by incomprehensible means. You knew that Carwin was there." But the voice had not told her who was in the closet. He then refers to the source of the voice as "my eternal foe; the baffler of my best concerted schemes" (102–3). The confusion here seems to spring from an attempt to rehabilitate Carwin. The latter's garbled description and explanation of what has just happened leaves the impression of two Carwins, where the better half is devoted to Clara's protection. But what is going on, and why, is unclear.[13]

The moral of the story, or rather the object of telling it, Clara says right at the beginning of her account, is to "inculcate the duty of avoiding deceit" (5). Carwin's mimicry is hard to disassociate from that deceit. The novel's epigraph is reminiscent of Jeremy Collier or William Law on the dangers of theater and clearly applies to Carwin:

From Virtue's blissful paths away
The double-tongued are sure to stray;
Good is a forth-right journey still,
And mazy paths but lead to ill.

Carwin and his double-tongued art are on the wrong side of the Socratic analogies of virtue and knowledge, vice and error. There is even an admission on Brown's part that the errors of religious enthusiasm have a theatrical, poetic cast. The Wielands are related to the German poet, Christof Martin Wieland, and Clara's paternal grandfather was connected to the "German Theater" (7). The rational mind, says Clara, is susceptible; much vigilance is required. And the implication is that mistaking the copy for the original in theater is not that different from mistaking enthusiasm for true religious fervor. The failure of reason then follows, with Clara's own case as the first example: she writes that she has been "transformed from rational and human into a creature of nameless and fearful attributes" (205)—not by religion but by Carwin's deceptions, which places those deceptions, to their detriment, next to Wieland's.

At one time Clara had the utmost faith in reason. On her father's mysterious death she says that she "could not deny that the event was miraculous, and yet I was invincibly averse to that method of solution." When her brother hears Catherine's voice, Clara says she herself "could not bear to think that his senses should be the victims of such delusion . . . The will is the tool of the understanding, which must fashion its conclusions on the notices of sense. If the senses be depraved, it is impossible to calculate the evils that may flow from the consequent deductions of the understanding" (39).

Note that Clara claims that trouble arises not because the understanding depends on the senses, but when the senses themselves are depraved, as they are in the case of her brother—when the brain gets overheated, as Locke said. This is an important distinction; but our lack of knowledge about Wieland makes it hard to assess. When Clara asks him if the "Divine Will" must always, as it had apparently done in the case of their father, "address its precepts to the eye," Theodore says, no, that "the understanding has other avenues." But there is no clarification as to what he means, or just how his own senses are depraved, other than the fact that they are so because they lead to bad results.

Clara has her own proudly rational mind shaken by the voices in her closet but still strives to understand Carwin: "I studied to discover the true inferences deducible from his deportment and words" (109). When mistakes pile upon misunderstandings Clara complains: "What is man, that knowledge is so sparingly conferred upon him!" (116). Pleyel's senses are normal enough, and yet he too is easily fooled. Having heard on his way home what he took to be the voices of Clara and Carwin whispering together by the riverbank, he makes the wrong inference, working inductively from one of his senses. "Evidence," he says, dashing a pair of socks into the trunk he is packing, "less than this would only have excited resentment and scorn . . . it would merely be an argument of madness. That my eyes, that my ears, should bear witness to thy fall! By no other way could detestable conviction be imparted" (118). The language of the courtroom, reminiscent again of *Caleb Williams*, takes over the discussion. Clara finds herself in the position of having to convince Pleyel not to believe his ears. She fails to do so, and when he leaves she asks herself what "evidence" he had, whether his opinion was "rational," and complains: "He had judged me without hearing. He has drawn from dubious appearances, conclusions the most improbable and unjust" (120). This sounds much like Caleb's complaint over the equally unjustifiable conclusions reached about him by Laura. The issue once again is the epistemological weight to be accorded to physical evidence. Going to her brother, Clara asks him if he believes in her "guilt" and gets the same kind of language. Theodore answers: "I have struggled . . . to dismiss that belief. You speak before a judge who will profit by any pretense to acquit you: who is ready to question his own senses when they plead against you" (124). Clara is disappointed in Pleyel, not realizing that his senses were indeed not depraved but accurate. It did not matter; he still came to the wrong conclusion. She wonders how to expose his "error" and what she can "throw in the balance against it" that would "outweigh the testimony of his senses" and regrets that she "cannot summon Carwin to my bar and make him the attestor of my innocence" (126).

Brown came to hate lawyers for using their rhetorical skills to make falsehoods look like truths. He believed that no one's senses were immune to the kind of falsehoods that Pleyel, Clara, and Wieland fall victim to. All the characters are driven, possessed by the need to know the truth. The word *curious* occurs regularly to describe Clara, but also to describe Wieland, who is searching for guidance. Carwin is curious about just how rational a mind Clara has; and indeed how rational they all are. By the end, standing in front of her brother who has come to murder her, Clara is ready at last to admit "the impotence of reason over my own conduct" and says: "I doubted whether any one could be stedfast and wise" (256). Brown thus makes a broader point than the one concerning just religious enthusiasm and its overpowering of reason with sensuous emotion. One's senses need not be depraved, as Clara claims, for this to happen. The senses of Clara and Pleyel are not depraved, as Wieland's are, but they believe the voices they hear as much as Wieland does. It is not that the voices are unreal, or the senses that register them depraved; only that knowledge based on them is inevitably uncertain. As a one-time lawyer himself, Brown knew just how susceptible everyone was to emotion and how good rhetoricians could elicit and direct it. Carwin's voice alone, for example, affects Clara powerfully the first time she hears it. The "tone," Clara says, was totally new to her; Carwin's voice has a "force" and "sweetness" that is irresistible, surpassing by far the musicality and energy of her brother's voice or Pleyel's. She goes on: "The voice was mellifluent and clear, but the emphasis was so just, and the modulation so impassioned, that it seemed as if an heart of stone could not fail of being moved by it. It imparted to me an emotion altogether involuntary and incontroulable. When he uttered the words, 'for charity's sweet sake,' I dropped the cloth that I held in my hand, my heart overflowed with sympathy, and my eyes with unbidden tears" (59).

But the association of Carwin and his art with the subjugation of reason—something that Clara explicitly insists on—never comes about. Clara calls him "a person with whose name the most turbulent sensations are connected"; that just thinking of him (at the time of writing) her "blood is congealed" and her "fingers are palsied" (56). But as events in her story proceed, Clara's description, or prediction, becomes complicated and compromised by events as she herself describes them. No real evil, for example, follows any of the occurrences of the voices. In the first two cases, when Catherine's voice is heard, the effects might even be interpreted as benign. Nor do the murderous voices Clara hears whispering in her closet produce any further effects. And when she runs to her brother's home and falls down on the step, it is a voice calling from outside that brings help. In Clara's dream in the arbor, the voice, calling "Hold!" appears to save her from danger offered her by Theodore, something it will later do in real life. The voice in the arbor warns her to stay away from that spot in the future, but tells her she will be safe elsewhere. This is the record Clara reviews quickly in her mind on the night she decides to ignore the voice warning her not to open the door to her closet. Although she does not think it all through, her decision to act against its advice is more reasonable than it looks, and Clara, at the time she is writing, can look back and say, "Yet my conduct was wise" (108) because she remembers the advice of the previous voice telling her she would be safe everywhere but in the arbor. She has reason to believe that the voices are somehow associated with her protection, even this one that tells her not to open the door.

When Carwin comes out instead of her brother, he tells her he planned to rape her but has been inexplicably "baffled" by the voice that warned her not to open the door; then he leaves. But if he had been going to rape her, it is not clear why he would be deterred by a voice. The next day he appears sorry and writes to ask for an interview. Simmering below the surface is a love story that Carwin is striving to break into. But Clara is destined for Pleyel. He, meanwhile, has told Clara that Carwin is an escaped murderer; Clara is uneasy, but agrees to meet Carwin at her house. Again, what seems irrational, even to her, is not really so, since there is still no direct evidence (always supremely important to Clara) that Carwin is dangerous. In fact, his previous night's performance, hardly in keeping with the behavior of an escaped murderer, gives Clara confidence, so that she grants him the late-night interview. Again we are left with the hint that at this interview Carwin may reveal his own feelings for her, opening a whole new direction in the story.

This, however, is the night of Catherine's murder, and when Clara walks into her house she not only hears a voice again telling her to "Hold!" but sees Carwin's face as well. This is followed by her discovery of the murder upstairs and, shortly after, of Wieland's guilt. Clara is now convinced that Carwin is responsible. He is "the grand deceiver," the playwright who has set this infernal machinery in motion. She calls him "the author of this black conspiracy . . . the enemy whose machinations had destroyed us" (217). But by this point such a characterization seems mildly incongruous.

The voices have so far done more good than harm; we have already read what Wieland's testimony was in court, and so has Clara. If Carwin is responsible, then he can produce visions as well as throw his voice.

At their next and final interview, as Clara visits her home one last time before leaving for Europe, and just before Wieland also appears for the last time, Carwin comes in and explains everything. In the first case of Catherine's voice calling back her husband, Carwin says he had been hiding in the summerhouse and only wanted to prevent Wieland from coming up. In the second, he had also been caught in the summerhouse, but this time had also given in to his "passion for mystery . . . and imposture" (229). He reveals that he had begun an affair with Judith, Clara's maidservant, shortly after arriving in the neighborhood, and this had given him complete access to her house (which, one suspects, was the point of it). Judith had bragged to him about Clara's reputation as a supremely rational person who was completely immune to superstitious fears. He had decided to test her: hence the dialogue between the two murderers in her closet. Alarmed by her alarm, he followed her in her flight to Theodore's, and his was the voice that summoned them to help her. Similarly in the arbor, he had been responsible for the voices—it was, apparently, just a coincidence that his trademark "Hold!" worked so well in her dream—but his only purpose had been to keep her away from the arbor, since it was his temporary home and where he was seeing Judith at night. The night that Clara caught him in her closet he had been merely snooping and found out. He offers no explanation for the odd performance, or why he preferred to be taken for a thwarted rapist rather than just a snoop, but there is a degree of swagger in it that seems designed to impress her. On his way back to the arbor he had seen Pleyel approaching along the riverbank and decided to hide and imitate the two voices that Pleyel heard in conversation. His motive again, he claims, was nothing much more than mischief; but it is hard not to see the amorous conversation he mimics between Clara and himself as wishful thinking. Instead, he admits to her merely that it gave him pleasure to trick Pleyel—"a man of cold resolves and exquisite sagacity" (239). He denies that he is an escaped murderer, and it turns out later that he is not.

In all, Carwin uses his ventriloquism nine times in the story. In seven of those instances it is to extract either himself or Clara from trouble.[14] Clara, however, is still overpowered by her brother's recent mad act and remains unconvinced. When Carwin has concluded the account of his ventriloquism, she comments: "The power that he spoke of was hitherto unknown to me: its existence was incredible; it was susceptible of no direct proof . . . his tale is a lie, and his nature devlish" (246). By this time, however, Clara's insistence that she will only believe what she has seen and heard with her own eyes and ears is beginning to make her look foolish. When Wieland enters he sends Carwin away. Clara's "grand deceiver . . . the enemy whose machinations had destroyed us" (217) quietly leaves the room, "striving in vain for utterance, his complexion pallid as death, his knees beating one against another" (251). Clara, it seems, has misjudged him. And Carwin proves it moments later, when Wieland again turns on his sister, by miming the voice of God to deter him.

Brown's outline makes it clear that Carwin is innocent. And in the end he saves Clara's life. This is the most remarkable "transformation" in the novel. In essence, it is the transformation of an older view of the novel as in league with ethical and epistemological failure to a view that clearly exonerates the mimetic form. This curious transformation of Carwin from "double-tongued" villain to misunderstood artist may be just an example of Brown not following through on his initial idea for the character, but the result is a more explicit treatment of what we saw both in Radcliffe's *Udolpho*, where flights of sensuous emotion were similarly rationalized, and in Godwin's more reluctant realization of elements of romance. Jay Fliegelman writes in his introduction to *Wieland* about the need that politicians and ministers had "to preach against the Lovelaces and Whitefields in order to divert attention from the similarity of their strategies" (xxxv). There is something of that in Brown's impulse here to treat Carwin initially as he does. But then, he cannot keep it up. The discourse of the novel in *Wieland* finally disengages itself from and stands over and against the evils of sensuous emotion that it is first associated with.

* * *

D.A.F. Sade's work is not only a culmination of the cult of sensibility in the eighteenth century, it is also a vivid portrait of what a materialist ethics can look like when taken to revolutionary extremes. The issue and role of *sensibilité* in Sade's work has been much debated, and Sade himself can occasionally seem contradictory on the matter: characters will mock and attack a sentimental heroine like Justine, on one hand, while on the other they demonstrate hypersensitivity to erotic stimuli. The paradox, however, is only apparent since Sade distinguishes between the original physical understanding of sensibility, which he wants to get back to, and the abstracted version that developed out of it—a division reminiscent of

Diderot's double definition of sensibility as both natural and moral in the *Encyclopedia*. Reading Sade one quickly becomes aware that like Laclos he considers the abstracted version of sensibility an empty liability, not a strength. In *Dangerous Liaisons* sentimental women like Mme de Tourvel and Cécile Volanges are naïve and shunted around brutally by events. Merteuil, by contrast, is informed—knows how things work in the world and controls her own destiny. Sade sees things in a like manner. His work is a pointed attack on sentiment and a brutal parody of the virtuous and feeling heroine whose weepy weakness really acts as a red flag for the males around her. Like Laclos, Wollstonecroft, and others, Sade wants to discredit this abstracted form of sentiment.

What makes Sade different, however, is that he wants to do so in favor of the original, concrete meaning of the word *feeling,* thus literally reincarnating sensibility in its original material state as pure sensationism. And he wants to make knowledge claims for it—knowledge claims that are impossible to make on behalf of the cognitively handicapped sentimental heroine. Alongside the vacuity of the heroine of sentiment, Sade thus gives us his erudite libertines, implying that this purely empirical brand of sensibility is the true handmaid of knowledge.

The comparison with Laclos sheds further light on the way Sade configures his discourse on knowledge. In Laclos the intelligence of Merteuil and Valmont is patent; they reject sentiment but do not stand for the more basic version of sensibility in the way Sade's libertines do. Their physical sensations are normal, they are in the world, and they have normal sexual relations with their various partners. Sade's characters, by contrast, have implausible physical sensitivities, are in no world that we can readily recognize, and they do not have normal sexual relations. At the same time, Sade wants to convince us of their erudition, that their sensibility is somehow allied to their knowledge, by articulating the two together. And if his characters were intelligent in the way Merteuil and Valmont are intelligent, his argument might be persuasive. But they are not. Instead, their logic and erudition are invariably specious. In what follows I want to demonstrate how this quirky epistemology stands in relation to the discourse of and on the novel in his work and point out some familiar juxtapositions. I will begin with the discourse of the novel, then look at how sensibility and knowledge are linked in his sexual tableaux.

Sade's writings fall into two broad categories: what might be called the therapeutic fiction, in which physical sensation plays a major role, and the conventional artistic fiction.[15] Sade is at all times about the body, more so in his therapeutic fiction, but always, inevitably about sensation.[16] He suffered, as we know, from algolagnia, the perversion in which sexual pleasure is obtained from the experience and infliction of pain, and had what appears to have been either a congenital defect, perhaps of the ejaculatory duct, or some blockage, stricture, cyst, or lesion in the seminal canal that made his ejaculations painful. He suffered from this most during lengthy periods of sexual abstinence, when forced to resort to masturbation and self-sodomy; in the Bastille he complained bitterly of the ailment to his wife. René Pélagie was forced to smuggle in to him various instruments for self-sodomy, and Sade claimed that the more frequent his ejaculations, the less painful they were. What Sade wrote in prison—*Les 120 Journées de Sodome* [*The 120 Days of Sodom*], the first version of *Justine*, and *Eugénie de Franval*—was thus in one way a therapeutic attempt to provide vicariously for his needs. And even when freed he did not abandon it, but continued with *Philosophie dans le boudoir* [*Philosophy in the Bedroom*]; *Juliette;* and further versions of *Justine*—all clandestine works either unpublished in Sade's lifetime, published anonymously or unavowed, and all of which devote themselves to the repetitive portrayal of algolagnic sexual encounters. So the relevance of a completely physical sensationism to this part of Sade's work is clear.

The artistic works are different, acknowledged, and more conventional, and include his plays, the novel *Aline et Valcour* [*Aline and Valcour*], and the stories in the four-volume *Les Crimes de l'Amour* [*The Crimes of Love*] to which his *Idée sur les romans* [*Reflections on the Novel*] (1800) serves as preface. In his discourse on the novel in *Reflections,* Sade praises literary realism and criticizes the gothic for dealing in implausible events. He attacks it in particular for its dependency on "le sortilège et la phantasmagoria" [the supernatural and phantasmagoria] and claims that Matthew Lewis and Anne Radcliffe both fall into this trap: "ici, nécessairement, de deux choses l'une: ou il faut développer le sortilège, et dès lors vous n'intéressez plus, ou il ne faut jamais lever le rideau, et vous voilà dans la plus affreuse invraisemblance" [here, necessarily, both come to the same thing: either one develops the supernatural, in which case the reader loses interest, or one never lifts the curtain, and there we have the most frightful lack of realism].[17] The distinction is not that easy to make out since Lewis both "develops the supernatural" and does not lift the curtain; while Radcliffe is all about showing that, once the curtain is lifted, there is no mystery. If one "develops" the supernatural (presumably the case of Lewis), Sade says, the reader's interest will flag. If one does not lift the curtain—also presumably the case of Lewis, who allows supernatural elements to remain supernatural—then the result is *invraisemblance*. For Sade, both come to the same thing.

Sadian logic is something I will return to; for the moment the point is that in his discourse on the novel Sade, like Diderot, praises verisimilitude as the sine qua non of narrative fiction. He liked Richardson, was a huge admirer of Laclos, and yearned for public success of the same sort himself. Again like Diderot, Sade has a fairly straightforward neoclassical side to his thinking. The writer of mimetic fiction must: "nous faire voir l'homme, non pas seulement ce qu'il est, ou ce qu'il montre, c'est le devoir de l'historien, mais tel qu'il peut être, tel que doivent le rendre les modifications du vice, et toutes les secousses des passions. Il faut donc les connaître toutes" [make us see the man, not only what he is or what he shows, which is the domain of the historian, but as he might be, as he might be shaped by vice and all the shocks of the passions. One must therefore know them all] (10.12).

A Johnsonian reader of this declaration would surely begin by agreeing, and hope that what Sade meant by what a man "might be" was perhaps good or noble. A shudder must follow, however, at the move from the universal to the particular, given Sade's own specialty. Still, Sade's thoughts on the novel are generally conventional here—as conventional, in fact, as his plays, which competed with and generally lost out to others only slightly less insipid in the cultural marketplace of the day. However, if we juxtapose Sade's commentary on the novel to the actual discourse of the novel in Sade's works, the connection is tenuous at best. In the more conventional artistic pieces Sade experienced many of the same formal difficulties with realism that had plagued Diderot.[18] He avoids the supernatural but the narratives are episodic, event-driven, full of implausibilities, and show little or no interest in detail or character development.[19] Sade writes in the *Reflections* that the novelist will only succeed "s'il entrouvre avec frémissement le sein da la nature" [if he opens with a shudder the breast of nature] (10.16–17), but *opening the breast of nature* had, for Sade, a much more literal and macabre connotation than this figure of speech suggests. Nature, especially in the therapeutic fiction, is a purely biological and material affair.

In the therapeutic fiction the discourse of the novel is limited. In it Sade goes beyond anything the century had hitherto seen in allegories of evil. It is a long way from Bunyan's Mr. Badman—who is after all not a very bad man—to Sade's Grand Inquisitor, don Crispe Brutaldi Barbaribos de

Torturentia—who is bad indeed. Gothic horror dominates, even though Sade claims he is just presenting, as Godwin said, "things as they are." He avoids the supernatural, but then for Sade the natural was always already supernatural.[20] The prison works especially are clearly situated within the discourse of romance and are redolent with psychological extremes undreamt of by his predecessors. It would be a cliché to say that although Sade's body was fettered, his imagination was boundless; in truth, his imagination in prison was as bound and tortured as his body. The mental reality he constructs in his prison works is more constricted and hallucinatory than anything in Lewis or Radcliffe. Radcliffe's Udolpho is a paradise compared to the nightmare of Silling in the 120 Days. And even Silling is preferable to the castle in Italy that Juliette, Sbrigani, and their servants visit in Juliette in the company of their host, Minski, Hermit of the Appenines.

Minski is "une espèce de centaure" [a kind of centaur] who is "haut de sept pieds trois pouces" [seven feet three inches tall] (Sade is always more concerned with precision than probability) who invites them all to his castle. After walking all day they get above the tree line and climb a rocky slope until, at the summit, they pass over and descend into a valley with a lake at the bottom, in the center of which is the island where Minski lives. They descend to the edge of the lake and embark in a black gondola that moves them noiselessly out toward the island. As they go Juliette gets a better view of the surroundings and sees that they are in a natural bowl, the sides of which rise up symmetrically around them. Minski's island castle is in the crater of an extinct volcano.

On the island, they first pass through an iron gate, then cross a moat on a drawbridge, which their host quickly draws up after them. They go through a second iron gate and enter an almost impenetrable black forest through which they must force a passage, only to come up finally on a ten-foot thick wall with no gate at all. Their host, a hearty eater, is strong and removes "une pierre de taille énorme et que lui seul pouvait manier" [a stone of enormous size that only he could manage].[21] A stairway is discovered; he invites them to precede him down it, and replaces the stone behind them before following. At the bottom they come into a long underground passage that they follow until their way is again blocked by a second stone slab. Reading the narrative of this descent and slow progress produces the discomfort of nightmare, but also makes us aware of just how much Sade felt he had to hide his perversity. Silling in 120 Days is similarly isolated from the world.

Minski now removes the last stone as he had the first, replacing it again behind them. They continue, climbing back up now until they emerge, as Juliette describes it, "dans une salle basse toute tapissée de squelettes; les sièges de ce local n'étaient formés que d'os de morts, et c'était sur des crânes que l'on s'asseyait malgré soi; des cris affreux nous parurent sortir de dessous terre" [in a low room all hung with skeletons; the seats in the place were made exclusively from the bones of the dead, and one was forced to sit on skulls; frightful cries rose up from below the ground] (8.556).

Minski kidnaps, imprisons, sodomizes, and finally devours young children, all for the sake of his health, his sexual health in particular, which he boasts about as a pure product of his diet. Again, Sade's case is only thinly disguised; he felt his own tastes to be monstrous, but also natural, a necessary diet, so to speak. The other characters in his prison fiction are usually allegories of extremes in the same mode. The Duc de Blangis in *120 Days*, for example, is essentially a list: "Né faux, dur, impérieux, barbare, égoïste, également prodigue pour ses plaisirs et avare quand il s'agissait d'être utile, menteur, gourmand, ivrogne, poltron, sodomite, incestueux, meurtrier, incendiaire, voleur" [Born false, hard, imperious, barbarous, selfish, as prodigal in his pleasures as stingy when it came to being useful, liar, gourmand, drunk, poltroon, sodomite, incestuous, murderer, arsonist, thief] (13.8).

So while Sade's discourse on the novel is conventional, and as full of praise for literary realism as Diderot's once was, the discourse of the novel per se in both the artistic and prison works is conspicuous by its absence. Sade, however, insists he is just following Nature. "First follow nature," Pope says in the *Essay on Criticism*, and Sade goes to some lengths to persuade us that this is what he is doing—that the polymorphous perversity he deals in matches the polymorphism we find in nature.[22] In *Aline and Valcour*, for example, Sarmiento tells Valcour that depravity is natural. "Lorsque le grain germe dans la terre, lorsqu'il se fertilise et se reproduit, est-ce autrement que par corruption, et la corruption n'est-elle pas la première des lois génératrices?" [When the seed germinates in the earth, when it fertilizes itself and reproduces, is it not a kind of corruption, and is corruption not the first law of generation?] (4.192).

When Léonore, in the same work, is informed by dom Lopès that she and Clémentine are to be sacrificed for political ends to Ben Mâacro, the sodomite and cannibal chieftan of the neighboring kingdom in East Africa, Léonore calls their *host* a tyrant. Dom Lopès responds: "Mais ces attentats mêmes que vous craignez parce qu'ils vous blessent, en quoi sont-ils contre la nature? Son étude la plus réflechie nous apprend chaque jour que le sacrifice de la faiblesse à la force est partout la première de ses lois ... Le loup dévore l'agneau, le riche énerve le pauvre, et partout la force écrase ce qui l'entoure sans que la nature réclame jamais en faveur de l'opprimé" [But these attacks you fear, even if they hurt you, how are they unnatural? A close study of nature teaches us each day that the sacrifice of the weak to the strong is everywhere the first of its laws ... the wolf devours the lamb, the rich wear out the poor, and everywhere power crushes those around it without nature ever raising its voice in favor of the oppressed].

Léonore asks how he can believe that tyranny is not an outrage against nature. Dom Lopès replies: "[La tyrannie] la sert, elle en est l'image, elle est empreinte dans le coeur de l'homme civilisé comme dans celui de l'homme naturel; elle guide les animaux, elle détermine les plantes, elle conduit les fleuves, elle maîtrise les astres: il n'est pas une seule opération de la nature dont la tyrannie ne soit la base" [(Tyranny) serves it, it is the picture of nature, it is imprinted in the heart of civilized and uncivilized man alike; it guides the animals, it determines plant life, it leads the river, it controls the stars: there is not a single operation of nature that is not based on tyranny] (5.70).

In *Juliette*, the government minister, Noirceuil, cites Machiavelli repeatedly in support of such a view (8.244, 305, 504; 9.44, 585). In *Aline and Valcour*, as Léonore and Clémentine travel across Portugal with Brigandos and his band, they come upon a law student about to rape a young girl he has tied to a tree. Brigandos seizes him and learns that the girl had left her work at the student's request to guide him through a difficult stretch of country. The student cooly defends himself:

> Seigneur chevalier, la nature en courroux n'est pas toujours très délicate: plus elle nous parle avec violence, plus elle efface en nous la loi des considérations. Avez-vous quelquefois vu déborder le Tage? Respectait-il en s'échappant ces superbes plans d'oliviers dont l'agriculture économe ombrageait à plaisir ses rives? Opposait-on un frein au fleuve, celui-ci, plus furieux encore, ne les franchissait-il pas avec plus d'impétuosité? ... la jeune fille résistait ... elle m'irritait davantage ... suivant les lois, j'allais commettre un crime, je vous proteste pourtant que je ne suivais que la nature.
>
> [Chevalier, nature's wrath is not always very delicate: the more violently it deals with us, the less are we given to be considerate. Have

you ever seen the Tage overflow its banks? Does it respect those wonderful olive orchards whose thrifty cultivation has lined its banks with pleasant shade? If we block it will it not become even more furious and break through even more tempestuously? . . . the young lady resisted . . . she even irritated me . . . according to the law I was about to commit a crime, I maintain to you however that I was only following the law of nature.] (5.148–49)

Sade was a fan of La Mettrie, and the notion of *l'homme machine* is utilized everywhere to justify and naturalize his perverse needs and desires. A materialist philosophy grounds his view of sensibility the same as it did in Diderot. As we saw there, it is part of the discourse of skepticism. Noirceuil, the Machiavellian minister in *Juliette*, delivers a dissertation on the subject: "On appelle crime toute contravention formelle . . . à ce que les hommes appellent les lois; d'où tu vois que voilà encore un mot arbitraire et insignifiant: car les lois sont relatives aux moeurs, aux climats; elles varient de deux cents lieues en deux cents lieues . . . Le crime n'a donc rien de réel; il n'y a donc véritablement aucun crime, aucune manière d'outrager une nature toujours agissante" [We call any formal contravention a crime . . . against what men call laws; so you see there a word that is arbitrary and fails to signify: because laws are relative to customs, to climates; they are different two hundred miles away . . . crime therefore has nothing real about it; so there is really no crime, no way to outrage a nature always in motion] (8.167–68).

In "Eugénie de Franval," Eugénie might be thinking of Montesquieu when she tells her father that his incestuous relations with her are no offense because "des usages qui, variant à chaque climat, ne peuvent avoir rien de sacré" [practices vary according to climate and therefore cannot have anything sacred about them] (10.441). The affiliations of Sade's relativism with some familiar lines of skeptical thought in the century are easy to see. Against the arguments for the existence of God offered by characters like Mme Lérince in "Florville et Courval"—the argument from design, or even Pascal's wager (10.225)—Sade offers those of the Dying Man in his *Dialogue entre un prêtre et un moribund* [*Dialogue Between a Priest and a Dying Man*], who protests, as did Saunderson in Diderot's *Letter on the Blind*, and Thomas in *Caleb Williams*, that he believes only what his senses tell him: "Je ne me rends q'à l'évidence, et je ne la reçois que de mes sens" [I only abide by the evidence, and I only receive it through my senses] (14.57).

The argument on motion we heard first in Diderot's *Philosophical*

Thoughts recurs here (see chap. 4). Diderot argued that the existence of God could be determined by looking at nature to see if "le mouvement soit essentiel ou accidentel à la matière" [motion in matter is inherent or accidental]. If accidental, and matter is initially inert, then there must be a prime mover, a God who gave it its initial impulse; if essential, then there is no need for God. Sade's Dying Man argues: "Mon ami, prouve-moi l'inertie de la matière, et je t'accorderai le créateur . . . Jusque-là n'attends rien de moi" [My friend, if you can prove to me that matter is inert, I grant you a Creator . . . Until then, don't expect anything from me] (14.56–57). And Dolmancé in *Philosophy in the Bedroom* states: "Si la matière agit, se meut, par des combinaisons qui nous sont inconnues, si le mouvement est inhérent à la matière . . . quel sera le besoin de chercher alors un agent étranger à tout cela?" [If matter is in motion, through combinations unknown to us, if motion is inherent in matter . . . what need do we then have to look for a mover outside all of that?] (3.394–95).

It is in the sexual tableaux where we see most clearly Sade's attempt to identify his materialist understanding of sensibility with the discourse of and on knowledge. The first thing one notes is that these tableaux are, again, not part of the discourse of the novel. Like Laclos, Sade was a man of the theater and always has a director in his stories arranging the various sexual groupings and performances.[23] Whether it is Silling in the *120 Days*, the boudoir of Mme de Saint-Ange, or one of the many stations of the cross Justine passes through on her way to annihilation, the characters are readied, the stage is set, and the curtain rises.[24] These interpellated performances are thus pieces of manifest fiction that function like pornography to objectify the consumer/reader and maximize his/her delectation, both within and outside the text. Illusionism or the suspension of disbelief is not part of the equation. In "Eugénie de Franval," for example, Franval has offered Eugénie for a few hours to his friend Valmont and arranged the scene as follows:

> Là, dans une salle décorée, Eugénie, nue sur un piédestal, représentait une jeune sauvage fatiguée de la chasse, et, s'appuyant sur un tronc de palmier, dont les branches élevées cachaient une infinité de lumières disposées de façon que les reflets, ne portant que sur les charmes de cette belle fille, les faisaient valoir avec le plus d'art. L'espèce de petit théâtre où paraissait cette statue animée se trouvait environné d'un canal plein d'eau et de six pieds de large, qui servait de barrière à la jeune sauvage et l'empêchait d'être approchée de nulle part. Au bord de cette circonvallation était placé le fauteuil de Val-

mont; un cordon de soi y répondait: en manoeuvrant ce filet, il faisait tourner le piédestal en telle sorte que l'objet de son culte pouvait être aperçu par lui de tous côtés.

[There, in a decorated room, Eugénie, naked on a pedestal, represented a young savage tired from the hunt, leaning against the trunk of a palm tree whose raised branches hid numberless lights arranged in a way to let their reflections fall only on the charms of this beautiful girl and highlight them in the most artistic way. The little scene containing this living statue was surrounded by a six-foot-wide moat that served as a barrier so the young savage could not be approached from any side. Valmont's armchair was placed at the edge of the moat with a silk cord attached, by means of which he caused the pedestal to turn in such a manner that the object of his cult could be seen by him from all sides.] (10.468)

Not all the tableaux are theatricalized to this degree, but there is usually a director in the action like Franval—or four of them, like the four masters of ceremony in the *120 Days*. Everyone is assigned a role and the play begins. The object is to obtain the maximum possible physical stimulation and sensation. The *120 Days* even has a list of "Dramatis Personae" and Sade then proceeds through his allegorical demonstration of perversions with the mathematical joie de vivre of a satyr-accountant.[25] "The Sadian group," Barthes writes, "is often pictorial or sculptural." Its figures are "arranged, architectured, but especially frozen, framed, lit."[26]

And it is these static, overmanaged settings that then serve as launching pads for Sade's discourse of sensibility and erudition. With all variables reduced to constants, the stage is fully occupied by two kinds of activity: discourse precedes, follows, and accompanies each coupling; sex produces discourse, and discourse, more sex. Dolmancé in *Philosophy of the Bedroom* becomes sexually aroused listening to Mme de Saint-Ange lecture Eugénie; and later, Mme de Saint-Ange offers herself as a writing desk (citing the scene in Laclos's novel): "me voilà toute nue: dissertez sur moi autant que vous voudrez!" [here I am completely naked: discourse upon me as much you like!] (3.383). The student-teacher model is the favorite. Learning occurs through imitation. Mme Saint-Ange shows Eugénie how to do things and says, "Imite-moi" (3.282). The sentimental Justine suffers "les malheurs de la vertu" [the misfortunes of virtue] for her inability to learn. As Jean Paulhan puts it, "Whatever happens, Justine is surprised. Experience teaches her nothing."[27] Knowledge is the valued commodity.

For three hundred pages she is mocked for her ignorance, repeatedly raped, brutalized, and finally immolated for it. Her sister, Juliette, by contrast, knows the world the way Mme de Merteuil did, and prospers. One type of sensibility involves physical pleasure and knowledge, the other, pain and ignorance.

When one puts the pieces together what emerges in Sade is the picture of a powerful discourse of skepticism—pure sensationism, subjectivism, solipsism, materialism, the failure of reason and logic—located firmly inside the language, not of the novel, but of romance. Sade insists that he is imitating nature in his tableaux, but their small worlds are as implausible as his arguments. As Maurice Blanchot puts it: "There is a lacuna in his thought, a lack, a madness." Despite his obsession with dissertations, Sade's theories are dominated by "irrational powers."[28] His position on religion, for instance, is that since there is evil in the world, God is responsible for it; but since it is contradictory to believe that a god who is all-good can be responsible for evil, God does not exist.[29] The dissertations of the libertines are always examples of such "irrational powers."

Pierre Klossowski likens Sade's fin de siècle mind to a ripened, decomposing fruit "that is detaching itself from the tree of society." It will fall, Klossowski says, because it is an "end, not a beginning, the end of a long evolution."[30] The "long evolution" in question is the evolution in the preceding hundred years of *sensibilité*. The "end" is the darkest part of the culmination Louis Bredvold talks about as the terminus ad quem of sensibility in the century—far darker than the end that Werther comes to. As such it is last word on the nescience of this particular form of skepticism in the century and its relation to the discourse of the novel.

7

Conclusion

Ends and the Means to Avoid Them

There are good reasons why scholarship on the eighteenth-century novel in recent years has become characterized by a strong interest in material, cultural history. A novel, as J. Paul Hunter writes, never comes into the world "altogether naked, new, or alone"; it comes with "its past, its author, the power of its cultural consciousness, its referentiality to some larger world of thing and event, and its interaction with readers who know and care about some of these extratextual matters."[1] The "larger [extratextual] world" of course contains more than things and events—it also contains ideas that readers also care about and which are as important to an understanding of novels as they were to the writing of them, as important, at least, as an awareness of shipping lanes, printing practices, or divorce laws. The latter are extremely important indeed to cultural historians of the novel—the pearls of new historicism, so to speak; but ideas too are part of history. In the form of different philosophies and aesthetic theories, they are—to borrow a Henry James metaphor—the string those pearls are strung on.

The idea that I have tried to put forward here with regard to the rise in popularity of British and French novels in the second half of the eighteenth century belongs first and foremost to the Duc de La Rochefoucauld, who inherited it from Machiavelli. In order to survive at the French court in the mid-seventeenth century Rochefoucauld insisted that one needed what he called *habilité*. The word meant more than *ability* for Rochefoucauld; in the way he uses it, it has something of the meaning of the Greek word *metis*, or cunning—as when Homer calls Odysseus "*polymetis* Odysseus," the man of "many wiles." For Rochefoucauld it is a kind of calculating intelligence that is the mark of the successful courtier. Rochefoucauld was not an advocate of courtly intrigue, only its reluctant apologist, and he often writes of what he calls *les finesses* as a kind of indignity that everyone at court in fact bewailed. But all agreed that if it was an indignity, it was a necessary one. Courtiers may have regretted the necessity of such deceptions but used them nonetheless to their own ends—and often to avoid those ends.

Rochefoucauld's idea—that deception is a form of survival—is one that I believe worked for the popularity of the novel in the latter half of the eighteenth century and probably continues to work in its favor today. The novel is a deception that out-maneuvers skepticism by asking for the suspension of disbelief; it promotes, demands belief, and did so in the eighteenth century at a time when belief itself was under siege. It was a deception that was looked on with suspicion at the time even by those who practiced it as a literary art. Richardson was ambivalent about it and only reluctantly endorsed it, as we have seen. But he was clearly aware of its necessity, especially when it came to saving his heroines. More direct praise is evident in the work of Laclos, Godwin, and Brown, where artifice is given a literary face and directly associated with intelligence.

In the preceding chapters we looked at how the discourse of the novel was represented in this light in the eighteenth century, from Pope to Sade, in various literary forms, and how it was set against different manifestations and representations of skepticism. It should now be clear that these two systems of expression stand over and against one another, and that the novel works against skepticism in a variety of ways. In one very simple way novels counteract Pope's "Universal Darkness" by offering a second-order reality that is by definition immune to real-world doubt. There was indeed an epistemological crisis in that world in the second half of the eighteenth century, so a novel reality where such a crisis was impossible had its attractions. The word *krisis* in Greek means both judgment and separation. In a skeptical climate judgment will perforce exist, but it will be a dissociated, fractured judgment without any consensus or basis in a singular truth, so *crisis* is an apt word to describe the condition of the episteme at the time. The vacuum created by the gradual delegitimation of reason was filled by sensationism, and in literature by a variety of skeptical, irrational, and pre-romantic forms that, like *Werther*, replaced *Vernunft* [understanding] with *Herz* [heart] as a basis for that judgment. The remedial role of realism in this *crisis* was clear to Pope, who early on equated the failure of knowledge to a failure of realism on the stage, and by the end of the century was even clearer to Godwin and Brown, who come as close as any in the century to allegorizing the novelist in encounters with incarnations, respectively, of romance and sensuous emotion.

Richardson's musing on the novel-as-sermon do not constitute a conscious theory of the novel at mid-century any more than Godwin's oblique allegory of genre in *Caleb Williams* does at the end. The sort of anxiety that Diderot expressed about Rameau-le-fou's mimicry in 1761 ran through the entire century. But readers and writers, like the courtiers of Rochefoucauld, enjoy plots for good reasons, even if they are unable to consciously formulate them. In times of disbelief there is an obvious pleasure in the suspension of that disbelief as we enter the second-order reality of a novelistic world, even if it is just for the period of reading. But more than this, the fictional worlds themselves that novel readers decide to believe in—if they are "worlds" of *substance*, as Shirley Brice Heath might say (see chap. 1)—are highly wrought products of the mind that demonstrate its power. When that power is in question, as it came to be in the age of Hume, it stands to reason that such "products" will give pleasure. The pleasure is Kantian in nature. It is the same one Shirley Brice Heath identifies today as the drawing attraction of novelistic discourse for modern readers: the connection of form-giving to the moral life. In periods of intense skepticism it is, after all, the ethical and moral life that is the first to suffer. Any display of the rational in such times will have a positive effect.

Kant understood this very well. When reason, and hence ethics, are under erasure, novels will give pleasure because of their high degree of organization. The reader will derive pleasure from the artwork's "purposiveness" as Kant calls it, and respond to the ethical nature of form-giving. Georg Lukács writes that realist fiction pleases not because it is a form of escapism, which in a way it always is; or because it mirrors the dissonance of its world, which it does; or because the stories teach us lessons; but because "in the novel . . . the ethical intention . . . is visible in the creation of every detail." The "ethical intention" is "an effective structural element of the work itself."[2] The key word here is *structural*. Lukács does not mean that the author's ethical intention informs her novel, which of course it must. What he means by saying that the "ethical intention" is in the "detail" and structure is that formally structuring or narrativizing a world is an essentially ethical act. A realist novel may promote vice or virtue, make a reader a better or worse person, but it is always an appeal to order, to a set of shared rules, always a call for consensus, for mutual understanding. As such it is in the purest sense of the word, ethical.

Shirley Brice Heath's study indicates that readers today still respond to novels in this way. Her respondents, she says, were not looking for escape or a quick, self-help fix in their reading, but for complexity and its resolu-

tion. "Reading serious literature," Heath writes, "impinges on the embed-
ded circumstances in people's lives in such a way that they have to deal
with them. And, in so dealing, they come to see themselves as deeper and
more capable of handling their inability to have a totally predictable life."[3]
The claim of her respondents, Heath reports, is that reading "enables me to
maintain a sense of something *substantive*—my ethical integrity, my intellectual integrity . . . Reading that book gives *me* substance."[4] One might
dismiss such language as impressionistic, Arnoldian, and uncritical, but to
do so would be foolish. It tells us something quite real about novels that
writers and readers are more in agreement on than we might like to admit.

Women were the main producers and readers of novels in the eighteenth century, and booksellers today still claim that roughly 70 percent of
all fiction sold is purchased by women.[5] If as Heath's respondents claim,
the pleasure in reading novels comes from the resolution of unpredictability, does this mean that women are more sensitive to unpredictability
than men? Women's lives today do seem more unpredictable than their
mothers', more unpredictable than the lives of women in the eighteenth
and nineteenth centuries, so there should be differences here, not similarities. And yet, in more patriarchal times young women like Pamela and
Clarissa had less control over their lives, and in that sense those lives were
indeed, at least from their own perspective, both unpredictable and a powerful source of anxiety. Also, as Heath claims, novel readers and writers
tend to be "social isolates." The reason the genre turned out, historically, to
be a feminine one is clear. The usual reason given is that women were and
are the more patient observers, better than men at seeing the nuances of
psychological and physical detail, and that this began in the eighteenth
century as a function of their increased leisure.[6] But there are better reasons. Heath provides a good one. But it is also logical that a genre like the
novel, whose principal effect is the creation of belief and the organization
of knowledge, would and should appeal to women, for whom knowledge
was traditionally considered unnecessary.

As I said at the beginning, the fact that novels act as an antidote to
skepticism hardly means that whenever skepticism characterizes an age,
novels will appear; or that when we have a golden age of literary realism,
skepticism must be a social problem (see chap. 1). It is true that our own
age, like Hume's, is a philosophically skeptical and antifoundational one.
But the nineteenth century was not; and women then were still the principal readers of novels. So there is no organic connection here. Literary
societies in Victorian London were societies of women; and as Kate Flint

notes, the large number of representations in the century of women reading, not only in novels but in paintings too, shows they were perceived quite clearly as the main consumers of fiction.[7] But none of this negates the possibility I have been arguing for that the sudden rise in the popularity of novels in the eighteenth century had much to do with the fact that they worked against the epistemological crisis of the age in the way I have been describing. A climate of antifoundationalism fosters "unpredictability," so it makes sense that a form that resolves it, as Heath points out, should be popular, especially with women.

I have also treated the literature of sensibility in the eighteenth century as a manifestation of skepticism. Novels of sentiment and sensibility became identified in the later eighteenth century with women, but this too was hardly through some sort of organic connection or necessity. The identification was, as we know, as restrictive for women as it was socially and politically advantageous for men, and men controlled publishing. The change in the writing of Eliza Haywood from vice to virtue is a good example of how this forced conformism worked. The switch from something like *Love in Excess* (1719) or *Anti-Pamela* (1741) to the conventional *History of Miss Betsy Thoughtless* (1751) can be understood as enforced by expectations. It will always serve the interests of the hereditary proprietors of the discourse of reason to keep women attached to a type of discourse that defines itself in terms of the heart rather than the head. Women like Mary Wollstonecroft eventually reacted against this, but not before the connection had been all but naturalized. Sensibility and sentiment are part of the discourse of skepticism, so the women-sentiment connection effectively ties down women writers and readers to the very failure of knowledge that their hunger for novels aimed to remedy.

Philosophical skepticism, as Christ said of the poor, is something we shall always have with us. In the West, as I said at the beginning, it has gone through three notable incarnations, from the early classical period, through the late seventeenth and eighteenth centuries, to our own age where post-Nietzschean philosophy has developed along some exciting but familiar skeptical lines. At its worst, skepticism is a kind of End, an epistemological terminus that, as Stanley Cavell says, is the last act of a self-devouring "demonic reason."[8] The damage it does is felt first and foremost in the area of ethics; and in the eighteenth century, beginning with Shaftesbury, the new ethics of feeling came in to fill the void. I would suggest, however, that the discourse of feeling and sensibility in the century was not a remedy, but a symptom of that void. What *was* a remedy, or at least a powerful force working against it, was narrative prose fiction. Writers at the time may not have consciously formulated the skepticism-novel dynamic in just these terms, but there are enough examples to show that they were well aware of it. When the logos is exposed as a fiction, one might expect fiction itself to benefit from the comparison and take on special importance, and this is what happened in the eighteenth century.

Notes

Chapter 1. Skepticism, Sensibility, and the Novel

1. On the "rise" in England see Hunter, "World"; and in France, see May, *Dilemme*. McKeon, *Origins*, 20, uses the phrase "epistemological crisis" for the pre-1740 period in a discussion of romance and realism where he asserts that the "instability of generic categories registers an epistemological crisis." Damrosch, *Fictions*, 4, refers to the Age of Hume and Johnson as "an age of epistemological crisis or destabilization [in which] skeptical empiricism had become the intellectual norm." Spitzer, *World Harmony*, 76, may overstate the case in claiming that the middle decades of the century marked a "great caesura" in the history of Western thought, but he is nonetheless referring to the same "crisis."

2. On deconstruction as skepticism, see the studies by Hiley, "Deep Challenge"; Butler, *Interpretation*; Wilmore, "Scepticism"; and Critchley, *Ethics*, 156–63. The description by Harris, "Critical Discussions," 318, of deconstruction as an "all-purpose solvent" also describes Pyrrhonism, the most radical form of skepticism, as I will demonstrate later in the chapter.

3. I follow Catherine Belsey's definition of realism in *Critical Practice*, 51–52, as "fictional forms which create the illusion while we read that what is narrated is *really* and intelligibly happening . . . Speaking animals, elves, or Martians are no impediment to intelligibility and credibility if they conform to patterns of speech and behaviour consistent with a *recognizable* system."

4. Heath is quoted in Franzen, "Perchance," 48–49.

5. McKeon, 20–22. Tavor, *Scepticism*, 1, writes: "The eighteenth-century fictions which twentieth-century criticism has characterized both as *novels* and as *good novels*, all grow out of the eighteenth-century sceptical tradition."

6. Mayer, "Middle Class," 279.

7. For the view that skepticism died in the Enlightenment, see Popkin, *High Road*.

8. This is what McKeon has in mind in his triple-rise and fall of "romance idealism," "naïve empiricism," and "extreme skepticism"—the Hegelian ruler along which he sees the eighteenth-century mind sliding back and forth.

9. See Young, *Religion*, 1.

10. Quoted in Willey, *Background*, 81.

11. Tillotson, Fussell, and Waingrow, *Literature*, 474.

12. Young, 2, draws attention to the Counter-Enlightenment strain of religious and visionary thought in England that continued—in spite of all this—through the century from Warburton, Law, and the Moravians, to Wesley and Blake.

13. Overton and Relton, *English Church*, 64. Porter, *English Society*, 169, speculates that the outpouring of devotional literature in the century registers this divisiveness, but it is hard to know how much of it was really due to demand.

14. Porter, ibid.

15. Berkeley, *Works*, 61, 129. In the preface to the first edition of his *Treatise*, Berkeley writes: "What I here make public has . . . seemed . . . not unuseful to be known, particularly to those who are tainted with skepticism" (*Works*, 63).

16. Young, 83, notes that the tendency to associate Locke with Newton has left an inaccurate picture of Locke's thinking as more secular than it was. See chap. 3, "Metaphysics before Physics." Young quotes Bacon: "Beyond the true Physics is divinity only," and rightly notes that "early modern epistemology was largely secured through religion's presuppositions which denied the possibility of a total absorption of metaphysics by physics."

17. Hume, *Dialogues*, 139.

18. Hume, *Enquiries*, 161.

19. Cavell, *Quest*, 138.

20. See Sextus Empiricus, *Outlines*. Cf. Wittgenstein's claim that philosophy leaves everything as it is. For the *no consequences* argument, see Clarke, "Legacy"; and Burnyeat, "Sceptic."

21. Popkin, *High Road*, 60.

22. See Gay, *Enlightenment*, 290–95.

23. For an attempt to read the relation between skeptic and man of feeling in Hume in a more dialectical fashion, see Livingston, *Hume's Philosophy;* and Norton, *Hume.*

24. See Popkin, *History*, 173.

25. Burnyeat, 3. See Descartes, *Principes*, pt. 1, sec. 43, p. 43, on clear and distinct ideas and the avoidance of error.

26. See Egan, *Gassendi's View*, 53.

27. See Tavor, 226; and Bolton, "Locke."

28. See Harrison and Laslett, *Library.*

29. See Jolley, *Leibniz*, 35–53. Leibniz's comments, in the *Nouveaux Essais*, bk. 1, chap. 1, are also discussed by Bolton. Aaron, *John Locke*, 31–32, mentions Lee's comment and claims that Locke "writes obviously in the spirit of Gassendi [and] appears disposed to approve of most of the objections which Gassendi has made to Descartes."

30. Lucretius, *Nature*, bk. 1, p. 29. Spellman, *John Locke*, 130–31, addresses the mistaken linkage of the *Essay's* sensationism to the materialism of Hobbes.

31. Yolton, *John Locke*, 115, remarks that the first criticisms were theological in nature.

32. Locke, 1.31. Jolley, *Locke*, 16–18, suggests that skepticism was Locke's target, as it had been Descartes'.

33. See Hutchison, *Locke*. Spellman, 123–24, discusses the selective appropriation of Locke to ends unrelated to the purpose of the *Essay*.

34. Quoted in Hampson, *Enlightenment*, 76.

35. Darnton, *Cat Massacre*, 195, discusses the language of the *Prospectus*.

36. Crane, "Suggestions." See also Green, "Latitudinarianism"; and de Bruyn, "Latitudinarianism."

37. Locke's connection to the discourse of sentiment has been well documented. Hutchison, 1, claims that Locke's philosophy was the foundation of French *sensibilité*. The same affiliation in England is noted, among others, by Todd, *Sensibility*, 24; and Brissenden, *Virtue*, 22.

38. For an early, well-balanced view of Shaftesbury as the popularizer but not inventor of sensibility, see Moore, "Shaftesbury."

39. The open affiliation of the two forms of discourse by 1750 is underlined by Mullan, *Sentiment*, who begins his study with Hume's *Treatise*.

40. See Todd, 129–46. Hegel writes that the "man of common sense who makes his appeal to feeling . . . tramples underfoot the roots of humanity . . . The anti-human, the merely animal, consists in staying within the sphere of feeling" (43).

41. Ellis, *Politics*, 24. See Warren, "Conscious Speakers"; and Claudia Johnson, "*Sweet Face*."

42. Vila, *Enlightenment*, 3, writes that "even the most hard-boiled philosophes prided themselves on their sensibility and saw nothing unmanly about cultivating this quality."

43. Vila, 111. In England, Cheyne's *English Malady* (1733) took a physiological approach to sensibility. For a discussion of Cheyne's influence, along with that of von Haller and Boerhaave in neurology, see Barker-Benfield, *Culture*, 15ff.

44. Vila, 286–88.

45. See Jameson, *Political Unconscious*, 152; Barthes, "L'Effet de reel"; and Humphries, "Flaubert's Parrot," 323.

46. "You may be certain, Sancho," says Don Quixote, "that the author of our history is some sage enchanter" (de Cervantes Saavedra, *Don Quixote*, 484). Boyd, *Reflexive Novel*, 17, writes that *Don Quixote* "parodies not only those romances that it replaces but also those novels which will follow it, follow it without questioning, as *Quixote* questions, their status with regard to the reality they purport to represent."

47. Kinkead-Weekes, *Samuel Richardson*, 455.

48. Ortega y Gasset, *Dehumanization of Art*, 57.

49. Paulson, *Satire and the Novel*, 5–7.

50. See Taylor, *Early Opposition*, 75, 93ff.

51. Porter, 308–9.

52. Locke, 1.203.

53. Hume, *Treatise,* 121. See also the "Essay of the Standard of Taste," in *Essays,* 236: "Many of the beauties of poetry, and even of eloquence, are founded on false-hood and fiction, on hyperboles, metaphors, and an abuse or perversion of terms from their natural meaning."

54. Barish, *Antitheatrical Prejudice,* 2, 5, 228.

55. See the letter to his son (Bath, October 19, O.S. 1748) in Tillotson, Fussell, and Waingrow, 863.

56. May, *Dilemme,* 29.

57. Cf. Bernard Harrison, *Inconvenient Fictions,* 11, who suggests that the plea-sure comes from unhinging and destabilizing "Great Truths."

58. Ingarden, *Literary Work,* 180–81.

59. McCormick, *Fictions,* 98. Käte Hamburger questioned the theory of quasi-judgments in 1957 in *Logik der Dichtung.* See Ingarden's reply, 64ff.

60. Another curative would be Adam Smith's impartial observer—a character-ization of conscience for a purpose.

61. Cassirer, *Language,* 8. Iser, *Fictive,* 12, 164–68, discusses fiction as cognition. Bender, *Penitentiary,* 1, notes Kenneth Burke's characterization of language as a mode of action, and refers to novels and visual arts as "advanced forms of knowl-edge" and "cognitive instruments."

62. The moral theory of both Spinoza and Hobbes rested on the belief (shared by Swift and other Augustinians) that Man was essentially an irrational animal. On the Machiavelli-Spinoza connection, see Feuer, *Spinoza;* for Machiavelli's influence on Hobbes, see Meinecke, *Machiavellism.*

63. For Hobbes, even government is a form of artifice. Leviathan is an automaton; sovereignty is its "Artificiall Soul," and so on. See *Leviathan,* 81.

64. Montesquieu, *Lettres Persans,* letter 137, 305 (my translation).

65. De la Rochefoucauld, *Maximes,* M. 124, p. 73 (my translation).

Chapter 2. Pope and Richardson on the Epistemology of Artifice

1. Cheyne wrote to Richardson saying that Pope had read the novel "with great Approbation and Pleasure." See Mullet, "Letters," 65.

2. Carole Fabricant, "Pope's Moral," for example, wonders how Pope could be so upset when he had little personally to complain about.

3. See chap. 1, p. 16, regarding Paulson.

4. *Essay on Man,* 2.4–5. "Man" is "A Being darkly wise, and rudely great: / With too much Knowledge for the Sceptic side." In Tillotson, Fussell, and Waingrow, 640.

5. See chap. 1 n. 15 above.

6. *Epilogue to the Satires, Dialogue II,* 1.73. In Pope, *Twickenham,* 4.317.

7. All quotations from the *Dunciad* will be from James Sutherland's volume in the *Twickenham Edition,* vol. 5., and will be cited parenthetically in the text by A (1729) or B (1743), book, and line number.

8. *Essay on Man*, 2.35–38, in Tillotson, 640. On Newton and Pope, see Nicolson, *Newton*, esp. chap. 6.

9. Sutherland, *Twickenham*, xxx.

10. Ibid., 176. Pope might have objected to the blasphemous nature of such representations, but uses words like *unintelligible* and *absurdity*.

11. In Marlowe's version, Faustus rejects offers of money and political power in favor of books. See Marlowe, *Faustus*, 5.170ff.

12. Sutherland, 252.

13. Pope had been a friend and advisor to authors like James Thomson and David Mallet, who had suffered under the act, and he had "played a role," as Maynard Mack puts it, "in the cluster of historical-allegorical Opposition plays" that were written in 1738 and 1739 to test the act. See Mack, *Alexander Pope*, 758.

14. See Mengel, "*Dunciad*." 161–78.

15. Barish, 234, quotes Law.

16. Cf. Steiner, *Death of Tragedy*, 264, which claims tragedy is impossible in an age of economic and bourgeois rationalism; and Cavell, *Disowning Knowledge*, 6, 8, which claims that tragedy in Shakespeare's time is "the display of skepticism" and "the working out of a response to skepticism."

17. See Goldstein, *Pope*, 79.

18. Fielding, *Works*, 206.

19. See Scouten, *London Stage*, 923–24.

20. Milhous and Hume, *Register*, 693.

21. On the dramatic quality of Richardson's writing, see Konigsberg, *Richardson*; Kinkead-Weekes; and Richetti, "Richardson's Dramatic Art."

22. See chap. 1 n. 52 above.

23. Richardson, *Vade Mecum*, 12–13.

24. Barish, 234.

25. In 1756 Richardson writes in a letter to Mrs. Watts (where the comment occurs) that playgoing once had been "a favourite diversion." Sherburn, "Richardson's Novels," 325, quotes from the letter.

26. Eaves, Duncan, and Kimpel, *Richardson*, 549, write that Richardson "was certainly no proponent of the freedom of the press: he regretted to Young that no legal authority stood sentinel over it, to prevent *infidelity, indecency, libel, faction, nonsense*."

27. See Crean, "Stage Licensing Act."

28. See Richardson, *Vade Mecum*, 9ff., for the quotations that follow in the next paragraph.

29. Collier, *Defence*, 10.

30. See Richardson, *Selected Letters*, 92.

31. Samuel Johnson, *Preface*, 330–31.

32. Taylor, 99, writes: "The very persons who had condemned fiction for untruth and unreality to life held in horror all realistic detail."

33. Samuel Johnson, "On Fiction," 325–27.

34. As writing in *Phaedrus*, 274–75; as knowledge in *Critias* in *Timaeus and Critias*, 106. On the play among the meanings of *pharmakon, pharmakeus,* and *pharmakos* in Plato, see Derrida, *Dissemination*, 95–134, esp. 124 and 127.

35. Richardson, *Clarissa*, 1.87. All future citations will be included parenthetically in the text by volume and page number.

36. Taylor, 54, notes that antinovel forces in the century were torn between the universally accepted belief that there was a need to improve female education and the fear of smart women.

37. Note Richardson's interesting comment in *Correspondence*, 2.298, that "I never wrote from what I saw by the bodily eye." Contrast this with his parallel claim in *Selected Letters*, 197, that Fielding's effects "are all drawn from what he has seen and known."

38. See Slattery, *Richardson-Stinstra Correspondence*, 16–17.

39. Richardson, *Selected Letters*, 197.

40. Cf. Doody, *Natural Passion*, 17, which argues that Richardson's concern with states of consciousness places him in the skeptical tradition.

41. McKeon, 363, repeats the fears of early critics of the novel that artifice is a symptom of relativism. There is an "undeniable turn toward extreme skepticism . . . implied in [Pamela's] fitful awareness of the projective and constructive powers of her own mind and its *contrivances*." Cf. Walker, "*Pamela*," which points out that this fails to account for her obvious knowledge.

42. De la Rochefoucauld, M. 124, p. 73 (my translation).

Chapter 3. Sterne and Laclos: Atropos or Dissemination

1. Sterne, *Works*, 2.12.129. All future citations of Sterne's works will be from the Florida Edition and included parenthetically in the text.

2. Tuveson, "Locke and Sterne," 265. Cf. Day, "*Tristram Shandy*," which warns that since almost everything in *Tristram Shandy* is borrowed it may be a mistake to make too much out of Locke.

3. Traugott, *Tristram Shandy's World*, 48.

4. Price, *Palace*, 204. Wasserman, *Subtler Language*, 170, also mentions the "failure of words" and claims that in Tristram's world meaning is "a function of each person's private, subjective concerns."

5. See Chézaud, "Language Naturel." On the destabilizing effect in *Sentimental Journey* of polysemic words like *remise* and *desobligeant* see Keryl Kavanagh, "Discounting Language."

6. Berkeley, 1.3, 78. Hume, *Treatise*, 215–18.

7. For the deconstructionist perspective, see J. Hillis Miller, "Narrative Middles"; and Lamb, *Sterne's Fiction*. Cf. New, "Sterne and the Narrative of Determinateness," who deconstructs the indeterminacy argument.

8. Lehman, "Of Time," 24; Damrosch, *God's Plot*, 296; Werner, *Diderot's Great Scroll*, 96, n. 13; Hunter, "*Tristram Shandy*," 624; Lamb, *Sterne's Fiction*, 11; Homer O. Brown, *Institutions*, 116.

9. Hume's comment dates from 1773. See Howes, *Sterne,* 147. Friedrich Nietzsche, *Human,* 239, writes of "a feeling of uncertainty" and that Sterne "wants to be in the right and in the wrong at the same time." On Nietzsche and Sterne, see New, *Free Spirits.*

10. Howes, 40, 385.

11. Showalter, *Evolution,* 112ff.; Booth, "Self-Conscious Narrator."

12. See New, "Sterne and Swift"; and Sterne, *Works,* 3.170ff. On Sterne's borrowings from Tillotson and Hall, see the Florida *Notes to the Sermons,* in *Works,* 5.23–26.

13. Lamb, "Sterne's System," suggests that the borrowing habit can be viewed as another facet of Sterne's Lockianism, since borrowing travels along associative lines.

14. See Wehrs, "Sterne"; Pellan, "Sterne's Indebtedness"; and Parnell, "Swift, Sterne, and the Skeptical Tradition."

15. Sterne, *Sentimental Journey,* 283–84. All future citations will be included parenthetically in the text.

16. See *Sermons,* in Sterne, *Works,* 4.276ff.

17. Quoted in Bredvold, *Natural History,* 84. R. S. Crane calls it the "pursuit of altruistic emotions for egoistic ends" (229–30).

18. See her introduction to Laurence Sterne, *A Sentimental Journey through France and Italy,* xiv.

19. Knox is quoted in Byrd, *Tristram Shandy,* 52. See also Auerbach, *Mimesis,* 401, who writes of Prévost's *Manon:* "The pleasure which the author endeavors to evoke in his readers by his representation of his lovers' childishly playful and unprincipled corruption, is in the last analysis a sexual titillation, which is constantly interpreted in sentimental and ethical terms while the warmth it evokes is abused to produce a sentimental ethics."

20. See New, *Sterne as Satirist.*

21. Battestin, "Sterne among the Philosophes."

22. See Barker-Benfield, 296–97.

23. Byrd, 52.

24. Lukács, *Soul and Form,* 148, writes on Sterne that there can be no "ethic of moments."

25. Oates, *Shandyism,* 10.

26. See Howes, 47.

27. Ibid., 106

28. Mullan, 158–60.

29. See Markley, "Sentimentality"; and Nuttall, *Common Sky,* esp. "The Sealing of the Doors," 1–44.

30. Alter, *Novel,* 41.

31. See Sterne, *Sentimental Journal.* Editor Stout, 291 n, adds that Sterne originally had a dash after "Chambre's" but deleted it, making the run-on obvious.

32. See Perry, "Words for Sex." Bloom, *Sterne's "Tristram Shandy,"* 2, writes that "a Freudian exegesis of *Tristram Shandy* therefore becomes a redundancy."

33. de Laclos, *Liaisons,* Lettre 81, 171. English translations are from *Les Liaisons*

Dangereuses, trans. Richard Aldington. For the sake of convenience all future citations will be by letter number only and will follow the English translation.

34. Merteuil tells Danceny that Valmont has seduced Cécile Volanges, knowing that Danceny will respond by challenging Valmont to a duel. She knows that Valmont will now arrange to make her letters to him public, so that whether he lives or dies she will be ruined. She will return the favor.

35. Seylaz, *Liaisons,* 31.

36. Byrne, "Valmont-Merteuil."

37. See Dowd, *Le Général.*

38. On the vanity explanation, see Palache, *Four Novelists,* 95, 97–98.

39. See Cusset, "L'Erreur."

40. Vartanian, "Marquise," 174.

41. Ibid., 172, 174.

42. On "représentation" as "hypocrisie" for the libertines, see Pommeau, *Laclos,* 11.

43. Aldington makes the mistake of translating "comédien" as "comedian."

44. For a reading of *Liaisons* as a "feminocentric" novel, see Nancy K. Miller, *Heroine's Text.*

45. See Barguillet, *Roman,* 199, on how Laclos arranges the letters to release information.

46. Hunter, *Before Novels,* 44.

47. Brooks, *Novel of Worldliness,* 175.

48. Seylaz, *Liaisons,* 129.

49. Vartanian, 173, 175. On Merteuil as a jealous woman, see Therrien, *Liaisons.*

50. See de Laclos, *Oeuvres,* 762.

51. Turnell, *Novel,* 61.

52. Seylaz, "Les Mots," 563, tells us that "the word *love* is not used in any more [of a] univocal sense than the word *heart* . . . what they designate is a complex reality where affection and sensation have ambiguous connections" (my translation).

53. On Merteuil's usurpation of male roles, see Nancy K. Miller, 144–46; Jones, "Literary," 163; and Thelander, *Laclos,* 92.

54. The English misses the sexual double entendre of "petite tête."

Chapter 4. Skepticism, Diderot, and the Novel

1. In *Diderot's Dream,* 11, Anderson notes that the literary writings are grounded in "a materialist theory of physical matter in motion."

2. Quoted in Mornet, *Diderot,* 57. Mornet, 6, sums up the problem in terms of Diderot's later philosophy: "In materialism there is no human freedom. Without freedom, without being able to choose between good and evil there is no morality. But Diderot has no more ardent desire than to organize and teach morality" (my translation).

3. Diderot, *Jacques le fataliste,* 49–50. All future citations will be included parenthetically in the text. Translations are my own.

4. Wilson, *Diderot,* 49, suggests that Diderot knew English by 1742. On Hobbes,

see Thielemann, "Diderot and Hobbes," 221, who finds a mention by Naigeon, a contemporary of Diderot's, that the latter had read Hobbes as early as 1732.

5. Shaftesbury's formal solution was important to Kant. See Cassirer, *Philosophy*, 312–31. Cassirer writes, "The nature and value of beauty [for Shaftesbury] do not lie in the mere emotional effect they produce on man, but in the fact that they reveal the realm of form" (326).

6. Diderot, *Oeuvres Complètes*, ed. Herbert Dieckmann et al., 1.295. All future citations to this edition will be included parenthetically in the text as *DPV*, followed by volume and page number. Translations are my own.

7. On Diderot's rewriting of Shaftesbury, see Adams, *Diderot*, 28–29. Adams writes that Diderot's piece was "not so much intended to explore a problem as to reduce an opponent to silence" (26).

8. Cooper, *Inquiry*, sec. 31.

9. Booksellers regularly hauled out remainders of other books for the flames, putting condemned books like Diderot's back on sale the next day.

10. Cooper, sec. 272.

11. See Dieckmann, "Diderot's *Promenade*," 427.

12. Ibid., 438.

13. Hume, *Dialogues*, 38. 128. See also Walmsley, *Rhetoric*, 89.

14. Furbank, *Diderot*, 53, 181–82.

15. Adams, *Bibliographie*, 3–4, 6, cites from writers of the early part of the century to show the general view. Good dialogues had to produce, as Rémond de Saint-Mard wrote, "une idée singulière et intéressante" [an idea singular and interesting]. They had to be tendentious, with a strict object in view. Adams notes that in the *Encyclopedia* article by Marmontel on "Dialogue" the links lead to "logique," "raisonnement," and "dispute."

16. Diderot, "Apologie de l'Abbé Galiani," in *Oeuvres politiques*, 112.

17. On the literary qualities of the *Promenade*, see Dieckmann, *Cinq Leçons*, 73–76; Pommier, *Diderot*, 39–54; and Venturi, *Jeunesse*, 108–19.

18. Diderot, "Entretien entre D'Alembert et Diderot," in *Oeuvres philosophiques*, 251.

19. On the materialist notion of the interconnectedness of phenomena, the *Encyclopedia* defines *beau* (DPV 6.156) as something that expresses "l'idée de rapports" [the idea of connections], a harmonious tendency between parts and "le tout" [the whole]. The idea also appears in the translation of Shaftesbury's *Essay* (DPV 1.321).

20. Naigeon, Diderot's contemporary, in the article on Diderot in his *Encyclopédie méthodique* (1792), also blamed the letter form for the disorderliness. On chance as the moving force of materialism see the *Pensées philosophiques* 21, DPV 2.28. Pommier, 97–98, blames Diderot's work habits; Venturi, 143, the conflictual nature of his models.

21. On philosophy-as-literature in the two *Lettres*, see Creech, *Thresholds*, 99–136.

22. Wilson, 84.

23. Diderot, *Les Bijoux Indiscrets*, 200–1.

24. Ibid., 201.

25. The play brought serious charges of plagiarism. Elie Fréron, editor of the *Année littéraire*, wanted to publish a mock letter of protest, purporting to be from Goldoni; but Malesherbes, in his capacity as official censor, forbade it as being a falsehood worse than plagiarism. See Furbank, 144. Ironically, it was a falsehood Diderot himself had already practiced four years earlier. In the midst of a religious scandal in 1752 surrounding the publication of a supposedly heretical thesis by the Abbé Jean-Martin de Prades, Diderot brought out an inflammatory piece called *Suite de L'Apologie de M. L'Abbé de Prades*, purportedly by de Prades and vindicating *philosophe* principles. Prades denied authorship but it brought down a further storm of troubles on his head. The *Encyclopedia* was also accused regularly of plagiarism, and Diderot and D'Alembert prefaced their second volume with an attempted explanation. See Wilson, 153–54. Fréron found a way around the interdiction by publishing a detailed act-by-act synopsis of Goldoni's play in one issue and then a detailed act-by-act synopsis of *Le Fils Naturel* in the next. Diderot was outraged and rallied his friends to defend him, including Grimm in his *Correspondance littéraire*, but the damage had been done. Furbank, 145, characterizes the whole episode as one in which Diderot was "caught in the toils of his own mystification."

26. The play itself was not performed until 1771 and was withdrawn after one performance.

27. *DPV* 10.143. The remaining citations from the *Entretiens* will be from this volume and included parenthetically in the text by page number.

28. In the preface to *La Religieuse*, 18 (my translation).

29. See May, *Diderot*.

30. Mauzi, preface to *La Religieuse*, 19, 21 (my translation). Mylne, *Eighteenth-Century*, 212, originally agreed but in "What Suzanne Knew" reverses her position and claims the "blunders" and inconsistencies in the novel are part of a different level of logic. Similarly, de la Carrera, *Success in Circuit Lies*, 58, says the inconsistencies are intentional.

31. Diderot, *Correspondance*, 3.40.

32. Furbank, 242–43, cites descriptions of him that match Diderot's. He was a friend of Diderot's and a "baffled genius."

33. Diderot, *Neveu*, 31. All citations will be from this edition and included parenthetically in the text; translations are my own.

34. Estimates vary on when Diderot first read Richardson; estimates from his letters to Sophie Volland indicate 1759. Prévost's translation of *Clarissa* appeared in 1751.

35. The comment occurs again later at the end of *Les Deux Amis de Bourbonne* [*The Two Friends of Bourbonne*] (1770). Page numbers for the *Eulogy* are from the Hermann *DPV* edition and will be included parenthetically in the text.

36. Anderson, 50.

37. See Smietanski, *Le réalisme.*

38. Loy, *Diderot's Determinist Fatalist,* 254.

39. Thomas M. Kavanagh, *Vacant Mirror.* Jack Undank, *"Jacques,"* 745; and Werner, 65, 23.

40. Anderson, 62–63.

41. Ibid., 53.

42. Dieckmann, "Presentation of Reality," 106–7, discusses the work's "inconsistencies and obscurities." Diderot, says Dieckmann, "seems to have jotted down his ideas somewhat hastily."

43. Diderot, *Paradoxe sur le comédien,* 127. All future citations will be included parenthetically in the text; translations are my own.

44. Collier, *A Short View,* 390.

45. Diderot, *Correspondance inédite,* 2.271.

46. Catrysse, *Diderot,* 123, 125.

47. "Sur le Génie" ["On Genius"] in *Oeuvres Complètes,* ed. J. Assézat, 26–27.

48. Quoted in Catrysse, 125.

Chapter 5. The Realization of Romance: Radcliffe, Godwin, and Goethe

1. See Bredvold's last chapter, "Culmination in Horror," 55ff. Howells, *Love, Mystery, and Misery,* 7, also claims that the gothic in particular "represents the extreme development of the eighteenth-century cult of sensibility."

2. Reeve, *Progress of Romance,* 2.7, dates its demise literally to "some thirty or forty years" before the appearance, in 1752, of Charlotte Lennox's *Female Quixote.*

3. Wollstonecroft, *Vindication,* 9.

4. Brissenden, 9, 114, 272, claims that *Udolpho* is indeed a sensationalized version of the sentimental novel. On Radcliffe's debt to novels of sensibility, see Murray, *Ann Radcliffe.*

5. Cf. Napier, *Failure of Gothic,* 5, who reads the back-and-forth shifting as a double movement of stabilization and fragmentation generic to the gothic.

6. Radcliffe, *Udolpho,* 5. All future citations will be included parenthetically in the text.

7. On the juxtaposition of the sacred and the sublime, see Otto, *Idea of the Holy.*

8. See Graham, "Two Endings," 1238.

9. The published ending seems to betray the novel's Jacobinism. Kramnick, 115, argues that Godwin's distaste for politics makes him "by no means a friend of reform." Cf. Dumas, "Things as They Were."

10. See McCracken, "Godwin's Literary Theory," 132.

11. Godwin, *An Enquiry Concerning Political Justice* in *Political and Philosophical Writings,* 20. Future citations will be included parenthetically in the text.

12. See McCracken, "Godwin's *Caleb Williams.*"

13. The letter was published as one of the seven letters by Mucius in *Political Herald and Review.* See Godwin, *Uncollected Writings,* 14.

14. On Godwin's concept of the ruling passion and its relation to moral philosophy, see Munro, *Godwin's Moral Philosophy*, 16.

15. Godwin, *Things as They Are; or, the Adventures of Caleb Williams*, 10. All future citations will be included parenthetically in the text.

16. Shakespeare, *Hamlet*, 3.2.22.

17. A re-presentation of the crime is integral to detection and prosecution; note how Wilkie Collins uses it in *Moonstone*, for example. On the *Hamlet* connection, see Graham, *Politics of Narrative*, 62–63.

18. See the foreword to *Sorrows*, xiii.

19. Von Goethe, *Werke*, 102; *Sorrows*, 138. All future citations to the German and English editions will be included parenthetically in the text.

20. Proescholdt-Obermann, *Goethe*, 51, n. 10.

21. On Goethe's debt to Rousseau, see Siebers, "*Werther* Effect."

22. See Prier, "Charlotte's Vicar."

23. Cf. Wellbery, "Mirrors," who argues that "in *Werther* nature is not an authoritative source . . . Nature claims no authority" (234–35, 236).

Chapter 6. Sensibility and the Moral Divide: Charles Brockden Brown and D.A.F. Sade

1. Jay Fliegelman writes in his introduction to the novel: "Even as it warns against seduction, the novel has seduction as its very essence and project." Charles Brockden Brown, *Wieland and Memoirs of Carwin the Biloquist*, xxiv. All future citations will be included parenthetically in the text.

2. Pattee, *Wieland*, x.

3. Quoted in Pattee, xxvi.

4. Allen, *Life*, 388–90.

5. Clark, *Charles Brockden Brown*, 163.

6. Dunlap, *Life*, 16.

7. Godwin, *Caleb Williams*, 4.

8. See Russo, "Chimeras."

9. Baym, "Minority Reading," 88. Cf. Grabo, *Coincidental Art*, x, on the numerous coincidences in the story, which he says are just too frequent not to have been intentional.

10. Clark, *Charles Brockden Brown*, 166, believes in his guilt; and so did Allen, 390–91, Brown's contemporary and biographer. The "Outline" to *Wieland*, found in Commonplace Book No. 14 among the Brown family papers in the manuscript collection of the Historical Society of Pennsylvania, makes it clear that Carwin is innocent. See Cowie, "Historical Essay," 320.

11. See O'Shaughnessy, "*Imperfect Tale*," 53, n. 18, who writes that "responsibility for Theodore's death cannot be definitively determined."

12. Locke, 2.432–33.

13. Hagenbüchle, "American Literature," 143, writes that Brown "made the act of

knowing the center of his work." Fliegelman, *Prodigals and Pilgrims*, 237, sees *Wieland* as a reaction against a new world of "epistemological dilemmas." On the obsession with knowing and interpretation in general in American literature, see Minter, *Interpreted Design*, 36–77; and Feidelson, *Symbolism*, 77–118.

14. On ventriloquism and/as mimesis, see Fussell, "*Wieland*," 174.

15. Sade classified his own works as L (lumière) and S (sombre).

16. Vila notes that any attempt to understand Sadian sensibility must take into account the burgeoning discourse of medicine late in the century. See chap. 1, and Vila, 287, where she talks about the "anthropological multiplication of types of sensibility" that would have been available to Sade.

17. D.A.F. Sade, *Oeuvres Complètes*, 10.15. All future citations will be included parenthetically in the text as volume and page number. Translations are my own.

18. Cf. Laborde, "Biography," 1, who divides Sade's work into the "conventional" stories, which "expose a mimesis of life and characters"; and the nonmimetic pornography, which "in no way is . . . representative of the world we know." For a discussion of *invraisemblance* in Diderot and Sade, see Waller, "Rhetorique," 48.

19. On Sade's lack of interest in setting and physical detail, see Ferguson, "Sade."

20. See Fabre, *Idées*.

21. Sade's descriptions of constricted, tortuous underground passages blocked by stones has its urological analogue in his medical condition. The labor and anguish of characters striving upward from underground tunnels to sites of sexual release is a trope for Sade's own physical strivings in prison. See Sade, *Letters*. Richard Seaver, who has translated the letters, comments on the famous *Vanilla and Manilla* Letter 97 (367–70), in which Sade describes to his wife the painful details of what he calls his "congenital defect," and says that "it is entirely possible that [Sade's] wild sexual fantasies are directly related to this dysfunction" (368 n). See also Weidmann, "Vox in Pace."

22. See Ilie, "Polymorphosis," 4.

23. On which, see Le Brun, *Sade*, 7–87.

24. Barthes, *Sade*, 32, catalogues the theater terminology in Sade's writing.

25. On the theatricality of the *120 Days*, see Le Brun, 95.

26. Barthes, *Sade*, 157 (my translation).

27. Paulhan, *Le Marquis*, 43 (my translation).

28. Blanchot, *Sade*, 13, 15.

29. Harari, "Sade's Narrative," 119, suggests that some of the disorder in Sade's thinking "is artful and willed," but calls the dissertations on religion an example of "mad logic." Cf. Le Brun, 34, who says it is merely Sade's "shuttling between the surface and the depths" that creates the illusion of illogicality.

30. Klossowski, *Sade*, 48.

Chapter 7. Conclusion: Ends and the Means to Avoid Them

1. Hunter, *Before Novels*, ix, xi–xii.

2. Lukács, *Theory of the Novel*, 72.

3. Quoted in Franzen, 46.

4. Ibid., 49.

5. Ibid., 47.

6. See Watt, *Rise of the Novel*, 47ff.; Ballaster et al., *Women's Worlds*, 64; and Turner, *Living by the Pen*, 13–15.

7. Flint, *Woman Reader*, 254–57.

8. Cavell, *Quest*, 138.

Bibliography

Aaron, R. I. *John Locke*. London: Oxford University Press, 1937.

Adams, D. J. *Bibliographie d'ouvrages français en forme de dialogue 1700–1750*. London: Oxford University Press, 1992.

———. *Diderot, Dialogue and Debate*. Liverpool: Francis Cairnes, 1986.

Allen, Paul. *The Life of Charles Brockden Brown*. New York: Scholars' Facsimiles and Reprints, 1975.

Alter, Robert. *The Novel as a Self-Conscious Genre*. Berkeley: University of California Press, 1975.

Anderson, Wilda. *Diderot's Dream*. Baltimore: Johns Hopkins University Press, 1990.

Auerbach, Eric. *Mimesis: The Representation of Reality in Western Literature*. Trans. Willard R. Trask. Princeton: Princeton University Press, 1953.

Ballaster, Ros, Margaret Beetham, Elizabeth Frazer, and Sandra Hebron. *Women's Worlds: Ideology, Femininity and the Woman's Magazine*. London: Macmillan, 1991.

Barguillet, Françoise. *Le Roman au XVIIième Siècle*. Paris: Presses Universitaires de France, 1981.

Barish, Jonas. *The Antitheatrical Prejudice*. Berkeley: University of California Press, 1981.

Barker-Benfield, G. J. *The Culture of Sensibility: Sex and Society in Eighteenth-Century Britain*. Chicago: University of Chicago Press, 1992.

Barthes, Roland. "L'Effet de reel." *Communications* 11 (1968).

———. *Sade, Fourier, Loyola*. Paris: Éditions du Seuil, 1971.

Battestin, Martin. "Sterne among the Philosophes: Body and Soul in *A Sentimental Journey*." *Eighteenth-Century Fiction* 7.11 (October 1994): 17–36.

Baym, Nina. "A Minority Reading of *Wieland*." In *Critical Essays on Charles Brockden Brown*. Ed. Bernard Rosenthal. Boston: G. K. Hall, 1981. 87–103.

Belsey, Catherine. *Critical Practice*. London: Methuen, 1980.

Bender, John. *Imagining the Penitentiary: Fiction and the Architecture of Mind in Eighteenth-Century England*. Chicago: University of Chicago Press, 1987.

Berkeley, George. *Philosophical Works*. London: Dent, 1975.

Blanchot, Maurice. *Sade et Restif de la Bretonne.* Paris: Éditions Complexe, 1986.

Bloom, Harold, ed. *Laurence Sterne's "Tristram Shandy."* New York: Chelsea House, 1987.

Bolton, Martha Brandt. "Locke and Pyrrhonism: The Doctrine of Primary and Secondary Qualities." In *The Skeptical Tradition.* Ed. Myles Burnyeat. Berkeley: University of California Press, 1983. 353–75.

Booth, Wayne. "The Self-Conscious Narrator in Comic Fiction before *Tristram Shandy.*" *PMLA* 67 (1952): 170–75.

Boyd, Michael. *The Reflexive Novel: Fiction as Critique.* London and Toronto: Associated University Presses, 1983.

Bredvold, Louis. *The Natural History of Sensibility.* Detroit: Wayne State University Press, 1962.

Brissenden, R. F. *Virtue in Distress: Studies in the Novel of Sentiment from Richardson to Sade.* London: Macmillan, 1974.

Brooks, Peter. *The Novel of Worldliness: Crebillon, Marivaux, Laclos, Stendhal.* Princeton: Princeton University Press, 1969.

Brown, Charles Brockden. *Wieland and Memoirs of Carwin the Biloquist.* Ed. Jay Fliegelman. Harmondsworth, England: Penguin, 1991.

Brown, Homer O. *Institutions of the English Novel from Defoe to Scott.* Philadelphia: University of Pennsylvania Press, 1997.

Burnyeat, Myles. "The Sceptic in his Place and Time." In *Scepticism from the Renaissance to the Enlightenment.* Ed. Richard H. Popkin and Charles B. Schmitt. Weisbaden, Germany: Harrassowitz, 1987. 13–43.

Butler, C. *Interpretation, Deconstruction and Ideology.* Oxford: Oxford University Press, 1984.

Byrd, Max. *Tristram Shandy.* London: Allen and Unwin, 1985.

Byrne, Patrick. "The Valmont-Merteuil relationship: coming to terms with the ambiguities of Laclos's text." *Studies on Voltaire and the Eighteenth Century* 266 (1989): 373–409.

Cassirer, Ernst. *Language and Myth.* Trans. Susanne K. Langer. New York: Doubleday, 1946.

———. *The Philosophy of Enlightenment.* Trans. Fritz C. A. Koelln and James P. Pettegrove. Princeton: Princeton University Press, 1951.

Catrysse, Jean. *Diderot et la Mystification.* Paris: Nizet, 1970.

Cavell, Stanley. *Disowning Knowledge in Six Plays of Shakespeare.* Cambridge, England: Cambridge University Press, 1987.

———. *In Quest of the Ordinary: Lines of Skepticism and Romanticism.* Chicago: University of Chicago Press, 1988.

Chézaud, Patrick. "Language Naturel et Art du Roman chez Laurence Sterne." *Bulletin de la Société d'études anglo-américaines des XVIIième et XVIIIième siècles* (November 1995): 113–22.

Clark, David Lee. *Charles Brockden Brown: Pioneer Voice of America.* Durham, N.C.: Duke University Press, 1952.

Clarke, Thompson. "The Legacy of Skepticism." *Journal of Philosophy* 69 (1972): 754–69

Collier, Jeremy. *A Defence of the Short View of the Immorality and Profaneness of the English Stage.* London, 1699.

———. *A Short View of the Immorality and Profaneness of the English Stage, Together with the Sense of Antiquity upon This Argument.* In *British Dramatists from Dryden to Sheridan.* Ed. George H. Nettleton and Arthur E. Case. Carbondale: Southern Illinois University Press, 1969. 389–91.

Cooper, Anthony Ashley, Third Earl of Shaftesbury. *An Inquiry Concerning Virtue, or Merit.* Ed. David Wolford. Manchester, England: Manchester University Press, 1977.

Cowie, Alexander. "Historical Essay." Bicentennial Edition of the Novels and Related Works of Charles Brockden Brown. Vol. 1. *Wieland* and *The Memoirs of Carwin.* Ed. Sydney J. Krause and S. W. Reid. Kent, Ohio: Kent State University Press, 1977. 311–48.

Crane, R. S. "Suggestions Toward a Genealogy of the *Man of Feeling*." *ELH* 1 (1934): 205–30.

Crean, P. J. "The Stage Licensing Act of 1737." *Modern Philology* 35 (1938): 239–55.

Creech, James. *Thresholds of Representation.* Columbus: Ohio State University Press, 1986.

Critchley, Simon. *The Ethics of Deconstruction: Derrida and Levinas.* Oxford: Blackwell, 1992.

Cusset, Catherine. "L'Erreur de Valmont: D'un libertin qui n'assume pas son libertinage." *L'Infini* 24 (1988–89): 84–89.

D'Alembert, Jean Le Rond. *Preliminary Discourse to the Encyclopedia of Diderot.* Trans. R. N. Schwab. Indianapolis: Bobbs-Merrill, 1963.

Damrosch, Leopold. *Fictions of Reality in the Age of Hume and Johnson.* Madison: University of Wisconsin Press, 1989.

———. *God's Plot and Man's Stories: Studies in the Fictional Imagination from Milton to Fielding.* Chicago: University of Chicago Press, 1985.

Darnton, Robert. *The Great Cat Massacre and Other Episodes in French Cultural History.* New York: Vintage, 1984.

Day, W. G. "*Tristram Shandy:* Locke May Not Be the Key." In *Laurence Sterne: Riddles and Mysteries.* Ed. Valerie Grosvenor Myer. London: Vision Press, 1984. 75–83.

de Bruyn, Franz. "Latitudinarianism and its Importance as a Precursor of Sensibility." *Journal of English and German Philology* 80 (1981): 349–68.

de Cervantes Saavedra, Miguel. *The Adventures of Don Quixote.* Trans. J. M. Cohen. Harmondsworth, England: Penguin, 1950.

de la Carrera, Rosalina. *Success in Circuit Lies: Diderot's Communicational Practice.* Stanford: Stanford University Press, 1991.

de Laclos, Pierre Choderlos. *Les Liaisons Dangereuses.* Paris: Flammarion, 1981.

———. *Les Liaisons Dangereuses.* Trans. Richard Aldington. New York: Signet, 1982.

——. *Oeuvres complètes*. Ed. Laurent Versini. Paris: Gallimard, 1979.

de la Rochefoucauld, François. *Maximes*. Ed. F. C. Green. Cambridge: Cambridge University Press, 1946.

Derrida, Jacques. *Dissemination*. Trans. Barbara Johnson. Chicago: University of Chicago Press, 1981.

Descartes, René. *Les Principes de la Philosophie*. In *Oeuvres de Descartes*. Vol. 9. Ed. Charles Adam and Paul Tannery. Paris: Vrin, 1957.

Diderot, Denis. *Les Bijoux Indiscrets*. Paris: Flammarion, 1968.

——. *Correspondance*. 16 vols. Ed. G. Roth and J. Varloot. Paris: Éditions de Minuit, 1955–70.

——. *Correspondance inédite*. 2 vols. Ed. André Babelon. Paris: Gallimard, 1931.

——. *Jacques le fataliste*. Paris: Bookking, 1993.

——. *Le Neveu de Rameau et autres dialogues philosophiques*. Ed. Jean Varloot. Paris: Gallimard, 1972.

——. *Oeuvres Complètes*. Ed. Herbert Dieckmann et al. 19 vols. to date. Paris: Hermann, 1975–.

——. *Oeuvres Complètes*. Vol. 4. Ed. J. Assézat. Paris: Garnier, 1875.

——. *Oeuvres esthétiques*. Ed. Paul Vernière. Paris: Garnier, 1965.

——. *Oeuvres philosophiques*. Ed. Paul Vernière. Paris: Garnier, 1964.

——. *Oeuvres politiques*. Ed. Paul Vernière. Paris: Garnier, 1963.

——. *Paradoxe sur le comédien*. Paris: Flammarion, 1981.

——. *La Religieuse*. Ed. Robert Mauzi. Paris: Gallimard, 1972.

Dieckmann, Herbert. *Cinq Leçons sur Diderot*. Geneva: Droz, 1959.

——. "Diderot's *Promenade du sceptique*: A Study in the Relationship of Thought and Form." *Studies on Voltaire and the Eighteenth Century* 55 (1967): 417–38.

——. "The Presentation of Reality in Diderot's Tales." *Diderot Studies* III (1961): 101–28.

Doody, Margaret Anne. *A Natural Passion: A Study of the Novels of Samuel Richardson*. Oxford: Clarendon Press, 1974.

Dowd, E. *Le Général Choderlos de Laclos*. Paris: Perrin, 1905.

Dumas, D. Gilbert. "Things as They Were: The Original Ending of *Caleb Williams*." *Studies in English Literature* 6 (1966): 576–97.

Dunlap, William. *The Life of Charles Brockden Brown: Together With Selections from the Rarest of his Printed Works, from his Original Letters, and from his Manuscripts Before Unpublished*. Vol. 1. Philadelphia: James P. Parke, 1815.

Eaves, T. C. Duncan, and Ben D. Kimpel. *Samuel Richardson: A Biography*. Oxford: Clarendon Press, 1971.

Egan, Howard T. *Gassendi's View of Knowledge: A Study in the Epistemological Basis of His Logic*. Lanham, Md.: University Press of America, 1984.

Ellis, Markman. *The Politics of Sensibility: Race, Gender and Commerce in the Sentimental Novel*. New York: Cambridge University Press, 1996.

Fabre, Jean. *Idées sur le Roman de Madame de Lafayette au Marquis de Sade*. Paris: Éditions Klincksieck, 1979.

Fabricant, Carole. "Pope's Moral, Political, and Cultural Combat." In *Critical Essays on Alexander Pope*. Ed. Wallace Jackson and R. Paul Yoder. New York: G. K. Hall, 1993. 84–102.

Feidelson, Charles, Jr. *Symbolism and American Literature*. Chicago: University of Chicago Press, 1976.

Ferguson, Frances. "Sade and the Pornographic Legacy." *Representations* 36 (1991): 1–21.

Feuer, Lewis Samuel. *Spinoza and the Rise of Liberalism*. Boston: Beacon Press, 1958.

Fielding, Henry. *The Works of Henry Fielding, Esq.* Vol. 10. Ed. Leslie Stephen. London: Smith Elder, 1852.

Fliegelman, Jay. *Prodigals and Pilgrims: The American Revolution Against Patriarchal Authority 1750–1800*. Cambridge: Cambridge University Press, 1982.

Flint, Kate. *The Woman Reader: 1837–1914*. Oxford: Clarendon Press, 1993.

Franzen, Jonathan. "Perchance to Dream: In the Age of Images, A Reason to Write Novels." *Harper's* (April 1996): 35–54.

Furbank, P. N. *Diderot: A Critical Biography*. New York: Alfred Knopf, 1992.

Fussell, Edwin Sill. "*Wieland:* A Literary and Historical Reading." *Early American Literature* 18 (1983): 171–86.

Gay, Peter. *The Enlightenment: An Interpretation*. 2 vols. New York: W. W. Norton, 1966.

Godwin, William. *An Enquiry Concerning Political Justice*. In *The Political and Philosophical Writings of William Godwin*. Vol. 3. Ed. Mark Philp. London: William Pickering, 1993.

———. *Things As They Are; or, the Adventures of Caleb Williams*. Ed. David McCracken. Oxford: Oxford University Press, 1970.

———. *Uncollected Writings (1785–1822)*. Ed. Jack W. Marken and Burton R. Pollin. Gainesville, Fla.: Scholars' Facsimiles and Reprints, 1968.

von Goethe, Johann Wolfgang. *The Sorrows of Young Werther*. Trans. Elizabeth Mayer and Louise Bogan. New York: Random House, 1971.

———. *Goethes Werke*. Hamburg: Christian Wegner Verlag, 1965, Band 6.

Goldstein, Malcolm. *Pope and the Augustan Stage*. Stanford: Stanford University Press, 1958.

Grabo, Norman S. *The Coincidental Art of Charles Brockden Brown*. Chapel Hill: University of North Carolina Press, 1981.

Graham, Kenneth W. *The Politics of Narrative: Ideology and Social Change in William Godwin's Caleb Williams*. New York: AMS Press, 1990.

———. "The Two Endings of *Caleb Williams:* Politics and Aesthetics in a Revolutionary Novel." *Studies on Voltaire and the Eighteenth Century* 265 (1989): 1238.

Green, Donald. "Latitudinarianism and Sensibility: The Genealogy of the *Man of Feeling* Reconsidered." *Modern Philology* 75 (1977): 159–83.

Hagenbüchle, Roland. "American Literature and the Nineteenth-Century Crisis in Epistemology: The Example of Charles Brockden Brown." *Early American Literature* 23 (1988): 121–51.

Hamburger, Käte. *Logik der Dichtung.* Stuttgart, Germany: Klett, 1957.

Hampson, Norman. *The Enlightenment.* Harmondsworth, England: Penguin, 1968.

Harari, Josué. "Sade's Narrative: Ill-logical or Illogical?" *Genre* 7 (1974): 112–31.

Harris, Wendell V. "Critical Discussions." *Philosophy and Literature* 11.2 (October 1987): 317–29.

Harrison, Bernard. *Inconvenient Fictions: Literature and the Limits of Theory.* New Haven: Yale University Press, 1991.

Harrison, John, and Peter Laslett. *The Library of John Locke.* Oxford: Clarendon Press, 1971.

Hegel, G.W.F. *Phenomenology of Spirit.* Trans. A. V. Miller. Oxford: Oxford University Press, 1977.

Hiley, David. "The Deep Challenge of Pyrrhonian Scepticism." *Journal of the History of Philosophy* 25 (1987): 185–213.

Hobbes, Thomas. *Leviathan.* Harmondsworth: Penguin, 1968.

Howells, Carol Ann. *Love, Mystery, and Misery: Feeling in Gothic Fiction.* London: Athlone Press, 1978.

Howes, Alan B., ed. *Sterne: The Critical Heritage.* London: Routledge and Kegan Paul, 1974.

Hume, David. *Dialogues Concerning Natural Religion.* Ed. Martin Bell. London: Penguin, 1990.

———. *Enquiries Concerning Human Understanding and Concerning the Principles of Morals.* Ed. L. A. Selby-Bigge. 3d ed. Revised P. H. Nidditch. Oxford: Clarendon Press, 1975.

———. "Essay of the Standard of Taste." In *Essays Moral, Political and Literary.* Oxford: Oxford University Press, 1963. 231–55.

———. *A Treatise of Human Nature.* Ed. L. A. Selby-Bigge. 2d ed. Revised P. H. Nidditch. Oxford: Clarendon Press, 1978.

Humphries, Jefferson. "Flaubert's Parrot and Huysmans's Cricket: The Decadence of Realism and the Realism of Decadence." *Stanford French Review* (Fall 1987): 323–30.

Hunter, J. Paul. *Before Novels: The Cultural Contexts of Eighteenth-Century English Fiction.* New York: W. W. Norton, 1990.

———. "*Tristram Shandy* and the Art of Interruption." In *Tristram Shandy.* Ed. Howard Anderson. New York: W. W. Norton, 1980. 623–40.

———. "The World as Stage and Closet." In *British Theatre and Other Arts 1660–1800.* Ed. Shirley Strum Kenny. Washington, D.C.: Folger, 1984. 271–87.

Hutchison, Ross. *Locke in France 1688–1734.* Vol. 209. Oxford: Voltaire Foundation, 1991.

Ilie, Paul. "Polymorphosis in Sade." *Symposium: A Quarterly Journal in Modern Literatures* 38 (1984): 3–12.

Ingarden, Roman. *The Literary Work of Art.* Trans. G. G. Grabowicz. Evanston, Ill.: Northwestern University Press, 1973.

Iser, Wolfgang. *The Fictive and the Imaginary: Charting Literary Anthropology.* Baltimore: Johns Hopkins University Press, 1993.

Jameson, Fredric. *The Political Unconscious.* Ithaca, N.Y.: Cornell University Press, 1981.

Johnson, Claudia. "A Sweet Face as White as Death: Jane Austen and the Politics of Female Sensibility." *Novel: A Forum of Fiction* 22.2 (1989): 159–74.

Johnson, Samuel. "On Fiction." *The Rambler* 4 (March 31, 1750). In *Critical Theory Since Plato.* Ed. Hazard Adams. New York: Harcourt Brace Jovanovich, 1971. 325–27.

———. "Preface to Shakespeare." In *Critical Theory Since Plato.* Ed. Hazard Adams. New York: Harcourt Brace Jovanovich, 1971. 329–36.

Jolley, Nicholas. *Leibniz and Locke: A Study of the New Essays on Human Understanding.* Oxford: Clarendon Press, 1984.

———. *Locke: His Philosophical Thought.* New York: Oxford University Press, 1999.

Jones, Shirley. "Literary and Philosophical Elements in *Les Liaisons Dangereuses:* The Case of Merteuil." *French Studies: A Quarterly Review* 38 (1984): 159–69.

Kant, Immanuel. *Critique of Judgment.* Trans. Werner Pluhar. Indianapolis: Hacket, 1987.

Kavanagh, Keryl. "Discounting Language: A Vehicle for Interpreting Laurence Sterne's *A Sentimental Journey.*" *The Journal of Narrative Technique* 22.2 (Spring 1992): 136–44.

Kavanagh, Thomas M. *The Vacant Mirror: A Study of Mimesis Through Diderot's Jacques le fataliste.* Vol. 104. Oxford: Voltaire Foundation, 1973.

Kinkead-Weekes, Mark. *Samuel Richardson: Dramatic Novelist.* London: Methuen, 1973.

Klossowski, Pierre. *Sade my neighbour.* Trans. Alphonso Lingis. Evanston, Ill.: Northwestern University Press, 1991.

Konigsberg, Ira. *Samuel Richardson and the Dramatic Novel.* Lexington: University of Kentucky Press, 1968.

Kramnick, Isaac. "On Anarchism and the Real World." *The American Political Science Review* 66 (1972): 114–28.

Laborde, Alice. "The Marquis de Sade's Biography Revisited." In *Sade: His Ethics and Rhetoric.* Ed. Colette V. Michael. New York: Peter Lang, 1989. 1–26.

Lamb, Jonathan. *Sterne's Fiction and the Double Principle.* Cambridge: Cambridge University Press, 1989.

———. "Sterne's System of Imitation." *Modern Language Review* 76 (1981): 794–810.

Le Brun, Annie. *Sade: A Sudden Abyss.* Trans. Camille Naish. San Francisco: City Lights Books, 1990.

Lehman, Benjamin H. "Of Time, Personality, and the Author." In *Laurence Sterne: A Collection of Critical Essays*. Ed. John Traugott. Englewood Cliffs, N.J.: Prentice-Hall, 1968. 21–33.

Livingston, Donald W. *Hume's Philosophy of Common Life*. Chicago: University of Chicago Press, 1984.

Locke, John. *An Essay Concerning Human Understanding*. Ed. Alexander Campbell Fraser. 2 vols. New York: Dover, 1959.

Loy, J. Robert. *Diderot's Determinist Fatalist*. New York: King's Crown Press, 1950.

Lucretius. *On the Nature of Things*. Trans. Cyril Bailey. Oxford: Clarendon Press, 1910.

Lukács, Georg. *Soul and Form*. Trans. Anna Bostock. Cambridge: MIT Press, 1971.

———. *The Theory of the Novel*. Trans. Anna Bostock. Cambridge: MIT Press, 1971.

Mack, Maynard. *Alexander Pope: A Life*. New York: W. W. Norton, 1985.

Markley, Robert. "Sentimentality as Performance: Shaftesbury, Sterne and the Theatrics of Virtue." In *The New Eighteenth-Century: Theory, Politics, English Literature*. Ed. Felicity Nussbaum and Laura Brown. New York: Methuen, 1987. 210–30.

Marlowe, Christopher. *The Tragical History of the Life and Death of Doctor Faustus*. In *English Drama: 1580–1642*. Ed. C.F.T. Brooke and N. B. Paradise. Lexington, Mass.: D. C. Heath, 1961. 171–91.

May, Georges. *Diderot et La Religieuse*. Paris: Presses Universitaires de France, 1954.

———. *Le Dilemme du roman au XVIIIième siècle: Etude sur les rapports du roman et de la critique (1715–1761)*. Paris: Presses Universitaires de France, 1963.

Mayer, Robert. "Did You Say Middle Class? The Question of Taste and the Rise of the Novel." *Eighteenth-Century Fiction* 12.2–3 (Jan.–April 2000): 277–307.

McCormick, Peter J. *Fictions, Philosophies and the Problems of Poetics*. Ithaca, N.Y.: Cornell University Press, 1988.

McCracken, David. "Godwin's *Caleb Williams:* A Fictional Rebuttal of Burke." *Studies in Burke and his Time* 11 (1969–70): 1442–52.

———. "Godwin's Literary Theory: The Alliance Between Fiction and Political Philosophy." *Philological Quarterly* 49 (1970): 113–33.

McKeon, Michael. *Origins of the English Novel 1600–1740*. Baltimore: Johns Hopkins University Press, 1987.

Meinecke, Friedrich. *Machiavellism: The Doctrine of Raison d'Etat and its Place in Modern History*. Trans. Douglas Scott. New Haven: Yale University Press, 1957.

Mengel, Chris. "The *Dunciad* Illustrations." *Eighteenth-Century Studies* 7 (73/74): 161–78.

Milhous, Judith, and Robert Hume, eds. *A Register of English Theatrical Documents 1660–1737*. Carbondale: Southern Illinois University Press, 1991.

Miller, J. Hillis. "Narrative Middles: A Preliminary Outline." *Genre* 11 (1978): 375–87.

Miller, Nancy K. *The Heroine's Text: Readings in the French and English Novel*. New York: Columbia University Press, 1980.

Minter, David L. *The Interpreted Design as a Structural Principle in American Prose.* New Haven: Yale University Press, 1969.

Montesquieu, *Lettres Persans.* Paris: Gallimard, 1973.

Moore, C. A. "Shaftesbury and the Ethical Poets, 1700–1760." *PMLA* 31 (1916): 264–325.

Mornet, Daniel. *Diderot.* Paris: Hatier-Boivin, 1941.

Mullan, John. *Sentiment and Sociability: The Language of Fiction in the Eighteenth Century.* Oxford: Clarendon Press, 1988.

Mullet, C. F. "The Letters of Dr. Cheyne to Samuel Richardson 1733–1743." *University of Missouri Studies* 18 (1943): 1–137.

Munro, D. H. *Godwin's Moral Philosophy.* Oxford: Oxford University Press, 1953.

Murray, E. B. *Ann Radcliffe.* New York: Twayne, 1972.

Mylne, Vivienne. "What Suzanne Knew: Lesbianism and *La Religieuse.*" *Studies on Voltaire and the Eighteenth Century* 208 (1982): 167–73.

Napier, Elizabeth. *The Failure of Gothic: Problems of Disjunction in an Eighteenth-Century Literary Form.* Oxford: Clarendon Press, 1987.

New, Melvyn. *Laurence Sterne as Satirist: A Reading of Tristram Shandy.* Gainesville: University of Florida Press, 1969.

———. "Sterne and the Narrative of Determinateness." *Eighteenth-Century Fiction* 4 (1992): 315–29.

———. "Sterne and Swift: Sermons and Satire." *Modern Language Quarterly* 30 (1969): 198–211.

———. "*Tristram Shandy*": A Book for Free Spirits. New York: Twayne, 1994.

Nicolson, Marjorie Hope. *Newton Demands the Muse: Newton's Opticks and the Eighteenth Century Poets.* Hamden, Conn.: Archon Books, 1963.

Nietzsche, Friedrich. *Human, All Too Human.* Trans. R. J. Hollingdale. Cambridge, England: Cambridge University Press, 1986.

Norton, David Fate. *David Hume: Common-Sense Moralist, Sceptical Metaphysician.* Princeton: Princeton University Press, 1982.

Nuttall, A. D. *A Common Sky: Philosophy and the Literary Imagination.* London: Chatto and Windus, 1974.

Oates, J.C.T. *Shandyism and Sentiment, 1760–1800.* York, England: Cambridge Bibliographical Society, 1968.

Ortega y Gasset, José. *The Dehumanization of Art and Notes on the Novel.* Trans. Helene Weyl. Princeton: Princeton University Press, 1948.

O'Shaughnessy, Toni. "An *Imperfect Tale:* Interpretive Accountability in *Wieland.*" *Studies in American Fiction* 18 (1990): 41–54.

Otto, Rudolf. *The Idea of the Holy.* Trans. John W. Harvey. New York: Oxford University Press, 1958.

Overton, J. H., and F. Relton. *The English Church: From the Accession of George I to the End of the Eighteenth Century 1714–1800.* New York: Macmillan, 1906.

Palache, J. G. *Four Novelists of the Old Regime: Crebillon, Laclos, Diderot, Restif de la Bretonne.* London: Jonathan Cope, 1926.

Parnell, J. T. "Swift, Sterne, and the Skeptical Tradition." *Studies in Eighteenth-Century Culture* 23 (1994): 220–42.

Pattee, Fred Lewis, ed. *Wieland, or the Transformation, together with Memoirs of Carwin the Biloquist of Charles Brockden Brown.* New York: Hofner Publishing, 1926.

Paulhan, Jean. *Le Marquis de Sade et sa complice.* Paris: Éditions Complexe, 1987.

Paulson, Ronald. *Satire and the Novel in Eighteenth-Century England.* New Haven: Yale University Press, 1967.

Pellan, Françoise. "Laurence Sterne's Indebtedness to Charron." *Modern Language Review* 67 (1972): 752–55.

Perry, Ruth. "Words for Sex: The Verbal-Sexual Continuum in *Tristram Shandy.*" *Studies in the Novel* 20 (1988): 27–42.

Plato. *Phaedrus.* Trans. C. J. Rowe. Wiltshire, England: Aris and Phillips, 1986.

———. *Timaeus and Critias.* Trans. Desmond Lee. Harmondsworth, England: Penguin, 1977.

Pommeau, René, ed. *Laclos et le libertinage.* Paris: Presses Universitaires de France, 1983.

Pommier, Jean. *Diderot avant Vincennes.* Paris: Boivin, 1939.

Pope, Alexander. *The Twickenham Edition of the Poems of Alexander Pope.* 3d ed. General Editor John Butt. New Haven: Yale University Press, 1963.

Popkin, Richard H. *The High Road to Pyrrhonism.* San Diego: Austin Hill, 1980.

———. *The History of Scepticism from Erasmus to Spinoza.* Berkeley: University of California Press, 1979.

Popkin, Richard H., and Charles B. Schmitt, eds. *Scepticism from the Renaissance to the Enlightenment.* Weisbaden, Germany: Harrassowitz, 1987.

Porter, Roy. *English Society in the Eighteenth Century.* Harmondsworth, England: Penguin, 1982.

Price, Martin. *To the Palace of Wisdom: Studies in Order and Energy from Dryden to Blake.* Garden City, N.Y.: Doubleday, 1964.

Prier, Raymond Adolph. "Charlotte's Vicar and Goethe's Eighteenth-Century Tale about *Werther.*" In *Narrative Ironies.* Ed. R. A. Prier and G. Gillespie. Amsterdam: Rodopi, 1997. 283–97.

Proescholdt-Obermann, Catherine Waltraud. *Goethe and his British Critics.* Frankfurt: Peter Lang, 1992.

Radcliffe, Ann. *The Mysteries of Udolpho.* Ed. Bonamy Dobrée. Oxford: Oxford University Press, 1966.

Reeve, Clara. *The Progress of Romance.* New York: Facsimile Text Society, 1930.

Richardson, Samuel. *The Apprentice's Vade Mecum and A Seasonable Examination of Playhouses.* New York: Garland, 1974.

———. *Clarissa. Or the History of a Young Lady: Comprehending The Most Important Concerns of Private Life.* Ed. Florian Stuber. 8 vols. New York: AMS, 1990.

———. *The Correspondence of Samuel Richardson.* Ed. Anna Laetitia Barbauld. 6 vols. New York: AMS Press, 1966.

———. *Pamela or, Virtue Rewarded*. Ed. T. C. Duncan Eaves and Ben D. Kimpel. Boston: Houghton Mifflin, 1971.

———. *Selected Letters by Samuel Richardson*. Ed. John Carroll. Oxford: Clarendon Press, 1964.

Richetti, John. "Richardson's Dramatic Art in *Clarissa*." In *British Theatre and Other Arts 1660–1800*. Ed. Shirley Strum Kenny. Washington, D.C.: Folger, 1984. 288–308.

Russo, James F. "The Chimeras of the Brain." *Early American Literature* 16 (1981): 60–88.

Sade, D.A.F. *Marquis de Sade: Letters from Prison*. Trans. Richard Seaver. New York: Arcade, 1999.

———. *Oeuvres Complètes*. 16 vols. Paris: Cercle du livre Précieux, 1966.

Scouten, Arthur H., ed. *The London Stage 1660–1800*. Vol. 2, pt. 3: 1729–1747. Carbondale: Southern Illinois University Press, 1961.

Sextus Empiricus. *Outlines of Pyrrhonism*. Trans. R. G. Bury. Cambridge: Harvard University Press, 1933.

Seylaz, Jean-Luc. *Les Liaisons Dangereuses et la création romanesque chez Laclos*. Geneva: Droz, 1965.

———. "Les Mots et la chose: Sur l'emploi des mots amour, aimer chez Mme de Merteuil et Valmont." *Revue d'Histoire Littéraire de la France* 82.4 (1982): 559–74.

Sherburn, George. "Samuel Richardson's Novels and the Theatre: A Theory Sketched." *Philological Quarterly* 41 (1962): 325–29.

Showalter, English, Jr. *The Evolution of the French Novel 1641–1782*. Princeton: Princeton University Press, 1972.

Siebers, Tobin. "The *Werther* Effect: The Esthetics of Suicide." *Mosaic* 26.1 (1993): 15–34.

Slattery, William C., ed. *The Richardson-Stinstra Correspondence*. Carbondale: Southern Illinois University Press, 1969.

Smietanski, Jacques. *Le réalisme dans Jacques le Fataliste*. Paris: A. G. Nizet, 1965.

Spellman, W. M. *John Locke*. New York: St. Martin's Press, 1997.

Spitzer, Leo. *Classical and Christian Ideas of World Harmony: Prolegomena to an Interpretation of the Word "Stimmung."* Ed. Anna Granville Hatcher. Baltimore: Johns Hopkins University Press, 1963.

Steiner, George. *The Death of Tragedy*. London: Faber and Faber, 1961.

Sterne, Laurence. *The Florida Edition of the Works of Laurence Sterne*. 5 vols. Ed. Melvyn New and Joan New. Gainesville: University Press of Florida, 1978.

———. *A Sentimental Journey through France and Italy*. Ed. Gardner D. Stout, Jr. Berkeley: University of California Press, 1967.

Sutherland, James, ed. *The Twickenham Edition of the Poems of Alexander Pope*. 3d ed. Vol. 5. General editor John Butt. New Haven: Yale University Press, 1963.

Tavor, Eve. *Scepticism, Society and the Eighteenth-Century Novel*. London: Macmillan, 1987.

Taylor, John. *Early Opposition to the English Novel: The Popular Reaction from 1760 to 1830.* New York: King's Crown Press, 1943.

Thelander, Dorothy R. *Laclos and the Epistolary Novel.* Geneva: Droz, 1963.

Therrien, Madeleine. *Les Liaisons Dangereuses: une interprétation psychologique.* Paris: Société d'éditions d'enseignement supérieur, 1973.

Thielemann, Leland. "Diderot and Hobbes." *Diderot Studies* 2 (1952): 221–78.

Tillotson, Geoffrey, Paul Fussell Jr., and Marshall Waingrow, eds. *Eighteenth-Century Literature.* San Diego: Harcourt Brace Jovanovich, 1969.

Todd, Janet. *Sensibility, an Introduction.* London: Methuen, 1986.

Traugott, John. *Tristram Shandy's World: Sterne's Philosophical Rhetoric.* New York: Russell and Russell, 1954.

Turnell, Martin. *The Novel in France: Mme de La Fayette, Laclos, Constant, Stendhal, Balzac, Flaubert, Proust.* London: Hamish Hamilton, 1950.

Turner, Cheryl. *Living by the Pen: Women Writers in the Eighteenth Century.* London: Routeledge, 1992.

Tuveson, Ernest. "Locke and Sterne." In *Reason and Imagination: Studies in the History of Ideas 1600–1800.* Ed. J. A. Mazzeo. New York: Columbia University Press, 1962. 255–77.

Undank, Jack. "*Jacques le fataliste* and the Uses of Representation." *Modern Language Notes* 101 (1986): 741–65.

Vartanian, Aram. "The Marquise de Merteuil: A Case of Mistaken Identity." *L'Esprit Créateur* 3.4 (Winter 1963): 172–80.

Venturi, Franco. *Jeunesse de Diderot.* Trans. Juliette Bertrand. Paris: Skira, 1939.

Vila, Anne C. *Enlightenment and Pathology: Sensibility in the Literature and Medicine of Eighteenth-Century France.* Baltimore: Johns Hopkins University Press, 1998.

Walker, William. "*Pamela* and Skepticism." *Eighteenth-Century Life* 16 (November 1992): 68–85.

Waller, Richard. "La Rhetorique du narrateur sadien." *Neophilologus* 77 (1993): 41–49.

Walmsley, Peter. *The Rhetoric of Berkeley's Philosophy.* Cambridge, England: Cambridge University Press, 1990.

Warren, Leland. "The Conscious Speakers." In *Sensibility in Transformation.* Ed. Syndy Conger. London: Associated University Presses, 1990. 25–42.

Wasserman, Earl. *The Subtler Language.* Baltimore: Johns Hopkins University Press, 1959.

Watt, Ian. *The Rise of the Novel: Studies in Defoe, Richardson and Fielding.* Harmondsworth, England: Penguin, 1957.

Wehrs, Donald. "Sterne, Cervantes, Montaigne: Fideistic Skepticism and the Rhetoric of Desire." *Comparative Literature Studies* 25.2 (1988): 127–51.

Weidmann, Paul. "Vox in Pace." *Chicago Review* 39 (1993): 53–64.

Wellbery, Caroline. "From Mirrors to Images: The Transformation of Sentimental

Paradigms in Goethe's *The Sorrows of Young Werther.*" *Studies in Romanticism* 25.2 (1980): 231–49.

Werner, Stephen. *Diderot's Great Scroll: Narrative Art in Jacques le fataliste.* Banbury, England: Voltaire Foundation, 1975.

Willey, Basil. *The Eighteenth-Century Background.* Boston: Beacon Press, 1961.

Wilmore, S. J. "Scepticism and Deconstruction." *Man and World* 20 (1987): 437–55.

Wilson, Arthur M. *Diderot.* New York: Oxford University Press, 1972.

Wollstonecroft, Mary. *A Vindication of the Rights of Woman.* New York: W. W. Norton, 1988.

Woolf, Virginia. Introduction to Laurence Sterne's *A Sentimental Journey through France and Italy.* London: Oxford University Press, 1928.

Yolton, J. W. *John Locke and the Way of Ideas.* London: Oxford University Press, 1956.

Young, B. W. *Religion and Enlightenment in Eighteenth-Century England: Theological Debate from Locke to Burke.* Oxford: Clarendon Press, 1998.

Index

William Donoghue is an assistant professor of literature at Emerson College in Boston. He has published a translation of a book of French poetry by the Quebec poet Anne-Marie Alonzo, has written on George Herbert, skepticism, and the fin de siècle, and has published his own short fiction in *TriQuarterly*, *Grain*, and other literary journals.